Bosnian Refugees
in Chicago

Bosnian Refugees in Chicago

Gender, Performance, and Post-War Economies

Ana Croegaert

LEXINGTON BOOKS
Lanham • Boulder • New York • London

Published by Lexington Books
An imprint of The Rowman & Littlefield Publishing Group, Inc.
4501 Forbes Boulevard, Suite 200, Lanham, Maryland 20706
www.rowman.com

6 Tinworth Street, London SE11 5AL, United Kingdom

Copyright © 2020 The Rowman & Littlefield Publishing Group, Inc.

All rights reserved. No part of this book may be reproduced in any form or by any electronic or mechanical means, including information storage and retrieval systems, without written permission from the publisher, except by a reviewer who may quote passages in a review.

British Library Cataloguing in Publication Information Available

Library of Congress Cataloging-in-Publication Data Available

ISBN 978-1-7936-2306-5 (cloth)
ISBN 978-1-7936-2308-9 (pbk)
ISBN 978-1-7936-2307-2 (electronic)

Contents

List of Figures	vii
Acknowledgments	ix
A Note on Language and Pronunciation	xi
A Note About Terminology	xiii
Gathering Grounds: An Introduction	1
1 Refugee Women and a Chicago Volag	27
2 Making Home and Family after War, and from a Distance	43
3 Ajla in Stolac	63
4 Shifting Time in the Social Life of Bosnian Coffee	73
5 American Balkanism and the Optics of Violence	95
6 A Trade in Stories	117
7 #BiHInSolidarity / Be in Solidarity	141
Gathering Grounds: A Reflection	163
Bibliography	169
Index	179
About the Author	183

List of Figures

4.1	Devon Market Coffee Shelves. October 2006. Photo by Ana Croegaert.	79
4.2	*Zambak* Magazine Ramadan 2004 cover shot with džezva and fildžan. Photo courtesy of Isak Berbić.	80
4.3	"Selma's" Restaurant Menu.	89
5.1	*Lana's Rain* Ticket Stub.	101
5.2	Teatr Biuro Podrozy *Carmen Funebre*.	104
6.1	"Women of Bosnia Tell Their Story" Announcement.	118
6.2	Daley Plaza Srebrenica Memorial 2005. Photo by Ana Croegaert.	122
6.3	BosFam Brochure.	127
6.4	BosFam Memorial Carpet with men's names. Displayed during International Woman's Day on Capitol Hill in Washington DC, 2009. Photo by Ana Croegaert.	129
7.1	Screenshot of tweet from twitter user Sons of Bosnia (SonOfBosnia) "#JusticeforZemir #Bosnian community wants to make this country better, we don't burn, we earn. #Nohandouts #ZemirBegic" Sons of Bosnia (SonOfBosnia) December 1, 2014.	150
7.2	Screenshot of tweet showing a sidewalk memorial for Zemir Begić in St. Louis Bevo Neighborhood. Sarah Kendzior (sarahkendzior) December 12, 2014.	153

7.3 Screenshot of tweet showing a photo of young mourners with R.I.P. sign for Zemir Begić. Francis Flandro (Fflandro) December 3, 2014.   153

7.4 Screenshot of tweet from twitter user Ida (idddaaa23): "I have to be really honest. Zemir's death is really triggering for me, as it is for many other Bosnians. #JusticeforZemir #BiHInSolidarity" December 1, 2014.   154

C.1 ŠTO TE NEMA Chicago 2017. Photo by Ana Croegaert.   164

Acknowledgments

The preparation for this book began a long time ago, in classrooms that inspired me to explore, ask questions, listen, and write. I am especially grateful to Bruce Mitchell at Evanston Township High School, Valerie Simms at Northeastern Illinois University, and Lynda Morgan, Lynn Morgan, Amy Kaplan, and Christopher Benfey at Mount Holyoke College for creating classroom experiences that were both rigorous and fun.

At Northwestern University Helen Schwartzman encouraged me to take seriously children's social worlds and use their insights to inform my scholarship on refugee migration. Katherine Hoffman's delight in everything "language"—poetry, song, text, archive, movement, discourse—is captivating, and she championed my efforts to value the significance of language across registers and genre. I am grateful to Mary Weismantel for sharing her endless enthusiasm for the politics and pleasures of food. D. Soyini Madison and the late Dwight Conquergood modeled how to cultivate scholarship that moves and inspires others, and Alaka Wali has been a constant source of inspiration for scholarship that makes meaningful conversations and contributions among publics outside of academic institutions. Micaela di Leonardo's passion for scholarship that centers the nuances of women's lives and her devotion to the craft of writing motivated me to be particularly attentive to the politics of representation. I am forever indebted to her mentorship in intellectual history, political economy, and feminist scholarship—always conveyed through her singular razor-sharp wit. Jim Spillane's mentorship in collaborative large-scale data collection deepened my appreciation for interdisciplinary research design, and Mary Patillo generously provided critical background for post-1970s housing and development on Chicago's north side.

I am grateful for the generous support of the Northwestern Alumnae Association Dissertation Fellowship, and research grants from the Buffett Institute for Global Affairs and the Mount Holyoke College Faculty Research Fund. Portions of chapters 4, 5, and 7 previously appeared in *American Anthropologist*, *Identities*, and the *Journal for the Anthropology of North America*.

This book would not have been possible without the support of Courtney Morales, Shelby Russell, and Della Vache, the excellent editors at Lexington Books and Rowman & Littlefield. Early parts of this work developed out of insights gained in graduate workshops at Northwestern University, the University of Chicago, and the University of Illinois at Champaign-Urbana. I am especially grateful for critiques offered by Tatiana Andronova, Umud Dalgic, Nicole Fabricant, Ruth Gomberg-Muñoz, Elissa Helms, Anneeth Kaur Hundle, Jean Hunleth, Larisa Jašarević, Andrea Muehlebach, José-Maria Muñoz, Öykü Potuoglu-Cook, Judith Singleton, and Craig Tower. Kathleen Adams and Bren Ortega Murphy were constant sources of support and inspiration during my time at Chicago's Loyola University. Renia Ehrenfeucht, Elizabeth Steeby, and the late Susan Mann provided crucial intellectual companionship at the University of New Orleans, and Dubravka Gilić, Isa Hinrichs, Kathy Namba, Tatjana Pavlović, Ozrenka Popović, jackie sumell, and Summer Wood introduced much-needed levity to my writing process while in New Orleans.

Ioana Szeman has been my intellectual companion throughout every stage of this work; her ethical sensibilities and keen eye for coupling performance analysis with ethnographic writing were indispensable to this book's contributions. There is no more creative and patient language tutor and consultant than Snežana Žabić: hvala, and rock on, Nana!

This work owes much to my teachers outside of the university: to Kathleen Alexander for introducing me to advocacy work, and to Suzanne Donoghue for sharing her passion for the concept of "fair trade" retail. Julie Hamos taught me about how public policy is crafted, legislated, and implemented, and Verna Barton and Jack Crane showed me the ropes at Shorebank and the nuances of Chicago's south side mortgage markets. Katiti Crawford, Tricia Hersey a.k.a. "The Nap Bishop," and Karen Thomson worked with me to promote literacy among Chicagoland's young parents, and to share our work with librarians, caseworkers, social workers, and teachers.

Thank you to Adela, Lara, Emir, Dženita, Ajla, Vedran, Mario, Elmina, Adnan, and Tony for your hospitality and friendship. Thank you to Tajma Hodžić, Jeanne Petrolle, Aida Šehović, Ida Sefer, Belma Sadiković, and Nitasha Sharma for your input and questions. Jordan Burton, Janalee and Jim Croegaert, Leilani Garrett, and Liz Lazar read drafts and, along with Jacob Croegaert, Jubal Croegaert, and Sean Croegaert-Key, rallied me to the final stretch.

Most of all, this book would never have been written without the women who bravely shared their vulnerability and steady determination with me. Your sorrows, laughter, creativity, desires, and resolve animate this book.

A Note on Language and Pronunciation

j	"y" like yes
c	"ts" like cats
č	hard "ch" tip of tongue
ć	soft "ch"=blade of tongue
ž	"zh" "s" as in "leisure"
dž	"dzh" tip of tongue
dj	"dzh" blade of tongue
š	"sh" as in show
nj	like "ne" in "news"
lj	"llio" as in million
a	"a" as in father
e	"e" as in bet
i	"e" as in she
u	"oo" as in food

I refer to the language spoken by the people in this book as "Bosnian," as this was the way they most commonly labeled their language.[1] "Bosnian," refers to a south Slavic variant that in the Socialist Federal Republic of Yugoslavia was glossed as "Serbo-Croatian." The Serbo-Croatian standard was based on the late nineteenth-century Bosnian Shtokavian variant, associated with the Herzegovina in particular. Bosnian is written with the principle that every sound corresponds to a letter, and every written letter ought to be heard when spoken, thus there are no "silent vowels," as found in English. Officially, Yugoslavs were to be conversant in both Cyrillic and Latin scripts, although this skill varied widely and was especially dependent upon the speaker's regional and class affiliations. When I took formal instruction in 2003–2004, the language was listed as "BCS" Bosnian/Croatian/Serbian, the label affixed to it by the United Nations. I never heard this term used by the people in this book. Although language is a sensitive issue for some and was a site of contest during and after the war, many people in the United States refer to the language with the encompassing label *naš jezik / our language*, especially in settings that include speakers from varied regional and ethnic backgrounds.

NOTE

1. These pronounciations were adapted from Alexander, Ronelle 2006, and Bringa, Tone 1995.

A Note about Terminology

Bosnia refers to the territory of Bosnia-Herzegovina (BiH), the borders of which have remained relatively the same since at least the fourteenth century. "[The] Herzegovina" is the southernmost region of the country and has its own topographic, historical, and cultural significance reaching back to the medieval era. The United States–brokered Dayton Peace Accords that delineated the terms of the end of the war in Bosnia maintained the state's pre-war territorial borders, but ceded an internal boundary of two "entities," the Serb Republic (RS) and the Federation that largely correspond to territories seized and occupied by the VRS during the war. At the time of this writing, Bosnia's external border is contested by ongoing secession efforts among some in the RS, and efforts by some in the Herzegovina to secede and join Croatia.

Bosnian / Bosanac may refer to varied "peoples" within Bosnia and/or those who trace their origins there. In the decades leading up to the 1990s wars, the term *Bošniak* had come to be increasingly claimed by and associated with Bosnian Muslims. But a longer view of the label's use shows that Bošniak (p. Bošnjaci) was sometimes used prior to and during the Ottoman period to refer to all of the state's inhabitants, regardless of religious community.[1] According to anthropologist Tone Bringa and historian Edin Hajdarpašić, the national concept of *Bošnjaštvo / Bosnian-ness* developed in the context of burgeoning Croatian and Serbian nationalisms in the second half of the nineteenth century. As these national identifications intensified, some of the Bosnian literati began to further identify with and use the Bošniak label, a move that was emphasized and encouraged during the forty-year period of Austro-Hungarian rule (1878–1918).[2] During the SFRY period, "Bošniak" was left out of the state-recognized official nationalities, unlike "Croat" and "Serb," with "Muslim" formally introduced as an ethno-national category in 1971. Oppositional Serb and Croat nationalisms surged again during the late 1960s and 1970s, and the dominant meaning of Bošniak increasingly was associated with Bosnian Muslims, many of whom connect their religious identification with Islam to the Ottoman period.[3] Among the Bosnian American diaspora, Bosnian/ Bosanac was most often used as the inclusive term for referring to people who trace their origins to Bosnia. In this book, I use Bosnian except where participants specified the use of Bošniak.

NOTES

1. Bringa, Tone. *Being Muslim the Bosnian Way*. New Jersey: Princeton University Press, 1995. Bringa, citing Fuad Saltaga (1991) writes that *Bošnjak* is first mentioned in documents relating to the medieval state in 1166 and that "Ottoman sources used Bošnjak sometimes to refer to any inhabitants of the Bosnian vilajet (province) and at others to Bosnian Muslims only." Bosnian Franciscans also supported the multifaith use of Bošnjaštvo movement to end Ottoman rule (Bringa 1995: pp. 34–35, n.33).

2. Bringa, "Being Muslim"; Hajdarpašić, Edin. *Whose Bosnia? Nationalism and Political Imagination in the Balkans, 1840–1914*. Ithaca: Cornell University Press, 2015.

3. Hromadžić, Azra. "Discourses of Trans-Ethnic Narod in Postwar Bosnia and Herzegovina." *Nationalities Papers* 41(2): 259–275, 2013: 266; Sorabji, Cornelia. "Islamic Revival and Marriage in Bosnia," *Journal of Muslim Minority Affairs* 9(2): 331–337, 332, 1988.

Gathering Grounds:
An Introduction

"Really? You just came from work?" Nasiha's raised eyebrows and tone registered surprise in—and disapproval of—my outfit. I had worn black jeans with black clogs to our late afternoon meeting at a cafe on a busy Chicago street, and my hair was loose and mussed from my black and red hoodie. Almost as if we had planned for the contrast, Nasiha arrived in a dusty pale rose dress with fitted bodice and full skirt with matching ballet flats. She wore a creme colored cardigan with 3/4 sleeves to cover her arms, and her fair hair pulled back in a tidy bun. I wrote later that evening in my fieldnotes, "Nasiha looked like a ballerina! Although she does not have the traditional figure of a ballerina, she moves with the grace of a dancer."

Nasiha had arrived in Chicago nearly a decade earlier, as a war refugee. She was among the more than two million people displaced by the 1990s wars in the former Socialist Federal Republic of Yugoslavia (SFRY) (Croatia 1991–1995, Bosnia and Herzegovina 1992–1995, Kosovo 1999) of whom at least 180,000 had arrived in the United States between 1992–2012.[1] I met Nasiha at The Community Center (TCC), a Voluntary Agency (Volag) serving Bosnian refugees on Chicago's north side where we both worked as volunteers between 2004–2006. She was accustomed to seeing me at TCC, casually clothed for my work with the seniors and children's groups. It hadn't occurred to me to change up my attire for our first meeting outside of TCC. Nasiha had agreed to meet with me for an informal interview about her refugee migration, away from the kids and the seniors we worked with at the center, and I wanted her to take me seriously! Flustered, I searched for an explanation: "Well, yes, I was at the library writing most of the day . . . I didn't teach today," I offered. She seemed somewhat satisfied with my response, but I made a note to be more attentive to my attire in our future meetings.

"Dress is embodied practice" writes Karen Tranberg Hansen, a reminder that my casual clothing might be interpreted as a reflection of a lack of concern for the occasion, or even for self.[2] Alternatively, Nasiha's carefully curated outfit could indicate her attentive self-care and preparation for the occasion. I would come to understand Nasiha's evaluation of my appearance as instructive of the ways refugee women drew on dress and comportment to convey and confer dignity, something that they were denied when they were forced to leave their homes and enter concentration camps in Bosnia, and during their routes out of Bosnia: via refugee housing in Germany, Italy, and in Chicago. And yet, Nasiha's self-presentation could not be understood solely as a response to her own personal experience with degradation during her forced migration. Her youthful stylish appearance also offered marked contrast to a more familiar image of Nasiha's refugee cohort: elder women wearing the patterned headscarf and loose, less structured clothing associated with the rural parts of her home country.

Like the majority of Yugoslav war refugees living in the United States, Nasiha was female, Muslim, and part of a multi-generational family unit that migrated in stages before reuniting at a more permanent new home country.[3] And, as was also the case for many Bosnian refugees in the United States, Nasiha belonged to a mixed family—she had a Catholic father and a Muslim mother.[4] Mixed families became increasingly common in the Yugoslav years, and Nasiha's home republic of Bosnia-Herzegovina was home to the highest percentage of these families. In some situations, people in mixed families identified simply as "Yugoslav" and in others more with one ethno-national heritage, as was the case with Nasiha. Nasiha's family were among those forced to leave when the political conflicts in Yugoslavia turned violent, sometimes referred to as organized campaigns of "ethnic cleansing," although many of the refugees I met rejected this terminology for its association of non-Serb ethnic groups and ethnic mixing with dirt and impurity. During the Serb military takeover in Nasiha's hometown of Prijedor, people were targeted for their ethno-religious identities, and Muslim Yugoslavs as well as those in mixed families like Nasiha's were depicted as "impure" traitors to the nation.

Prijedor is a small city known for steel production located in the republic of Bosnia-Herzegovina (BiH) in the heart of the SFRY. Bosnia is not only at the geographical center of the former SFRY but was also a central cultural site for the development of nineteenth century nationalist political movements. The most widely used language in SFRY, Serbo-Croatian, was standardized around the Herzegovinian variant, and, in the decades prior to and during Austro-Hungarian rule (1840–1914), the province figured prominently in the development of European transnational political projects when the reorganization of Ottoman, Russian, and Austro-Hungarian empires involved contested claims to the small territory.[5] Despite numerous political and economic precipitating factors contributing to the First World War, American high school history textbooks continue to narrate the beginning of World War I as beginning with the 1914 assassination of Austria's heir to the throne by anti-imperialist activists in Bosnia's capital city, Sarajevo. A century later, the 1990s conflicts over political power in the SFRY brought the most intensive violence to Bosnia (1992–1995) through genocidal campaigns that included mass displacements and the destruction of homes, systematic rapes, and mass executions of civilians including the massacre of at least 8,372 Muslim men and boys in the eastern province of Srebrenica over the course of several days in July 1995.[6] Unlike tens of thousands of female survivors, Nasiha and her mother had not personally been sexually victimized during the wars, but they overheard others being attacked. Regardless of their particular experiences with victimization, the wartime violence and its aftermath was harrowing to all survivors.

How does one remake a life after such violent political confrontations? What was it like to be a citizen-turned-refugee confronted with the ruination of a country, an economy, and a way of life that was part of Yugoslavia's experiment with socialism? What was it like to leave Yugoslavia, which had been introducing neoliberal reforms since the 1970s, and relocate to the United States during the 1990s intensive neoliberal restructuring? What is it like to be persecuted for one's Muslim identity in Yugoslavia and arrive in the United States during an intense uptick in American Islamophobia? And, what is it like to be a woman in this postwar diaspora? While studies of Yugoslav refugee diaspora have focused primarily on men and their transnational activities, this book explores these questions through the experiences of women survivors living in the United States, in Chicago.[7] I argue that their efforts to refashion their lives after wartime migration and the myriad meanings attributed to their circumstances constitutes living through injury, *injured life*, a mode of approaching the aftermath of forced wartime migration that insists on the inseparability of material and social injury.

BECOMING A REFUGEE

Nasiha's story and refugee experience is significantly shaped by the aspirations of her single mother, Enisa. When Enisa was pregnant with Nasiha in the mid-1970s, economic inequalities among and within different regions of the SFRY were increasingly apparent. The SFRY had begun its socialist experiment in worker self-management where state enterprises were turned over to workers' associations. At the same time, the country became simultaneously more dependent on Soviet trade and more reliant upon financial relationships with the International Monetary Fund (IMF), and the World Bank (WB)—economic instruments of western democracies. In order to retain access to IMF and WB support, SFRY leadership was required to implement neoliberal Structural Adjustment Policies (SAPs) and austerity programs that further decentralized state responsibility and re-oriented development toward free market-based growth and solutions to social well-being. This led to what Susan Woodward has described as the SFRY's "faustian bargain," wherein development paradigms placed the poorer republics and regions associated with extraction and processing of raw materials, including Bosnia and Kosovo, in the service of wealthier republics with more developed manufacturing operations and closer ties to western markets, namely Slovenia and Croatia. As a young woman in her early twenties, Enisa saw the writing on the wall and went to university in the Slovenian capitol, Ljubljana. And, when she became pregnant with Nasiha, she decided to give birth there, in Slovenia, rather than returning to Bosnia. This meant that Nasiha had a Slovenian birth certificate. Enisa's decision would later prove to be beneficial to Nasiha in ways Enisa could never have anticipated. Enisa would come to find Nasiha's father to be a neglectful partner who drank too much and she divorced him when Nasiha was quite young. After the divorce, Enisa took Nasiha and moved back to her hometown in Bosnia, nearer to her parents and brothers.

Nasiha grew up in Prijedor, where her grandparents had moved during the SFRY's massive urbanization and industrialization programs in the early 1960s. Enisa found a good job as an accounts manager at a local bank and the family enjoyed a life of material stability in the midst of increasing political unrest and rising ethno-nationalism. When the Bosnian Serb Army (VRS), with the support of the republic of Serbia, began a brutal military campaign in northern Bosnia in the spring of 1992, Nasiha was in her mid-teens, and she and Enisa, along with Nasiha's two uncles, one of her uncle's wives, her grandmother, and her six-year old cousin spent the next several months holed up in the Trnopolje concentration camp.[8] The VRS takeover of her city began the process of stripping away Nasiha's family's Bosnian citizenship. Further, Slovenia (1990) and then Croatia (1991) declared independence from the SFRY, meaning that Nasiha's Bosnian family would be considered refugees rather than citizens in these former republics and would need to apply for Temporary Protected Status (TPS) or political asylum in the newly autonomous countries, just as they would if they had sought refuge in Turkey, the United States, or Sweden.

Trnopolje was one of four concentration camps established in the region.[9] Initially the camps were presented as "check points" where non-Serb civilians seeking to escape the violence could gather in safety and register themselves for refugee status. With this understanding, Nasiha's family voluntarily entered the camp, which was set up in a school that bore the name of the Yugoslav-era motto: "Brotherhood and Unity." Here they stayed for several months, a school-turned-detention-center with 40–50 people living in each classroom.

When Nasiha spoke about the time in Trnopolje, she carefully told me that she was "so grateful we all made it through alive and whole . . . we made it through without being abused . . . as women." This reference to "abuse as women" was her way of letting me know that none of her family, as far as she knew, were raped in the camp. I found that this protective way of discussing sexual violence was the approach people preferred when addressing the profound violations and humiliations of sexual attacks, which were a widely deployed wartime strategy that led the International Criminal Tribunal for the former Yugoslavia (ICTY) to declare wartime rape as a "crime against humanity," and thus a war crime.

Documented abuses at Trnopolje led to a Red Cross takeover in August. Although Nasiha's family members had escaped the more violent crimes perpetrated against detainees at Trnopolje, they had seen and heard things done to others and feared the VRS strategy of separating men from women and children. Nasiha's family decided to leave the camp and await permission to cross the border into Croatia from their apartments in the city. Yet when they returned to their home, they found a Serb family occupying it. Enisa and Nasiha went to Nasiha's grandma's apartment and from there, Enisa went on a mission to expedite their exit to Croatia. To satisfy VRS requirements, she was forced to settle their accounts, sign away the rights to their property, and await the arrival of the "guarantee letter" her sister—a Croatian resident—sent from Croatia by way of Enisa's father who was already there. This "guarantee letter" was similar to a "sponsor" agreement in U.S. immigration procedures that pledged and proved that Nasiha's aunt was willing, and had the means, to care for them. Nasiha recalled this as a horrifying time: the VRS disappeared entire families, sometimes executing people in the streets and leaving the bodies there to terrorize the rest of the residents.

During this time, buses would make the trip weekly from a refugee outpost in Karlovac, Croatia across the border to Prijedor to pick up people who had all their paperwork in order and transport them back across the border, to Croatia. Enisa and her brothers had taken care of everything, and they were able to board one of these buses in January and take the two hour ride to Karlovac. The intimidation and humiliation continued en route, when the driver stopped the bus, and the military ordered all of the men off the bus at gunpoint, requiring the women to bribe the soldiers in order to get the men back. Nasiha's grandfather met them at the Karlovac bus station and accompanied them to Zagreb, where they registered with Merhamet and the Red Cross—two of the primary international humanitarian organizations managing the refugees' migration.

In Zagreb things were also tense. The city had become home to the largest number of refugees fleeing the conflict in northern Bosnia, and from the Serbia-led offensive against non-Serbs in the Krajina region of eastern Croatia. And in 1993, a new conflict was brewing between Croatia-supported separatists and Bosnian unionists in the Hercegovina region of western Bosnia. The Croatian government made it clear that the country was just a stopping point along refugees' routes; there was no offer of permanent residency to Muslim refugees from Bosnia. Once in Zagreb, they began to hear more and more reports of mass killings of men and sexual violence against women in Bosnia. Nasiha remembered this as a time when "we were seeing just all of these women . . . these women without men." Nasiha's uncles left for refugee programs in Germany and Sweden in less than two weeks after their arrival in Zagreb.

But Enisa wanted to wait things out a bit longer in Croatia with the hope that things would return to "normal." Foremost in her mind was Nasiha's schooling. Nasiha had already missed nearly a year of high school due to the situation in Prijedor, and Enisa didn't want her missing any more. Furthermore, refugees were not permitted to attend schools with citizen children, and she'd heard bad things about the makeshift schools assembled for the refugee children.

This is where Enisa's decision to give birth to Nasiha in Slovenia became a critical factor in their refugee trajectory. Croatia had implemented a different residency policy for Slovenian versus Bosnian nationals. Because Nasiha had a Slovenian, rather than a Bosnian, birth certificate, she was eligible to attend a regular high school in Croatia. Thus, they remained in Croatia for two more years while Nasiha completed her schooling in a northwestern city where her aunt lived. Refugees also were not permitted to hold jobs, so Enisa like many others, found what work she could in the informal economy in order to ease the burden on her sister who, according to the state's refugee policy, was officially responsible to support them all on the modest income she earned as a hairdresser and beautician, along with the modest refugee stipend Enisa received through the state and humanitarian agencies. Enisa found work in Zagreb where she remained during the week, and then spent the weekends at her sister's place. While in Croatia, Enisa and the family waited on another letter of guarantee from one of the volags in Chicago, and from an aunt who was already living in the city. Once this paperwork was in order and Enisa and Nasiha had completed the extensive screening process with the refugee agency officials in Croatia, they flew to Chicago in 1995.

INJURED LIFE

When I followed up with Nasiha to make sure I had accurately recorded the details of her refugee journey, she recounted for me again the radical alterations of her everyday life at the onset of war. She recalled how the self-declared Bosnian Serb government and military took over all aspects of municipal government in her city. Those directing the coup used the state radio and began broadcasting warnings to all non-Serbs that they must mark their homes with white sheets and prepare to enter "checkpoints" where they would be registered for immediate relocation. She remembered how, upon entry to the "checkpoint," her family discovered it was in fact the Trnopolje concentration camp. She repeated their encounters with multiple scenes of humiliation, and then, as if to remind us both, clarified for me again that, unlike many of the people who were detained in Trnopolje and the surrounding camps, she and her family made it out; none of them were killed, and none were raped. In her re-telling of these horrors, Nasiha repeated over and again, "it was just the bare life Ana, really, the bare life." Surprised to hear her use a phrase that to me was most familiar in the context of academic scholarship, I asked Nasiha if she was familiar with philosopher Giorgio Agamben's use of that term, "bare life"? "No, I'm not familiar [with his use] but that's what it was: just the bare life," she replied.

Agamben's theory of state sovereignty posits that processes related to the exercise of modern state power often produce situations that deem the lives of some human subjects to be expendable. According to Agamben, events like the VRS coup of Prijedor establish a "state of exception" whereby the rule of law is selectively suspended to enable the intensification of political power. This intensification transforms places such as the Trnopolje concentration camp into "spaces of exception" wherein state agents seek to render certain people dehumanized to the point of "bare life," stripped of all social and affective features.[10] Too often, however, scholarly accounts take bare life as an end point rather than using its insights to lead to the recognition that, even in the cases of those for whom bare life leads to death, people's lives leave traces on the world through what exists of their memory and material life among those who remain.[11] I argue that "bare life" is a useful concept only so far as it brings into view those social, sensual, and material lives that are regarded as expendable.[12] In fact when I mentioned Nasiha's phrasing to Mira, another wartime refugee and also a language scholar, she remarked that in Bosnian the phrase "bare life" translates as "goli život," and is heard most often in the phrase, "borba za goli život," which translates to "the struggle/fight for bare life." This phrasing emphasizes the fight and struggle to live that is missing from accounts of "bare life" that center abjectness and victimhood. I take my cue from Nasiha, Mira, and the women in the pages that follow and propose that their circumstances are better described as "injured life."

As does Laurence Ralph in his ethnography of people living with violence and injury in a south side Chicago African American neighborhood, I understand injury to encompass more than bodily harm or physical disability, and to include structural injuries brought about by political and economic policies that may—even despite good intentions—enact social violence and material hardship on particular populations.[13] Ralph sketches a conceptualization of injury that includes "historical emotions like nostalgia and philosophical sentiments like authenticity."[14] Nostalgia and authenticity entered the worlds of Bosnian refugee women in ways that provided commentary on, and evaluation of, their postwar, post-migration situations. Refugees' affective responsibility to remember pre-war Yugoslavia and the wartime dead, and to care for other survivors—including members of the diaspora and those who remain in the postwar state—were ever-present in social exchanges and economic decisions. These sensibilities also governed women's efforts to manage their public image in the United States. *Injured life* captures the ways that women used the injuries of material, physical, and psychological violence, forced migration, family separation, and status-loss as tools to diagnose the aftermath of the harms they endured and to develop their visions for the future.

ENTERING "THE FIELD"

I grew up twelve blocks north of the street that divides Chicago's Rogers Park neighborhood where numerous refugees lived, from Evanston, where I had an unusual upbringing in a Christian faith-based commune that promoted social justice issues in its early years. Providing refuge to war survivors was among these issues, and our community began hosting refugees from Cambodia and El Salvador when I was ten years old. My friendships with peer children who found themselves in our community as a result of transnational political confrontations taught me not only about the horrors of war, but also about the inequalities embedded in the refugee-sponsorship model practiced by my church. These early experiences made me especially attuned to the inequalities in programs guided by good intentions that fail to consider dynamics of power.

When I first began the field research for this book, many people were reluctant to talk with me. I had tried to prepare myself for this: I knew I would be viewed by many as yet another outsider poking about with questions concerning the intimate and painful details of their lives. They'd done this all before; starting with the humanitarian workers in Europe who conducted the interviews and medical exams in the extensive U.S. refugee vetting process, followed by the arrival interviews and medical exams once they'd made it to the United States, and then the interviews endured at numerous social service agencies in order to access assistance with employment, food, housing, schooling, and healthcare. I volunteered at TCC for six months before learning that I wasn't even the first *researcher* to ask people about their migration experiences.

Ajša, who ran a group for senior women at TCC, was the one who finally enlightened me about this aspect of my research context. Five years prior, a researcher from a European University had come to study whether or not Bosnians in Chicago had constituted a "transnational community" in the early years of their migration. According to Ajša, and corroborated by others I followed up with, the researcher had enlisted the help of TCC staff and community leaders to administer a survey and identify interview subjects for her study. In exchange for this assistance, the survey administrators were promised a modest payment (a common practice in social science research protocol) and would receive a copy of the paper once it was published. But people had not received payment, and they had never received a copy of the paper. I did not know whether or not this account was "true," or whether it was the result of miscommunication or intentional lack of communication, but what mattered was that this experience shaped people's perceptions of researcher conduct. I was able to locate the paper, written in the genre popularly referred to as "white papers," or research papers that are written for the purposes of informing public policy. It was clear that the paper's intended audience were those involved in European immigration policy and in designing Bosnia's postwar development. In Bosnia, such individuals are referred to as members of "The International Community," but more commonly, as *stranci / foreigners* they were often perceived as occupiers whose primary objectives related more to external interests rather than with sincere investments in the country's postwar development.[15]

I was dismayed. I did not want to be considered to be an insincere aid worker like the Internationals! The people at the TCC knew I was not a refugee, and although many mistook me for having Bosnian heritage, I do not. My parents and their parents were born in the United States, and our antecedents were primarily from the region in Europe that is now Belgium. I shared this information often, as I was asked repeatedly, "Where are you from?" and quickly learned that many found my response: "here, Chicago," to be unsatisfactory. They would push, "but where are your parents from?" "Illinois," I offered. Increasingly exasperated, people would continue the line of questioning, "Where were your people *before* they were in the United States?!"

My inability to place myself in clear kinship to Bosnia sometimes brought suspicion: Why did I want to learn about their lives? What was I about? With whom was I sharing what I learned about their experiences? In part, I understood these inquiries as arising from people's awareness of the relationship between World War II and the 1990s wars. Historical memories of World War II played a part in political rhetoric, media campaigns, military recruitment, and in orchestrating specific acts of violence during the 1990s conflicts. At least one million Yugoslavs died during World War II, some at the hands of Italian and German fascist soldiers, but many perished in conflict with Yugoslav Nazi collaborators, Partisan resistance fighters, or Serbian royalists. Some of the most extensive conflicts took place in Bosnia, and some of the survivors had found their way to Chicago.

During the 1990s wars, long-time neighbors, co-workers, friends, and even family members betrayed one another. In Chicago, second generation members of this earlier diaspora were sometimes forbidden by their parents to socialize with friends from another Yugoslav ethnic group. Yet the "International Community" of United Nations peacekeepers had also broken trust with Bosnians during the war, most notably in the failure to protect the nearly 30,000 civilians who had fled to the UN "safe haven" in Srebrenica in summer 1995, to escape the encroaching VRS. These questions about my family origins were one strategy whereby women sought to recalibrate the relationship between researcher and participant, citizen and refugee, turning the tables so to speak, by asking me the same questions I put to them.

My lack of awareness regarding the previous researcher's efforts to study the refugees' lives was not the only teaching moment I encountered early on. In writing out a script for my "lay summary," a spoken explanation of my research project for participants, I had been careful to describe my interests broadly as wanting to learn about people's experiences, after migrating, of living and working in Chicago. I followed this by stating that I was "especially interested in women's experiences." It took months of listening to and participating in conversations similar to that between me and Nasiha before I realized that among many of the war survivors, "women's experiences" was a euphemism for women's sexual assault during the war, and that people interpreted my phrasing as meaning that I wanted to interview women who were sexually assaulted during the wars. I was embarrassed by my initial lack of sensitivity to this nuanced meaning. I have experience as a court-trained victim-witness advocate for domestic violence survivors and enough of a background to know that asking victims to re-tell their stories of abuse can be re-traumatizing without the appropriate social supports in place to do follow-up care. I purposefully had not directly asked women refugees about personal experiences with sexual violence for precisely this reason. I did not have the means to provide such care, and I would learn that such supports were severely lacking for Chicago's refugee community. I revised my script to say that I was interested in women's experiences of migration, locating jobs and housing, learning English, and other more specific aspects of building a livelihood after being forced to migrate.

I learned to not ask directly about violence, or even about the war.[16] People explicitly directed me away from these topics, often telling me they were happy to talk with me, but that they did not want to talk about the war. And yet, once I got to know people, they would bring up wartime memories. While the aftermath of collective violence is one of this book's themes, these pages do not contain descriptions of specific acts of violence. Such accounts can be found elsewhere, and in many ways their reproduction further harms, rather than heals, survivors. I follow Hariz Halilovich in his critique of the overuse of "trauma" and "PTSD" diagnoses applied to Bosnian war refugees that too often have stigmatized and pathologized refugees' remembering of wartime events.[17] Rather than codifying such remembering within a psychological trauma rubric, I understood such acts as socially mediated historical productions.[18] That is, women's accounts of the war and migration were shared and thus became part of a larger oral, and sometimes written, archive that could be consulted and interpreted by others. Women shared their experiences within varied settings including home spaces, TCC, and public memorial events, and each of these sites were governed by distinct social conventions. In home-sites, the "audiences" for these memories were limited to other family members and me, at TCC it included peers, and, in many memorial events, the audience extended to Yugoslav diaspora, international human rights organizations, and a more general "American" public. I draw on performance theories to examine these sites as co-productions forged by speakers and audience alike. In this way, I aim to illustrate the ways of speaking and remembering that survivors offered to me, to one another, and to these other audiences. As people told me over and again when they spoke about the difficulties of war and refugee life, "Everyone has their own story."

A CRITICAL DESIGN

> Ethnographies are fictions, but they are about material realities, realities that may be socially apprehended and historically contingent but can be checked, challenged, debated, and reconsidered.[19]

This project draws on critical ethnography—an approach to writing ethnography that has a long history in the Anthropology of the United States and centers on "the cultural, political, and economic complexities of the United States itself," rather than the more familiar practice of U.S. anthropologists traveling far away to study "exotic Others."[20] As Jasna Čapo notes, Anthropology in Yugoslavia also developed through studies "at home," rather than abroad, albeit with a predominantly rural focus on "village" life. I found that my participants rarely questioned my focus on the United States while Americans did—and do—express surprise at learning that I work primarily on and in the United States rather than a different country.[21] Critical ethnography presents participants' lives in relation to broader historical, cultural, political, and economic systems that shape the circumstances from which they (re)create their everyday lives. Performance ethnographer D. Soyini Madison further defines critical ethnography as generated by ethical commitments to attend to injustice and suffering, and to not only document the social world that is, but also to help envision social worlds that "could be."[22]

I use critical ethnography with a feminist lens to highlight the challenges faced by Bosnian women refugees living in the United States, and to foreground their perspectives on their postwar circumstances. As Dána-Ain Davis and Christa Craven note, in questioning the diminishment and marginalization of women's experiences in, and contributions to, political and economic domains, feminist scholarship also emphasizes a critical approach.[23] I build on a particular insight of this work that illustrates how gendered division of labor in the home, household, and family relations illuminate key aspects of women's economic and political lives. Susan Gal and Gail Kligman's analyses of "Gender after Socialism" in Central Europe shows how socialist reforms created greater professional and employment opportunities for women as workers, yet failed to address gender inequalities in household labor, thus women in socialist countries contended with the "second shift" of home labor in addition to workplace demands.[24] In a related vein, Heidi Hartmann's U.S.-based work on household economies during the "Women's Liberation Movement" showed that women's unpaid household-based labors provided critical—and unrecognized—value to the workings of capitalist economies, and similarly placed women in a "double-bind" of workplace and home-based labor obligations. Gender Studies scholars extended these analyses of household labor to make apparent the gender dimensions of emotional labor, demonstrating how care for family members and the maintenance of family relations through hosting practices and sustained correspondence across distance is also a significant form of labor, most often performed by women.[25]

Many women of Enisa's generation faced these multiple labor expectations, expectations that were further complicated by obligations to family and friends who remained in Bosnia. One woman, Hana, cited the expectation that she cook for extended family as among her reasons for resisting her husband's pleas to make a return trip to Bosnia after the war had ended. Hana and her husband Damir each worked two jobs in the United States, but it was

Hana who performed the bulk of home labor in addition to her wage labor outside of the home. While her husband framed the return trip as a "vacation," Hana felt her experience would be far from it, as she would be required to use Damir's mother's kitchen to prepare and host daily meals and coffee for at least ten people and any neighbors who happened to stop by.[26] In taking the social organization of home life seriously I aim to question rather than reproduce a public/private, male/female binary and emphasize the gendered connections and differences between home space and public space.

Outside of households, one of the key sites in this project was The Community Center (TCC). While Chicago's Progressive-Era settlement houses were primary sites of socialization and incorporation in previous migrations, during the 1980s, faith-based refugee resettlement agencies known as Volags / Volunteer Agencies were the primary administrative centers for managing refugee incorporation into the city's social fabric. TCC was an outgrowth of one of these agencies, and I volunteered there with the senior and youth programs during 2004–2006. At the time, TCC was the only volag in the city focused primarily on serving refugees from former Yugoslavia. Notably, TCC was also primarily staffed by Bosnian women refugees. I met people through TCC, and some of these contacts led to others, as when Nasiha introduced me to her mother, Enisa, and to Enisa's friend Danijela.

In addition, I relied on my existing social networks and knowledge of the city, its north side neighborhoods, and its non-profit and social services networks to recruit participants. Prior to entering graduate school, I spent five years working in Chicago's public and non-profit sectors, and prior to attending college, I worked for four years in domestic service as a live-in nanny and housecleaner, and before that, as an administrative assistant at a light industrial manufacturing operation on the city's northwest side. This previous knowledge of the city and of these sectors of the economy was helpful in gaining access to local institutions and assisted me in connecting with participants.

This book is based on more than a decade of multi-sited ethnography, with the most intensive periods in summer 2003, 2004–2006, summer 2009 in Bosnia, and follow-up visits to Chicago in summers 2010–2013, and 2017. Although I sought women participants, I met many of the men and children who were part of these women's lives, and I include them here. I also encountered Americans working in some capacity with refugees and immigrants in the city, primarily as social workers and program administrators. These American individuals are presented in composite characters in order to protect the anonymity of their work and their sites of employment.

With the exception of Amina, a socially active member of Chicago's Bosnian diaspora community, the remaining people in this book all entered the United States as refugees of the 1990s conflicts. The senior women who appear in these pages highlight one of the key demographic features of the Bosnian refugee cohort; this was a multi-generational group, reflecting the violent displacements of entire families and communities, but also the activation of "family reunification" policy in U.S. immigration protocol.

The majority of the interviews were conducted in English, with the exception of those with seniors, who preferred Bosnian. I met with people in their homes, and cafes, and at worksites. When not interviewing and conducting home visits, I assisted with ESL tutoring at TCC, served as a field trip chaperone for TCC's children's group, volunteered with TCC's senior women's group, and co-founded the annual Chicago Festival of Bosnian-Herzegovinian Film. I spent a significant amount of time attending events meant to depict and/or memorialize the wars. I also socialized with people in transit, sometimes on the bus, or El train, and sometimes as a car passenger or driver. To capture the experiences of migrants moving through urban space, and in a world where modes of citizenship are rapidly shifting, the settings in this book also shift. Thus, I enrich the study by accompanying women activists to Capitol Hill in Washington D.C. in spring 2009, and by a visit to one Chicago-based family's hometown in Bosnia-Herzegovina, near Mostar, during the following summer.

Bosnian American women living in Chicago are involved and invested in the future of the Bosnian state, whose borders at the time of this writing are contested by some ethno-nationalist political groups. Further, there has been a vocal resurgence of genocide-deniers who seek to portray the political confrontations in former Yugoslavia as "civil war," despite abundant evidence that unarmed civilians comprised the majority of wartime deaths and among these, the majority were Bosnian Muslim. Thus, I have taken many steps in these pages to protect people's privacy. Following ethnographic convention, I use pseudonyms for the people and some of the places in this book. I also de-identify some participants by altering individually identifiable information about Bosnian origins, as well as work and home sites. People who are public figures and whose public actions appear in this book retain their public names.

Finally, this ethnography is also shaped by my own situated history and social locations. Not only am I a professional researcher and a writer; I am also a member of a racially mixed white and African American family. As a young, white, female single parent in the 1990s, I learned how to advocate for myself and my child in a public assistance system that was rapidly diminishing, and in the midst of increasingly hostile racist popular discourse about "welfare queens" accused of scamming the system. As the continuation of Nasiha's story shows in the next chapter, most Bosnians in the United States also relied on public assistance at some point during their 1990s migrations and were keenly aware of the gendered and racialized stigma associated with this public good. This shared familiarity with economic vulnerability, stigmatized public assistance, parenthood, and mixed ethno-racial intimacies shaped my relationships with the women in this book. This is not to suggest a parity in our circumstances—to do so would be foolish and insensitive at the very least. Rather, I aim to highlight particular points that formed some of the notable intersubjective aspects of our ethnographic encounters.

"PEOPLE LIKE US"

The category of "refugee" varies widely in application and in experience. The formal classification of "refugee" is a modern category, created in conjunction with the nation-state and international institutions like the United Nations. Following World War II, the United Nations defined a refugee as,

> [S]omeone who, owing to a well-founded fear of being persecuted for reasons of race, religion, nationality, membership of a particular social group or political opinion, is outside the country of his nationality, and is unable to, or owing to such fear, is unwilling to avail himself of the protection of that country.

Thus, refugee-ness both troubles and reproduces a "national order of things," wherein the logic of citizenship is coterminous with "national" belonging and even with personhood.[27] Nasiha's and Enisa's forced migration from Bosnia illustrates loss of the protection of the state. They simultaneously lost their Bosnian and Yugoslav rights of citizenship and became first Internally Displaced Persons (IDPs) within Bosnia, then refugees in Croatia and in the United States.

While the UN definition is the most commonly used across western democracies, this conceptualization of refugee status has been roundly critiqued as ahistorical and falsely universal, obscuring the particularities of refugee cohorts and the international and transnational politics that create them.[28] Perhaps most significantly, by excluding socio-economic concerns, this definition of refugee status erases the cumulative effects of persistent economic exploitation from consideration in an individual, or group's, plight. Not only does refugee status efface the problem of economic inequalities, but the selective granting of refugee status contributes to a hierarchy of citizenship statuses. So, for example, while refugees of the much more protracted "civil wars" in Guatemala and El Salvador—conflicts in which the United States played a significant role—sought safety in the United States during the same time Bosnians did, Central Americans overwhelmingly were denied refugee status. This distinction meant that Central Americans who made it to the United States often were not eligible for citizenship, could not take advantage of family reunification policies, and were thus far more likely to become undocumented and subject to all of the vulnerabilities that arise from that status.

As Yén Lê Espiritu demonstrates, these legal aspects of the "refugee" designation are related to yet distinct from the varied social meanings of the refugee label.[29] Among Bosnians in the United States, these social meanings were imbued with gender, racial, age, and class undertones. For example, when I interviewed Nermina, one of TCC's staff members, I asked, "What do you think it's important for people in the United States to know about your experience?" She replied, "They don't think this can happen to people like us." I sought further clarification, "What do you mean, 'people like us?'"

Nermina proceeded, ". . . you know, they, Americans, and, like, the other refugees, from Africa, from Asia [at the time Chicago was also a resettlement site for refugees of Sudan and Bhutan] don't think this can happen to people like us," repeating the phrase, but this time brushing the bare skin of her forearm to emphasize its color.[30] Bosnians belong to Balkan peoples that some critical race scholars describe as "white but not quite" and "conditionally white, conditionally European."[31] While many Bosnians may appear to be "white," and are classified as such according to U.S. census records, their "off-white" experiences of Otherness, marked by ethnicity, refugee status, language, socialist principles, and adherence to Islam meant their identifications did not fit neatly into taken-for-granted American racial classifications.[32]

Bosnians' experiences with the refugee label were also tinged by gender and class. When I asked Amer, a young Bosnian American man, whether he thought Angelina Jolie's Hollywood 2011 film based on the wars in Bosnia, *In the Land of Blood and Honey*, affected the way Americans view Bosnian immigrants in the United States, Amer replied, "Bosnian immigrants are no different than other East European immigrants, but people don't know about Yugoslavia. They think we are poverty-stricken poor immigrants, refugees—they think of poverty-stricken women with headscarves. . . ." His remarks indicated Amer's discomfort with the refugee label as a symbol of "poverty," of "women," condensed in the image of the headscarf worn by elder rural women associated with the countryside rather than the covering styles associated with the city, and with modernity. His impression of Americans' [mis]perceptions of Bosnians' lives is one that readily fits into the homogenized subcategory of "woman" that miriam cooke and Lila Abu-Lughod describe as "the Muslimwoman," a subject who, following the attacks in the United States of September 11, 2001 has been objectified as emblematic of "unfreedom" and "uncivilization," and thus in need of "saving."[33] The legal and social nuances of their refugee status in the United States at times privileged Bosnians in relation to other non-white groups *and* represented their own racialized oppression as Muslims or as "mixed" family members.

INVITATION

Bosnian women refugees have overwhelmingly been depicted as victims—as wounded rape survivors, or as elder mothers mourning lost sons. Yet such depictions barely begin to touch on women survivors' lives, on the jobs they hold, on the decisions they make about spending money, investments, and their political involvements. It obscures the social ties and tensions women forge and negotiate among one another and with the men in their lives. In many ways, these depictions also efface the variations in women's suffering and of their responses to injustices. Younger Bosnian Americans, those who were children when they arrived in the United States, expressed frustration with these one-dimensional portraits of their refugee experience. After recounting to me her experience with being interviewed by a *New York Times* reporter, Elmina, for example, wanted to know "Why don't people ask us about our lives before the war?" conveying a sense that the war overdetermines how Bosnians are received in the United States. These American preoccupations with Bosnians' wartime suffering are enabled by what Sherene Razack describes as the "slipperiness of empathy," in her treatment of Canadians' consumption of European imagery and narrative accounts of the 1994 genocide in Rwanda.[34] Influenced especially by Susan Sontag's investigation of "the pain of Others" through photojournalists' images of war, Razack argues that this process of consuming others' pain through narrative and image—what she refers to as "stealing the pain of others"—is a "national one" that allows Canadians to identify with humanitarianism and connect it to their national identity by empathically viewing others' suffering. Razack argues that ultimately such identifications further dehumanize and differentiate the "Other" through a "politics of rescue."[35]

This book invites readers to engage and unsettle such sentiments. Consider how you interact with the stories presented in this book: how do you receive and understand them? Are you consuming them passively? Are you making connections to your own experiences? What elements feel familiar to you, and what feels unfamiliar? This chapter's title, "Gathering Grounds," draws on the literal and metaphorical meanings of the words "gathering" and "grounds." In addition to describing the earth beneath one's feet, "ground" can also refer to the foundation upon which people find something in common which may serve as the basis to "gather" with others. "Gathering Grounds" also has a more mundane meaning that refers to the traditional work of preparing Bosnian coffee, or prava kafa / "the real coffee." Bosnian coffee is a type of stove top coffee process that spread from coffee-house to household in Ottoman territories during the late nineteenth century, producing variants such as "Turkish coffee" "Greek coffee," "Ethiopian coffee," and was ever-present throughout my fieldwork. Prior to the introduction of mechanized processing methods in Bosnia, adults would gather together and sort imported beans and then grind them with heavy handmills until they produced finely powder-like grounds that were then brewed on the stove top or over another heat source. Bosnian coffee making and coffee drinking is considered to be a social ritual and has its own extensive lexicon including terms for *work coffee / radnu kafu, wedding coffee / svadbena kafa, Aunties' coffee / tetkine kafe*. Depending on a household's means, coffee service might be reserved primarily for hosting guests, or, served daily among household members. Very rarely is Bosnian coffee prepared and consumed while one is alone. My discussions with Elmina, Nasiha, and others in this book led to the development of a companion project that builds connections among refugees and expands awareness of the Yugoslav region's diverse histories and global diaspora by recording their stories and images of these coffee rituals and making them available in a digital archive.

Of course, not everyone in the postwar diaspora drinks this sort of coffee. It is more often associated with elder generations and with those who have a penchant for nostalgia. But everyone is familiar with the practice, and I found it to be integral to the ways many people marked time and established social space. Refugees' many references to returning to a "normal life" were a reminder that the significance of time and space intensify and shift in the context of forced migration. The myriad meanings in "gathering grounds" highlight Bosnian refugees' ongoing efforts to establish social and material well-being in the wake of their displacements.

CHAPTER DESCRIPTIONS

Chapter 1: Refugee Women and a Chicago Volag

This chapter describes how the shift to a decentralized state and an expanded role for the market in guiding social and material relations began in Yugoslavia decades prior to the war, and before the U.S. intensive version of this shift in the 1990s. Contrary to United States popular discourse that juxtaposes Socialism and Capitalism as distinct and opposing modes of social organization, post-1970s American state capitalism and Yugoslav socialism—sometimes called "laissez-faire socialism" or "market socialism"—are better understood as political projects that are related through international economic institutions and transnational political realignments. I address the still-common mischaracterization of the wars as "ethnic wars" by beginning with a brief sketch of Yugoslavia's experiment with socialism and the political economic context leading up to the 1990s wars. I then return to Nasiha and TCC to better describe the American volag and NGO structure and argue that the Yugoslav system of worker self-management provided women of Enisa's generation with a common framework through which they interpreted the NGO volag form and operated the small organization with an entirely all-woman, all-Bosnian refugee staff.

Chapter 2: Making Home and Family after War, and from a Distance

This chapter introduces the significance of the concept of home / kuća to understanding refugees' economic and political relationships to their former, and their new, homes. We move from The Community Center to households and center our attention on kinship dynamics that appear to generate layers of debt relations. Here I explore these debt connections as linked to the U.S. housing "bubble" leading up to the 2008 recession—what many Bosnian Americans referred to as "the crisis"—and the postwar reconstruction economy in Bosnia. In particular, I describe the family expectations and obligations between generations, and the increased credit card and mortgage debts that people accumulated in order to meet and exceed these expectations. These debt relations are nested in a larger system of exchange in which the Bosnian government and economy are beholden to the "Internationals"—development and reconstruction loans from the International Monetary Fund, the World Bank, and the NGO-entities of the United States, the Netherlands, and Sweden.

Chapter 3: Ajla in Stolac

This short chapter recounts a visit to Stolac, a mountain village in the Herzegovina region. It follows the hopes and dreams of Ajla, the young cousin of Edin. When their village was violently attacked by HVO forces in 1993, Edin's family had relocated to Chicago as refugees, while Ajla's family remained in Bosnia during the war and returned to their village after 1995. The chapter describes the transnational connections between Edin's and Ajla's families and examines Ajla's efforts to increase her range of mobility even as Bosnia remained outside of the Schengen Zone, and her family depended on her for day-to-day caretaking.

Chapter 4: Shifting Time in the Social Life of Bosnian Coffee

This chapter argues for a focus on commodity-use and consumption practices to explore the nuances of refugees' political and economic lives in relation to dimensions of time. I take coffee—and coffee making and drinking practices as particularly gendered activities—as my subject. I present a brief history of coffee in Bosnia that includes its introduction in urban coffeehouses, and then into village homes and bars during the Ottoman Era. I argue that because coffee condenses myriad traditions, histories, and places—Ottoman cosmopolitanism, Islam, village, city, and the gendered spaces of the coffeehouse and the home—it serves as a strong symbol for both Bosnian national, and pan-Balkan identities. Finally, I discuss the discourse of "tired bodies" and the concept of "ćejf" that accompanies coffee-drinking among the diaspora in Chicago. In contrast to the mainstream American approach to coffee—purchase it outside the home and drink it alone, on the way to work, or while one works (e.g., Starbucks and Dunkin' Donuts)—Bosnian coffee practices create spaces that emphasize service, individual reflection, leisure, and collective evaluation. In addition to providing a critique of neoliberal time, Bosnian coffee preparation also forwards neoliberal taste aesthetics as a type of "slow food."

Chapter 5: American Balkanism and the Optics of Violence

This chapter juxtaposes close narrative readings with audience reception of several theater productions and film screenings and describes these raced and gendered portrayals of Bosnians in Chicago as an extension of what Maria Todorova calls "Balkanism." I place these representations in the broader context of a Bosnian counterpublic (Warner 2002) concerned with depictions of immigrant "success stories" and domestic violence in "the community" to illustrate the stigma of violence and refugee status felt by some among the 1.5-er generation (those who became refugees and migrated as children).

Chapter 6: A Trade in Stories

In this chapter, we see what happens when Bosnian women take up the image of "the refugee woman" in the context of high-profile genocide deliberations at the ICTY (International Criminal Tribunal for the former Yugoslavia) and ICC (International Criminal Court). I examine women's survivor narratives at U.S.-based political events in Chicago (2005) and on Capitol Hill (2009), and the resilience and resistance narratives women share in less formal settings, among family and friends. While these stories share topics—war, physical violence, survival—their differently situated narrators and audiences index gendered power differences in the refugee and migration circuit. I draw on feminist scholarship of Non-Governmental Organizations along with linguistic anthropology and performance paradigms to analyze these narrative events as sites of exchange governed by differential "framings" and "footings," and ask: What is being traded here? This exploration of survivor narratives reveals ideological tensions about the functions of speech and its potential to liberate the speaker through public testimonials. Tracing these stories' symbols and their circulation illustrates the critical value of participant observation to understanding how women negotiate and accrue power under adverse circumstances.

Chapter 7: #BiHInSolidarity / Be in Solidarity

This chapter examines the racial positioning of Bosnians in the United States through encounters in Chicago and the murder of a Bosnian refugee in St. Louis. Six days after the Ferguson jury's non-indictment of police officer Darren Wilson for the murder of unarmed teenager Michael Brown, Zemir Begić, a 32-year-old Bosnian immigrant, was brutally murdered near Bevo Mill, St. Louis, 20 miles away from Ferguson. Almost immediately, white supremacist groups started a media campaign to portray the murder as racially motivated, positing Zemir as white, and his attackers as Black. This chapter engages in "hashtag ethnography" (Bonilla and Rosa 2015) of the racialized debate that occurred over social media among Bosnian Americans regarding their racial positioning in the wake of the killings of Michael Brown and Zemir Begić, with particular attention to the ways participants linked their arguments to broader questions of security and safety, global inequality, race, and the status of Muslims in the west. Notably, Bosnian women forward the most public anti-racist stance.

Gathering Grounds: A Reflection

This concluding chapter reflects on the 2017 installation of Bosnian American artist Aida Šehović's annual "nomadic monument" memorial commemorating the Srebrenica genocide, ŠTO TE NEMA. The 2017 installation occurred in Chicago's Daley Plaza.

NOTES

1. The SFRY included six republics: Bosnia, Croatia, Macedonia, Montenegro, Serbia, and Slovenia, and two semi-autonomous provinces: Kosovo and Vojvodina. Each of the republics and Kosovo are now separate countries. Vojvodina is part of Serbia.

2. Hansen, Karen Tranberg. "Introduction," In *African Dress: Fashion, Agency, Performance*, Karen Tranberg Hansen and D. Soyini Madison, Eds. London: Bloomsbury, 2013, 3.

3. Accurate gender statistics for the Bosnian refugee population are difficult to obtain, but see for example sociologists Silva Meznarić and Jelena Zlatković Winter 1993 report drawing on UNHCR data and Slovenian and Croatian census records showing women accounted for 58.8 percent of Bosnian refugees who fled to Slovenia and Croatia, the initial destination for the majority of refugees prior to third sites such as Germany, Austria, Sweden, Turkey, Canada, and United States (Meznarić, Silva and Jelena Zlatković Winter. "Forced Migration and Refugee Flows in Croatia, Slovenia, and Bosnia-Herzegovina: Early Warning, Beginning and Current State of Flows." *Refuge* 12(7):1–5, February 1993).

4. Nasiha identified as Muslim, with her mother's family. The cases of mixed families I was acquainted with among the U.S.-based Bosnian diaspora negotiated these arrangements individually, situationally, and through a variety of accommodations. Children sometimes opted, or were encouraged, to identify more fully with one parent's family, as was the case with Nasiha. In other cases, children identified with both parents' families as was the case with Ena, whose mother was Bosnian Muslim and father was Bosnian Christian (Orthodox, Serb). Further, some family members might vehemently oppose such cross-ethnic unions, while other members of the same family accept them, or even see them as desirable. As seen later in the chapter, Nasiha and her mother were estranged from Nasiha's father early in Nasiha's childhood, and their ties to his family were weak.

5. Hajdarpašić, *Whose Bosnia?*

6. At the time of this writing, The Federal Commission for Missing Persons in Bosnia places the number of those murdered in the Srebrenica genocide at 8,372, but this is only a working number, as forensic remains are still being analyzed and identified. I cite this number out of respect to survivors for whom individuating their loved ones within the collective attack is a critical part of their grieving processes. Beginning in 2013, mass graves have been found in the Prijedor region, largest being Tomašica. The search for human remains continues with 6,500 individuals still classified as "missing" after the wars.

7. See for example Hockenos, Paul. *Homeland Calling: Exile Patriotism and the Balkan Wars*, Ithaca, NY: Cornell University Press, 2003; Skrbiš, Zlatko. *Long-Distance Nationalism: Diasporas, Homelands, and Identities*. Brookfield, VT: Ashgate, 1999; Winland, Daphne. "The Politics of Desire and Disdain: Croatian Identity between 'Home' and 'Homeland,'" *American Ethnologist* 29(3): 693–718, 2002.

8. Independence votes took place in Slovenia (1990) Croatia (1991) and Bosnia (1992). Bosnia voted overwhelmingly for independence, although there was voter intimidation in areas closest to Serbia, keeping voter turnout low. The breakaway Bosnian Serb republic allied with Serbia began declaring "autonomous zones" in the north and was occupied by the VRS shortly after the vote (Gagnon, Phillip Jr. *The Myth of Ethnic War: Serbia and Croatia in the 1990s*. Ithaca: Cornell University Press, 2004. Helms, Elissa. *Innocence and Victimhood: Gender, Nation, and Women's Activism in Postwar Bosnia-Herzegovina*. Madison: University of Wisconsin Press, 2013).

9. The other camps were Omarska, Keraterm, and Manjaca.

10. Agamben, Giorgio. *State of Exception*. Translated by Kevin Atrell. Chicago: University of Chicago, 2005 and *Homo Sacer: Sovereign Power and Bare Life*. Palo Alto: Stanford University Press, 1998. As it is for Hannah Arendt, the "camp" is Agamben's exemplary site for theorizing this process. But scholars have also analyzed racial segregation (Du Bois, W.E.B. *Darkwater*, New York: Harcourt, Brace and Company, 1920 and *Dusk of Dawn*, New York; Oxford: Oxford University Press, 2007[1940]; Fanon, Frantz. *Wretched of the Earth*, New York: Grove Press, 1991[1963]) and the United States prison industry (Gilmore, Ruth. "Fatal Couplings of Power and Difference: Notes on Racism and Geography," *The Professional Geographer* 54(1): 15–24, 2002 and Wacquant, Loic. "The Penalization of Poverty and the Rise of Neoliberalism," *European Journal on Criminal Policy and Research* (9): 401–412, 2001) as modern sites for the production of dehumanized life. For a related discussion see Mbmembe's discussion of "necropower," as the creation of worlds of "the living dead" (Mbembe, Achille. "Necropolitics," *Public Culture* (15)1: 11–40, 2003).

11. Jason De León beautifully illustrates this phenomenon in his forensic and ethnographic account of one family's efforts to locate their loved one who died in the Sonoran desert while attempting to enter the United States without legal documentation of U.S. residency (De León, *The Land of Open Graves*, Berkeley, CA: University of California Press, 2015). See also Sarah Wagner's detailed and evocative account of Srebrenica survivors contributing bodily fluids for DNA analysis to be entered into a database and matched to forensic evidence unearthed from the mass graves where the men massacred at Srebrenica were callously hidden (Wagner, Sarah. *To Know Where He Lies*, Berkeley, CA: University of California Press, 2008).

12. In this sense, my approach is aligned with that of anthropologist Ćarna Brković in her sensitive ethnography in a refugee camp located in urban Montenegro for politically persecuted and displaced Albanian-speaking ethnic Roma, Ashkalias and Balkan Egyptians (Brković, *Südosteuropa* 66(1): 10–26, 2018). Anthropologist Michael Jackson's in-depth portraits of migrants and ethics offers this reflection of "bare life": "Life is never simply bare survival, but rather a matter of realizing one's humanity in relation to others, and death never a physical extinction but only the nullification of the relationships that sustain one's life among others" (Jackson, *The Wherewithal of Life*, Cambridge, MA: Harvard University Press, 2013: 228). Paul Gilroy illustrates a similar approach in his discussion of Black cultural productions in the context of the Trans-Atlantic slave trade (Gilroy, *The Black Atlantic*, Cambridge, MA: Harvard University Press, 1993).

13. See also Kleinman, Das, and Lock for a discussion of "social suffering" (Kleinman, Das, and Lock. *Social Suffering*, Berkeley, CA: University of California Press, 1997), and Kidron for a non-pathological approach to intergenerational "lived memory" of Holocaust survivors in Israel (Kidron, Carol. "Toward an Ethnography of Silence: The Lived Presence of the Past in the Everyday Life of Holocaust Trauma Survivors and Their Descendants in Israel," *Current Anthropology* 50(1): 5–27, 2009).

14. Ralph, Lawrence. *Renegade Dreams*, Chicago: University of Chicago Press, 2015: 5.

15. See Coles, Kimberly. *Democratic Designs: International Intervention and Electoral Practices in Post-War Bosnia-Herzegovina*, Ann Arbor, MI: University of Michigan Press, 2007; Helms, *Innocence and Victimhood*, 2013.

16. Charles Briggs refers to this part of participant observation as "learning how to ask" (Briggs, Charles. *Learning How to Ask: A Sociolinguistic Appraisal of the Role of the Interview in Social Science Research*. Cambridge University Press, 2012).

17. Halilovich, Haris. *Places of Pain: Forced Displacement, Popular Memory and Trans-local Identities in Bosnian War-torn Communities*, Oxford: Berghahn, 2013: 12–13. Mimi Thi Nguyen frames Vietnamese refugee experiences in the United States as characterized by "the diagnosis of abnormality," a process that involves a "racialized rhetoric of anachronism," that places the refugee as perpetually outside of the present through what she calls "the refugee condition," Nguyen, Mimi Thi. *The Gift of Freedom: War, Debt, and Other Refugee Passages*. Durham, NC: Duke University Press, 2012: 53. See also Kidron, "Toward an Ethnography of Silence," for exploration of "non-pathological" "lived memory" among Jewish survivors' tacit experiential and embodied ways of remembering the Holocaust, practiced among surviving family members in Israel. Richard Mollica uses his therapy treatment sessions with refugees to identify shortcomings in the PTSD-pathology model and posits that survivors must be treated as "experts" in their own lives and meaning-making in order to develop a sense of "healing." Mollica, Richard. *Healing Invisible Wounds: Paths to Hope and Recovery in a Violent World*. Nashville: Vanderbilt University Press, 2009[2006].

18. See Trouillot for discussion of how historical conventions have "silenced the past" wherein he develops an expanded conceptualization of history as constantly being (re)produced through genre that include but is not limited to academic scholarship. See also Comaroff and Comaroff reworking of Mills' "sociological imagination" to propose "imaginative sociology" as a methodology for exploring social worlds and history-making (Trouillot, Michel-Rolph. *Silencing the Past: Power and the Production of History*. Boston: Beacon Press, 1995; Comaroff, John and Jean Comaroff. *Ethnography and the Historical Imagination*. Taylor & Francis, 1992).

19. di Leonardo, Micaela. *Exotics at Home: Anthropologies, Others, American Modernity.* Chicago: University of Chicago Press, 1998: 74.

20. See Maskovsky, Jeff. "Critical Anthropologies of the United States," In *Handbook of Sociocultural Anthropology*, edited by James Carrier and Deborah Gewertz. London: Berg Press, 2013.

21. Čapo, Jasna. "Ethnology and Anthropology in Europe: Toward a Trans-National Discipline," *Cultural Analysis* 13(2014): 51–76, 2015: 60. Earlier studies in SFRY focused primarily on rural peasant communities, while urban studies became more prevalent during the 1970s. Some of the elder women participants assumed I would want to learn about rural practices and traditions rather than their urban contexts in Yugoslavia and the United States.

22. Madison, D. Soyini. *Critical Ethnography: Method, Ethics, and Performance*. Los Angeles: Sage, 2012: 5.

23. Davis, Dana-Ain and Christa Craven. *Feminist Ethnography: Thinking Through Methodologies, Challenges, and Possibilities*. Lanham, MD: Rowman & Littlefield, 2016.

24. Gal, Susan and Gail Kligman. *The Politics of Gender after Socialism: A Comparative Historical Essay*. Princeton, NJ: Princeton University Press, 2000a; Gal, Susan and Gail Kligman. *Reproducing Gender: Politics, Publics, and Everyday Life after Socialism*. Princeton, NJ: Princeton University Press, 2000b. See Arlie Hochschild for U.S.-based analysis of this phenomenon (Hochschild, Arlie. *The Second Shift*. Viking, 1989).

25. Grigoryeva, Angelina. "When Gender Trumps Everything: The Division of Parent Care Among Siblings," *The Center for the Study of Social Organization* (*CSSO*), Working Paper #9, April 2014.

26. Scholars of home-life in pre- and postwar Bosnia have noted the centrality of women's hosting practices to how individuals situated themselves as moral beings in relation to family members and neighbors, a point I discuss further in chapter 4.

27. Malkki, Liisa. "Refugees and Exile: From 'Refugee Studies' to the National Order of Things," *Annual Review of Anthropology* 24: 495–523, 1995.

28. Malkki, Liisa. "Speechless Emissaries: Refugees, Humanitarianism, and Dehistorization," *Cultural Anthropology* 11(3): 377–404, 1996; Ong, Aiwha. *Buddha is Hiding: Refugees, Citizenship, the New America*, Berkeley: University of California Press, 2003.

29. Espiritu, "Toward a Critical Refugee Study: The Vietnamese Refugee Subject in US Scholarship." *Journal of Vietnamese Studies*, 1(1–2): 410–433, 2006.

30. Catherine Besteman's study of Somali Bantu refugee resettlement to Lewiston, ME demonstrates how U.S. immigration policy reproduces racialized hierarchies and discriminates against refugees from Sub-Saharan Africa (Besteman, Catherine. *Making Refuge: Somali Bantu Refugees and Lewiston, Maine*. Durham, NC: Duke University Press, 2016).

31. Alcoff, Linda Martín. What Should White People Do? *Hypatia* 13(3): 6–26, 1998, 9; Baker, Catherine. *Race and the Yugoslav Region: Postsocialist, Post-Conflict, Postcolonial?* Manchester University Press, 2018, 123.

32. See Brodkin, Karen. *How the Jews Became White Folks and What That Says About Race in America*. New Brunswick, NJ: Rutgers University Press, 1998, 1–2.

33. cooke, miriam. "The Muslim woman," *Contemporary Islam* 1: 139–154, 2007; Abu-Lughod, *Do Muslim Women Need Saving?* Cambridge, MA: Harvard University Press, 2013; Abu-Lughod, "The Cross-Publics of Ethnography: The Case of the 'Muslimwoman,'" *American Ethnologist* 43(4): 595–608, 2016.

34. Razack, Sherene. "Stealing the Pain of Others: Reflections on Canadian Humanitarian Responses," *The Review of Education, Pedagogy, and Cultural Studies* 29:4(375–394), 2007, 376.

35. Razack, "Stealing the Pain" 381; Sontag, Susan. *Regarding the Pain of Others*. New York: Farrar, Straus and Giroux, 2003.

Chapter One

Refugee Women and a Chicago Volag

After evaluating my too-casual attire, Nasiha reached into a creme-colored cloth bag and pulled out a small bound weekly planner. She opened the planner and removed a photo of herself and Enisa upon their arrival in 1995 at Chicago's International O'Hare Airport. The mother and teenaged daughter stand in front of "Baggage Claim #2" and behind donated blue vinyl duffle bags from the International Organization for Migration (IOM) bearing the women's refugee numbers for processing with U.S. Customs agents. The bags contain the only belongings they were able to leave with from Bosnia. Nasiha is standing next to Enisa and smiling directly at the camera. She is thinner, her hair is shorter, but her smile is recognizable, unmistakable. The distant Chicago relatives there to welcome them cast warm looks at Nasiha and her mom, while Nasiha's young girl cousin follows Nasiha's lead and smiles directly at the camera. Enisa is much thinner than I know her to be. Her jeans and t-shirt are several sizes too big for her angular frame. She is not looking at the camera, the Aunties, Nasiha, nor the girl-cousin. Her gaze is elsewhere.

Nasiha remembers their first year as a time filled with confusion. "It was a big shock—in other countries where people were going into the system as refugees [there was a process] . . . here [United States] no one explained the system—we weren't awarded any special status as refugees—just public aid, which we didn't want anyway." In fact, the United States did have a "system," for resettling refugees. The 1980 Refugee Act for the first time formalized federal policies for screening, accepting, and resettling refugees. The act created the Office of Refugee Resettlement (ORR), in the Department of Health and Human Services, along with the institutional infrastructure—offices, jobs, administrative trainings and protocols—needed to receive and resettle refugees. Yet, there was great variation in local applications of these policies.[1]

The ORR coordinates with international agencies like the Red Cross, which screens people for refugee status, and grants contracts to U.S.-based non-profit and private organizations that can help refugees gain access to such basic resources as housing, employment, health care, and language classes. These organizations are called "volags," an abbreviation of "voluntary agencies," which are by and large faith-based, primarily affiliated with Christian and Jewish sects. TCC for example was incorporated and registered as a 501(c)(3) non-profit organization and subsidized by a private liberal arts religious university. In their applications for government contracts volags must show they have the capacity to provide the resources above, and, if their bid is successful, the federal government reimburses the volag a fixed per capita fee for providing these services. Thus, this policy established the basis for a public-private alliance built on existing institutions and social relations embedded in principles of faith-based humanitarianism. By the start of the Bosnian Wars in 1991, this structure was ten years old, and Chicago was home to the largest and most well-established refugee-service contracting agencies in the country; only New York City and Los Angeles have resettled more refugees than Chicago.[2]

But TCC had not yet been established in 1995 when Nasiha and Enisa arrived in Chicago and they were resettled by a much larger volag. The lack of institutional supports Nasiha describes was the result of broad shifts in normative approaches to governance that extended far beyond the Chicago region, the United States, or even capitalist democracies. This chapter describes how the shift to a decentralized state and an expanded role for the market in guiding social and material relations began in Yugoslavia decades prior to the war, and before the U.S. intensive version of this shift in the 1990s. Contrary to United States popular discourse that juxtaposes Socialism and Capitalism as distinct and opposing modes of social organization, post-1970s American state capitalism and Yugoslav socialism—sometimes called "laissez-faire socialism" or "market socialism"— are better understood as political projects that are related through international economic institutions and transnational political realignments. I address the still-common mischaracterization of the wars as "ethnic wars" by beginning with a brief sketch of Yugoslavia's experiment with socialism and the political economic context leading up to the 1990s wars. I then return to Nasiha and TCC to better describe the American volag and NGO structure and argue that the Yugoslav system of worker self-management provided women of Enisa's generation with a common framework through which they interpreted the NGO volag form and operated the small organization with an entirely all-woman, all-Bosnian refugee staff for two years.

YUGOSLAVIA'S LATE TWENTIETH CENTURY SOCIALISM

The Yugoslav state that emerged after World War II was initially aligned with the Soviet-style socialist system characterized by nationalizing companies and substituting centralized planning for markets. Yet by 1948, the Stalinist-dominated Cominform uniting the Communist Parties of Eastern and Western Europe "dramatically expelled Yugoslavia" over ideological differences and the Yugoslav state would go on to establish an approach to national development that served as a model for political economic projects around the world. Joanna Bockman writes that the Yugoslav approach incorporated a critique of "both the state socialism of the Soviet Union and the state capitalism of the U.S. as hopelessly bureaucratic and monopolistic," and sought to encourage "the withering away of the state . . . to move closer to communism."[3] This approach emphasized worker self-management and decentralized state and economy and envisioned a new ordering of economic relations between the global North and South through the Non-Aligned Movement (NAM) of formerly colonized countries including India, Indonesia, and Egypt. The NAM countries hoped to create an alternative geopolitical framework in the midst of the Cold War through their refusal to align neither with American-style state capitalism, nor with Soviet-style state socialism.

As soon as the Communist League of Yugoslavia (LCY) left the Soviet Cominform, the United States initiated international relations overtures with the newly independent country. The first U.S. loan to the SFRY (1949) removed the trade ban on U.S. imports and United States investment grew over the next decade with $1.2 billion in military and economic aid to Yugoslavia between 1949–1955 followed by $632.1 million between 1955–1960. In exchange for these trade relations, Yugoslavia was to develop its own standing military and serve as the security bulwark for NATO's "southern flank." Yugoslavia also maintained more tenuous trade relations with the Soviet Union. The SFRY economy thrived during this period, as did its foreign relations. Yugoslavia was a founding member and the only European member country of the Non-Aligned Movement, hosting the alliance's first meeting in the capital city Belgrade, 1961, and it was also an original signatory of the World Bank, the primary financial institution of Cold War capitalist states.

Bockman describes the Yugoslav-style socialism as characterized by 1) decentralization of the state and economy, 2) worker-based economic democracy, 3) movement away from state ownership of the means of production, and 4) toward an expanded role for markets.[4] While nineteenth century economic development models centered on transition from peasant to industrial economic production, many twentieth century development economists theorized transitions from capitalism to communism by way of socialism. In its pursuit of market socialism, SFRY leadership also developed a complex "national key," based on state-sanctioned categories of "nation," "nationality," and "ethnic" group belonging that served as a rubric for government administration and socialized employment. This system institutionalized axes of unequal difference through these classifications: "Nations" included Yugoslav groups with territories (Croats, Serbs, Macedonians, etc.), "nationalities" included nations with external territories (ethnic Germans, Hungarians, etc.), and "ethnicities" included groups without European territories such as Jews and Roma. As with labor identities, these national identities were theorized to ideally "wither away" along with the state.

Since the Yugoslav system had already "transitioned" to market socialism, it was viewed as more evolved in development schema and was declared a "success" by the World Bank in 1972.[5] In Yugoslavia, workers' councils acted as entrepreneurs and increasingly relied on banks for finance while central planning was abolished. The pursuit of worker self-management fostered a system of social ownership whereby "one's place of work was the center of one's social universe," although admission to public sector employment was not universally accessible to all SFRY citizens.[6] Worker's councils governed factories, schools, hospitals, groceries, banks and foreign trade firms and were comprised of a "labor aristocracy" belonging to the country's most highly skilled workers. This system of socialist full employment in fact also included "socialist unemployment" and depended both on household economies, which Susan Woodward describes as "in essence, a private sector," and labor migration and remittances to mask social and material shortcomings and inequalities in employment.[7]

By the early 1980s this system reached a crisis point as people struggled to contend with a global economic downturn made especially apparent in World Bank and International Monetary Fund imposition of austerity measures and Structural Adjustment Program (SAP) reforms that demanded intensive privatization and radically restructured exchange relations between Yugoslavia and the western financial institutions. As the Yugoslav republics endeavored to meet restructured debt obligations and the promise of full employment, political reactions came most loudly from those who were for the first time threatened with unemployment and were expressed through a language of nationalism that turned virulently ethno-nationalist by the late 1980s. Serb ethno-nationalists used anti-Muslim racist language to refer to Yugoslav Muslims with the racist epithet "balija," and as "Turks," a derogatory displacement projecting Bosnian Muslims as former Ottoman occupiers of the region. "Exploitation" was no longer discussed in Marxist terms but transmogrified to characterize economic exploitation as between nations in the federal system. According to Woodward, this shift to ethno-nationalism "can only be explained once international conditions are taken into account."[8]

With the end of the Cold War, Yugoslavia's stability was no longer seen as integral to U.S./NATO security and in spring of 1991 neither the United States nor the European Community countries were willing to loan SFRY the necessary funds to meet its foreign debt obligation. This despite the fact that these countries continued to extend such loans to Hungary, Czech Republic, and Poland. Austria, Germany, Switzerland, and Italy led international support for Slovenian and Croatian independence while the western democracies instituted a military weapons embargo on Bosnia when the republic followed Slovenia and Croatia with its own independence referendum. What remained of "Yugoslavia"—Serbia and Montenegro—had control of much of the Yugoslav National Army artillery and received weaponry from non-western countries that made it possible for the Bosnian Serb Army (VRS) to perpetrate extraordinary violence against civilians and the multi-ethnic population's cultural infrastructure, targeting historic Ottoman-era bridges and religious sites. Croatian militia mirrored these attacks in northwest Bosnia beginning in 1993 as both Serbia and Croatia sought to extend their new states into adjacent Bosnian territory, only stopping when NATO finally intervened in late August 1995.

In her study of gendered victimhood in postwar Bosnia-Herzegovina (BiH), Elissa Helms documents the ways that "ethnic war" functions as what Arjun Appadurai famously labeled "gate-keeping" concepts that largely structure and funnel popular and scholarly accounts of a particular region, blinding researchers to social forces and relations that don't comport to the gate-keeping concept.[9] In the case of the Yugoslav region, Woodward locates this phenomenon in the shift from Cold War to its aftermath: "Wars during the Cold War came to be called ideological wars whereas those occurring since 1989–1990 are labeled ethnic wars, or wars of identity."[10] The Yugoslav Wars of the 1990s were never solely "ethnic wars," and to gloss them as such obscures the transnational origins of the conflicts and the complex local interactions of class, region, gender, and ethnic differences through which individuals experienced and interpreted their situations.

SINGLE MOMS MARK THE MARGINS

In the introduction to their reappraisal of Yugoslavia's demise, Archer, Duda, and Stubbs use the dire circumstances of a single mom living in 1980s Belgrade to "bring class back in" to discussions of Yugoslav society. The story of "Zora" is published in the woman's magazine, *Bazar* and describes her as among more than 2,000 poor Belgrade residents who have had their electricity cut off because they cannot afford to pay the bill. Following Zora's factory worker husband's death in a traffic accident, she is left alone to support four daughters and cannot sustain employment because she is chronically ill, and she endeavors to earn what she can by selling needlework she makes at home. Her husband's meager pension barely covers the cost of the minimal monthly electricity payment, but apparently disqualifies the household from receiving any subsidy. Trade unionists take up Zora's story as cause to shame the electricity distributor for failing to provide service to the city's poor residents, and the authors note that her account centers on increasingly common concerns among pre- and post-war Yugoslavs:

> Worries about limited and differential access to education and housing, a concern with falling living standards and reduced social mobility, deficient social welfare and unpredictable responses by the authorities, and reflections on the individual's relation to the state and society.[11]

Such concerns are increasingly voiced by many residents of the United States, as they were by Bosnian Yugoslavs when they arrived in the United States as refugees. As some have argued, Yugoslavia's market socialism by the 1990s may be understood as providing an opening for neoliberal projects. Bockman, for example, characterizes late Yugoslav socialism as an environment amenable to neoliberalism that she defines as advocating for competitive markets, smaller authoritarian states, hierarchical firms, management, and owners, and capitalism and joins Collier in calling for more attention to how some political projects of the left relate to neoliberalising forms of governance.[12] Yugoslavia's introduction of neoliberal reforms may be seen as coinciding with, or perhaps even preceding, neoliberal reform in the United States. As in Yugoslavia, these reforms were often debated in public fora through gender, class, and racialized/ethnic depictions of the deserving and undeserving poor.

Bosnians began entering the country as refugees just as the United States government was implementing neoliberal reforms to social welfare programs that would radically alter social support systems for those who found themselves in precarious circumstances. Unlike the Yugoslav media's championing of Zora's single-mom pleas for assistance, the U.S. media campaigns promoting welfare policy changes centered on barely disguised racist and sexist stereotypes of female single parents as decidedly undeserving of assistance. Dorothy Roberts describes how this public attack on poor women promoted a racialized image of the so-called "welfare queen"—also assumed to be a single mom—by relying on recycled racist tropes that deny and stigmatize Black women's labor and kinship ties. Nasiha's attitude toward public aid, "we didn't want it anyway," illustrated the ways that many Bosnians encountered the stigma associated with receiving public aid, and sought to distance themselves from this form of government assistance.[13] Thus many, like Nasiha, came to adopt this attitude of stigma themselves. Yet, as she continued to recount her experiences, she expressed a more nuanced view, pointing out that situations arise wherein people need help that their social networks of family and friends may not be able to provide:

> We had public aid for a month and we went to work right away. The agency [volag] caseworker sent people to factories, hotels ... within a month I had a job at a clothing store, and my mother had a hotel job in housekeeping. And then they denied us public assistance! Together our check was $800 and our rent was $500! And they said we made too much money! We couldn't believe it!

Like Zora the Belgradian mom, Enisa learned that what little income she did have disqualified her household from receiving much-needed subsidies for basic needs.

Nasiha's and Enisa's accelerated placement in low-wage service jobs illustrates the coordination among volags, local public assistance offices, and employers as defined by the new policy reforms known as the Personal Responsibility and Work Opportunity Reconciliation Act (PRWORA 1996) and the Workforce Investment Act (WIA 1998). Jane Collins notes that in the American Midwest "rust belt," these policy strategies were shaped by structural changes in the deindustrializing labor market where off-shored manufacturing jobs are replaced by the addition of jobs that are by and large low-wage, rely on devalued labor of women, racial and ethnic minorities, and immigrants, and offer few benefits—for example, stocking shelves at retail outlets, and vacuuming hotel rooms.[14] Between 1980–1990 the Chicago metropolitan region saw a devastating net loss of 150,000 manufacturing jobs, and Bosnian refugees who began arriving at the end of this decade provided a vulnerable, skilled and semi-skilled, labor force in this radically altered jobs landscape in which the state, employers, and the city were increasingly divesting from worker training, compensation, and well-being.[15]

Collins further examines this neoliberal policy shift as the "precarity fix," building on geographer David Harvey's "spatial fix." Harvey uses the "spatial fix" to illustrate how contemporary globalization arises from the problem of overaccumulation within capitalist economic systems: "Overaccumulation, in its most virulent form (as occurred in the 1930s, for example) is registered as surpluses of labor and capital side by side with seemingly no way to put them together in productive, i.e., 'profitable' as opposed to socially useful ways."[16] Geographic expansion and market reconfiguration, for example, to new commodity markets, or to new or newly restructured labor markets provides a temporary "spatial fix" to these problems. According to Collins, we can understand the new "gig economies" and people's efforts to patch together numerous employment strategies in the face of increasingly unstable labor markets as a "precarity fix" for the problem of overaccumulation, and the problems brought about by the spatial fix of globalization. Privatizing public assets (for example electricity/energy sources, water) and programs (education and schools, hospitals and healthcare) and selling them back to people for a fee may be seen as an extension of the precarity fix. Like Zora's efforts to manage her household's vulnerability by combining home-based needlework and her deceased husband's meager pension, many Bosnians arriving in America had similarly been developing such coping strategies prior to the onset of war as employment brought fewer benefits as early as the 1970s.

During the neoliberal reforms in the United States, municipalities across the country have drawn on the labor of their communities' most materially and socially vulnerable individuals to fill the least desirable jobs. Barbara Franz's interviews with Bosnian refugees resettled during this same time period in New York City reveal a pattern similar to that described by Nasiha: discouragement from accessing public aid and pushed into low-wage jobs, with caseworkers sometimes taking advantage of refugees' language barriers and lack of knowledge of the social welfare system in the United States and denying them altogether, even though the refugees qualified for assistance.[17]

In Chicago, Nasiha and Enisa were assigned to a studio apartment in a part of Uptown that was known for absentee landlords who willingly rented to refugees and poor immigrants and, similar to the public aid caseworkers, took advantage of refugees' language and cultural barriers and lack of familiarity with local tenants' rights to avoid adequately maintaining their properties. Within several months, Enisa had moved them out of that apartment and into a one-bedroom apartment in a better building, albeit in the same neighborhood. "My mom wouldn't stand for that, regardless of the language barrier," recalled Nasiha.

"My mom wanted to make a normal life . . . we had a good apartment, we had jobs, I got another job at Jewel (regional grocery chain), and then Old Navy, and I started figuring out the different options for college . . . all of this helped with the healing. There was a sense that life continues." Nasiha benefited greatly from Enisa's determination to "make a normal life," a "normal" that was notably drawn from Enisa's expectations for social well-being as established in Yugoslavia, where prior to the war she had held a good socialized job in a bank and Nasiha was enrolled in their city's best local high school. By the time I met her in 2004 Nasiha was in her third year of employment as the Assistant Director of a local non-profit organization.

As Nasiha wondered aloud at her mom's spirit, she also remarked at how lucky they were in comparison to so many others. She had co-migrant friends who had never finished high school because of the war, and whose parents were so traumatized by the war and their displacements that they were unable to work. Their parents were not able to learn English well enough to advocate for themselves the way that Enisa had. When I asked Ena, a young teenaged girl I met at TCC, to tell me what she remembered about the first apartment her family lived in upon arrival in Chicago, she held up her hand to show me a finger with a severed tip. She explained that she'd lost the fingertip when a window suddenly shut on it. The pulley rope in the window had worn so thin that it snapped, and her small toddler-hand was holding onto the windowsill at the time. When I expressed alarm, she laughed and said, "That apartment was a mess! There were maybe fourteen of us living there with one bedroom . . . we had a fire too! The electricity wires in the wall caught fire and burned a hole in the wall!" For Ena, the catastrophe-ridden apartment represented a different sort of "normal" than that envisioned and achieved by Enisa and Nasiha, highlighting the inequalities within this refugee cohort.

TCC: A VOLAG OPERATED BY REFUGEE WOMEN

Chicago is home to several large volags, some with dozens of staff members, occupying multi-room offices on the city's north side. I had visited several of these and in the end settled on TCC, a more modest operation, as one of my field sites. Americans occupied the senior staff positions in the other volags I'd visited, while some refugees who possessed professional skills and English language proficiency were employed as assistant caseworkers to assist with housing and job placements, and I was struck by the fact that TCC was staffed entirely by Bosnian refugee women. Most of the women had arrived during the war and thus had been in the United States for nearly a decade. All had held what Nermina described as "good jobs," in socialized professional positions in Yugoslavia, prior to the war.

As with all volags, TCC was incorporated through the state as a non-profit 501(c)(3) tax exempt organization because of their service and education objectives and pledge not to profit from providing these services. TCC depended on federal, state, and city contracts and philanthropic donations from foundations and individuals to pay salaries for an Executive Director, three full-time, and one part-time staff members tasked with providing youth and senior programming, English as a Second Language (ESL) classes, and assistance with social services. Their mandate was to provide these services to any eligible refugee-immigrant, but in my two years there I rarely observed anyone who was not Bosnian, and not European seeking services. TCC had no one on staff who could speak languages other than Bosnian and English and was located just a short walk from a volag serving primarily Central American refugee-immigrants and another serving primarily refugee-immigrants from

South Asia and the Middle East, in particular Muslim immigrants from these regions. The other volags both had staff members who spoke at least one of the languages used by the majority of their service population.

Volags are a form of non-profit organization, and non-profits are a form of Non-Governmental Organization, a corporate form that has proliferated globally since the 1990s, so much so that it is often referred to as the "third sector" because it blends both "public" and "private" economies and modes of operation. Scholars of NGOs have noted that "what constitutes an NGO is profoundly gendered."[18] NGOs often provide social services such as training and education, domestic and sexual violence survivor services, health and wellness, that are less frequently provided by the state and often cannot be provided at the household level. Because NGOs tend to serve primarily female populations, and are often primarily staffed by women, it is considered a "feminized" sector of the economy. This was the case at TCC where the vast majority of "clients" served were women and children.

Scholars of volags have noted how the form may exploit ethnic, political, and class differences among refugee populations. For example, in her study of volags serving Cambodian refugee-immigrants in 1990s California, Aihwa Ong found that staff—some of whom were white, others who were Chinese American—often saw their jobs assisting refugees as "ridding cultural Others" of their "primitive-ness," a process she describes as a form of "ethnic cleansing." Caroline Brettell notes a different use of the volag form which she sees as amenable to the accrual of varied forms of social capital. She argues in her study of Asian Indian immigrants in early-aughts Texas that immigrants used volags to grow their social capital. Brettell isolates two forms of capital that she differentiates as "bonding capital" through which immigrants intensified their religious and regional social networks via intra-group social events, and "bridging capital," through which immigrants participated in inter-group social events and developed Pan-Asian social networks.

The TCC staff by and large were very committed to embracing Bosnians of all class and regional backgrounds, however, it was sometimes more difficult for refugees in mixed-status families to be heard at TCC. For example, during the senior women's group discussion of what constituted an appropriate emblem of "Bosnian culture" for display at the city's winter holiday celebration, "Christmas Trees From Around The World," Ajša and Zumreta wanted to include dolls wearing replicas of the traditional folk dress of various Bosnian ethnic groups, but their suggestions were side-lined by others who said that TCC should include only the doll dressed in the flowing dimije pants and women's fez that were reminiscent of provincial Muslim women's festive wear in the nineteenth century. The volag, then, is also an institutional form that may produce ethnicity.

Historically NGOs arose as a challenge to "state" forms, in the sense that it is "defined by something it is not—in other words, it is assumed *not* to be the state."[19] NGOs are also assumed not to be "the market," but in seeking competition for funding, grant-seeking, and donations, NGO staff must engage in significant entrepreneurial activities.[20] Thus, similar to the "worker-self-managed" firms of Yugoslav market socialism, the American volag/NGO relies on market relations to maintain its operations. In fact, the "Christmas Tree Festival" was foremost on Nermina's mind (TCC's Executive Director) because it was hosted by the Cook County Commissioner's office and she was advised by a contact at the Illinois Coalition for Immigrant and Refugee Rights that the event was an opportunity to increase TCC's "visibility" among potential state funding agencies.

Critics of NGOs identify the pressure to marketize and compete for funding as a primary structural flaw in the form. Because donors' mandates drive programming and staffing, and donor mandates can change according to shifts in state policy, or philanthropic trends, programming and staffing lack stability. In this sense, the NGO form differs from the ideal of worker-self managed firms where workers were guaranteed their job, could not be fired at-will, and did not have to continuously raise their own salary.

Although many Bosnians still could not safely return to their pre-war homes in the early aughts, their priority refugee status was much-reduced by the end of the 1990s, and by 2005, their efforts to continue to receive funding as a refugee-serving volag were met with far less success. Refugees fleeing more recent conflicts were arriving in Chicago and the state had canceled Bosnians' priority status. Not only was funding re-directed; there was also less of it. As were the public assistance offices, volags were subject to the neoliberal shrinking of funding for social welfare services and had to compete over a smaller and smaller "pie," while larger volags with advertising budgets packaged the dire stories of the newest refugee cohorts in glossy brochures and mailers in efforts to expand their philanthropic donor base, thereby increasing the "visibility" of a different refugee population's plight. This competitive market for refugee services led to pressure to hold onto "refugee" status, a development that became especially apparent during a performance of Eve Ensler's play, *Necessary Targets* in 2005.

ARE WE REALLY REFUGEES ANYMORE?

On a gusty fall day, Nasiha and I fought the headwinds on Chicago's Sheridan Road, at the curve by Devon Avenue. The road follows the southwestern shore of Lake Michigan, whose roiling gray waves were crashing in, bringing sandy sediment ashore. On this particular evening, gusts from the wind-tunnels created by the university's multi-story buildings blasted our cheeks as we approached the campus theater. It was the opening night of a student production of feminist playwright Eve Ensler's drama, *Necessary Targets*, based on Ensler's experience visiting a Red Cross refugee camp in Croatia, during the 1990s wars. When the play's director contacted TCC in search of a Bosnian language consultant, Nasiha volunteered. She had told me she was nervous about doing the translating since she is not a language specialist, and also because she feared working on the play might bring back bad memories. But she also felt connected to the play because of her direct experiences as a refugee in Trnopolje. We approached the building and fought against the wind to open the door and stepped quickly inside as the door blew shut behind us.

Nasiha saw her friend Dženi waving to her from the middle of the audience. We made our way over to Dženi and settled in to watch the performance, which centers on interactions among two western feminist professional volunteers (a psychologist and a journalist) and a diverse group of Bosnian and Croatian women refugees. The play was followed by an all-female panel discussion, "Creating Community Across Cultures: Women in Bosnia and Local Responsibility," among a student who volunteers with a local refugee resettlement agency, a documentary filmmaker, professors of theater, communication, and women's studies, and Nermina, from TCC.

Nermina was in her late forties, Nasiha's and Dženi's mothers' generation. Nermina was very concerned about potential budget shortfalls at TCC and welcomed the panel as a platform to remind the audience about TCC's work. Nermina was introduced first, and she used the play as a springboard to discuss her personal experiences as a refugee. She launched into a vivid narrative recounting the horrors of the war. She related how she and her family were forced from their homes and jobs, held in concentration camps, then transferred to refugee camps, and then once in the United States struggled with language barriers and cultural differences. She concluded with general observations on the war, drawing analogies between the experiences of Bosnian Muslims during the 1990s wars in the SFRY and those of European Jews during World War II.

I had heard Nermina give her wartime account before, when I first interviewed her. She would tell it later that month at the annual benefit dinner for TCC, and in letters to the local alderman, a state representative, and congressional representatives. I wondered if it was difficult for her to keep re-telling such a painful story, and if she felt pressure to do so in order to make the case for TCC's funding, but when I had posed this question to her she brushed it aside, saying only that "it was important that people know that this happened . . . that it happened in Europe." After Nermina's introduction, the remaining panelists introduced themselves and offered some brief observations about the play and then invited questions from the audience comprised primarily of university students. Rather than offer a question, one of Nermina's co-workers from TCC, Biba, added her own personal narrative of wartime victimization, enduring threats, violence, and the trauma of their aftermath. Biba also ended her narrative with an analogy to the World War II Holocaust.

Nasiha, seeming agitated, leaned over to me and said, "I think I'm gonna say something," and then stood up. She told the audience that wartime experiences differed by time and region. The mass killings and concentration camps set up in and around Prijedor in 1992 were distinct from the siege of Sarajevo in 1992–1996, and from the assaults carried out between Muslim and Catholic Bosnians in Mostar in 1994. Nasiha continued on and said that many Bosnian war refugees reject victimhood and instead embraced survivorhood and want to emphasize their resilience, illustrating her claims through examples of refugees who had found "success" in Chicago: "good jobs, good apartments, and education." She ended by noting that "It has been ten years" since the war in Bosnia had ended and asked, "Are we really refugees anymore?"

According to United States refugee policy in 2005, Bosnians were no longer considered priority status refugees. But according to Nermina, and Biba, they were still refugees—at a very a practical level, their "good jobs" depended on their ability to persuasively present Bosnians as refugees in need. Further, efforts at "return" were often met with hostility, particularly in the RS entity and in the Herzegovina region. For many, the formal "right of return" was not a realistic possibility, and thus "refugee" status remained an appropriate characterization of their situation. The pressures Nermina and Biba may have felt to narrate trauma stories, and the impetus behind Nasiha's reworking of their stories' formulaic modes into collective regional diversity of wartime experiences: Prijedor versus Sarajevo versus Mostar, and change: we were refugees / we are no longer refugees connect to writer Susan Sontag's reflection on objections to a war photography exhibit in Sarajevo that was mounted during the war.

Sontag famously visited Sarajevo many times during the war and recalls a story shared by one of her photojournalist friends, Englishman Paul Lowe. Lowe had been living in the besieged city for nearly a year when in 1994 he mounted an exhibit of Sarajevo photographs along with those he'd taken a few years earlier during political violence in Somalia. Lowe describes to Sontag how the Sarajevans who attended the exhibit expressed offense at his inclusion of the Somalia photos. In Songtag's understanding, Lowe saw his exhibit materials as a body of work that he was proud of while the Sarajevans took issue with having their experiences appear as wartime typology rather than nuanced by time and space. She reflects on the possibility of interpreting the Sarajevans' responses as imbued with racism, but also focuses on how the erasures of particularities can also be experienced as a form of violence:

> The atrocities taking place in Sarajevo have nothing to do with what happens in Africa, they exclaimed. Undoubtedly there was a racist tinge to their indignation—Bosnians are Europeans, people in Sarajevo never tired of pointing out to their foreign friends—but they would have objected too if, instead, pictures of atrocities committed against civilians in Chechnya or in Kosovo, indeed in any other country, had been included in the show. *It is intolerable to have one's own sufferings twinned with anybody else's.*[21]

Nermina's and Biba's efforts to continue to raise funds for TCC depended on the persuasive power of seeing Bosnian refugees as a distinct group, unified by their wartime plight. But Bosnians' traumas were no longer defined as urgent in U.S. refugee policy, and neither were they among American donors, nor by some Bosnians themselves—as Nasiha's post-performance rejoinder illustrated.

CONCLUSION

Since at least 1955, the Socialist Federal Republic of Yugoslavia had long-standing international economic relations with the United States in the form of development loans, security agreements, and economic planning models. In the years leading up to and following the end of the cold war, governments in both Yugoslavia and the United States responded to global economic shifts with policies that intensified and expanded social inequality among their residents, and poor women's experiences were coopted in public discourse through claims to who was "deserving" and "undeserving" of state benefits. During this same period, the worker self-management model in Yugoslavia faltered and the Non-Governmental Organization was on the rise globally, fully integrated into the American refugee resettlement system by the time Bosnians began to arrive in the early 1990s.

Bosnian refugee women with socialist employment histories were able to establish some worker autonomy through the NGO-form in Chicago. Yet the donor-based NGO volag funding demands required Bosnians to emphasize their refugee-ness and ethnic identities in order to continue operations. This dynamic had the effect of crowding out the variety of experiences among the wartime diaspora and functioned also to produce the appearance of ethnic coherence among Bosnians, and ethnic difference between Bosnians and other refugee cohorts, and other Americans. The TCC leadership's coupling of refugee-ness and ethnicity in the context of an American

NGO illustrates how ethnicity and refugee identities were reworked in response to the erosion of social and material well-being. While TCC was a resource for Chicago's Bosnian diaspora, many struggled at the household-level to maintain transnational family obligations to those in Bosnia where struggles with post-war reconstruction compounded the challenges of making a living for those who remained.

NOTES

1. Notably ORR is located in the Department of Health and Human Services (DHHS) while United States Citizenship and Immigration Services (USCIS) is now located in the Department of Homeland Security (DHS), created in 2001, after the September 11 attacks.

2. During the aughts, Chicago ranked #3 in U.S. municipalities' refugee populations, after New York City and Los Angeles (Singer, Audrey and Jill H. Wilson. "Refugee Resettlement in Metropolitan America," Migration Information Source March 1, 2007 last accessed 9.20.2019, http://www.migrationpolicy.org/article/refugee-resettlement-metropolitan-america).

3. Bockman, Johanna. *Markets in the Name of Socialism: The Left-Wing Origins of Neoliberalism*. Stanford: Stanford University Press, 2011, 78.

4. Bockman, *Markets*, 77.

5. Bockman, *Markets*, 101.

6. Woodward, Susan. "The Political Economy of Ethno-Nationalism," *Socialist Register*, 2003, 76.

7. Woodward, "Political Economy," Woodward writes that in SFRY, "Unemployment was high (and largely structural), but it was largely invisible," 84.

8. Woodward, "Political Economy," 85.

9. Helms, *Innocence and Victimhood*, University of Wisconsin Press: Madison, 2013, 37–40; Appadurai, Arjun. "Theory in Anthropology: Center and Periphery," *Comparative Studies in Society and History* 28(2): 356–361, 1986. See also Gagnon, Phillip Jr. *The Myth of Ethnic War: Serbia and Croatia in the 1990s*. Ithaca, NY: Cornell University Press, 2004.

10. Woodward, "Political Economy," 74.

11. Archer, Duda, Stubbs, Eds. "Bringing Class Back In: An Introduction" in *Inequality and Discontent in Yugoslav Socialism*, New York: Routledge, 2016, 3.

12. Bockman, Johanna "The Political Projects of Neoliberalism" and Collier, Stephen "Neoliberalism as Big Leviathan, or . . . ?" In *Social Anthropology* 20(3): 310–317, 2012.

13. Numerous scholars have critiqued these racialized attacks on public welfare programs, delineating their origins in policies premised on underclass ideology, and their extension to non-Black public aid recipients. In addition to Roberts, Dorothy. *Killing the Black Body: Race, Reproduction, and the Meaning of Liberty*. New York: Vintage, 1998, see also Collins, Jane. "What/Where Is the Working Class?" paper

presented at *Mellon Humanities Without Walls Global Work and Working-Class Community* in the Midwest Symposium, Northwestern University, Evanston, IL: 28 Sept. (2014); Davis, Dana-Ain. "Manufacturing Mamies: "The Burdens of Service Work and Welfare Reform among Battered Black Women." *Anthropologica* 46(2): 273–288, 2004; and Kingfisher, Catherine and Jeff Maskovsky, "The Limits of Neoliberalism," *Critique of Anthropology* 28(2): 115–126, 2008.

14. Collins, Jane. "The Specter of Slavery: Workfare and the Economic Citizenship of Poor Women," in *New Landscapes of Inequality: Neoliberalism and the Erosion of Democracy in America*, Jane Collins, Micaela di Leonardo, and Brett Williams, Eds. Santa Fe: School of American Research, 2007, 148. Collins is building here on Jamie Peck's analysis in Peck, Jamie. *Work-Place: The Social Regulation of Labor Markets*. New York: The Guilford Press, 1996.

15. Ranney, David. *Global Decisions, Local Collisions: Urban Life in the New World Order*, Philadelphia: Temple University Press, 2003.

16. Harvey, David. "Globalization and the 'Spatial Fix,'" *Geografische Revue* 2/2001, 26.

17. Franz, Barbara. *Uprooted and Unwanted: Bosnian Refugees in Austria and the United States*, Eugenia and Hugh M. Stewart '26 Series on Eastern Europe, United States, 2005.

18. Bernal, Victoria and Inderpal Grewal. "Introduction: The NGO Form: Feminist Struggles, the State, and Neoliberalism," in *Theorizing NGOs: States, Feminisms, and Neoliberalism*. Raleigh, NC: Duke University Press, 2014, 3.

19. Bernal and Grewal, "Introduction," 7. My italics.

20. See Elyachar 2002 for marketization and NGOs, Elyachar, Julia. "Empowerment Money: The World Bank, Non-Governmental Organizations, and the Value of Culture in Egypt," *Public Culture* 14(3): 493–513, 2002.

21. Sontag, Susan. *Regarding the Pain of Others*, New York: Picador, 2003, 87–88.

Chapter Two

Making Home and Family after War, and from a Distance

I sat at Hana's kitchen table peeling carrots and potatoes while she stood at the counter quartering a small chicken for the late afternoon meal. Her husband Damir would be returning home soon from his six o'clock morning shift at a plastics manufacturing factory. The factory had recently fired a number of its employees in efforts to reduce cost but had not adjusted productivity levels to match the loss of workers. This meant that those who remained, like Damir, faced increasing pressures to turn out the same quality and quantity of parts, albeit with far fewer resources. Hana had just arrived home after a day of cleaning houses, one of her three jobs at the time. In addition to working outside of the home, Hana prepared all of the daily meals for her family, and I found this to be the best time for visiting with her, as I could work alongside her prepping food and washing dishes.

I met Hana through Shawn, an American staffer at a local university who had worked with an NGO in Bosnia after the wars and offered to introduce me to some of the Bosnian refugees he had come to know in Chicago. During my initial visits with Hana, we discovered that we shared some significant life circumstances. Hana's eldest son by her first marriage was the same age as my son, we'd both become parents as teenagers, and we each left our sons' fathers because of physical abuse. We developed a friendship and I occasionally acted as a liaison between the family and local institutions, as when her preteen younger sister Sara got into trouble at school for being consistently late to class because she was in the school bathroom putting on makeup and changing out of her jeans into miniskirts—things their mother, Vehida, explicitly forbade.

In addition to helping Vehida and Sara manage Sara's adolescence in a new city where Vehida felt like an outsider because she did not possess the language, status, and customs that were foremost in Sara's American enculturation, Hana was also negotiating pressures from Damir to make another return visit to Bosnia. She had gone once, after they'd gained their U.S. citizenship in 2001, and Damir took their son Haris and went without her in 2003, but he was insistent that she return with him this time. She was equally insistent that she would not join him. One of the primary reasons Hana gave for not journeying to Bosnia was the expense involved. Money—how to manage it, and how to find more of it—was a common topic during my conversations with Hana and others. I grew accustomed to being asked by people I had only recently met how much I earned and how much I paid in rent. Although refugees were eligible for public assistance, the 1990s public aid reforms introduced a lifetime limit of five years, and, as we saw with Nasiha and Enisa, refugees entered a political climate that was increasingly hostile to people in need, and in which they were discouraged from seeking assistance. Enisa's and Hana's peer Nina, for example, told me, "I felt bad with [accepting] foodstamps because all the older people had it," and explained that she used public aid for only a few months following her arrival.

The refugees I met were also eager to work. The war had interrupted their working lives for years, and having a job provided some semblance of a return to "normal life." Yet many among Hana's generation arrived with limited English language competencies and did not possess comparable American degrees and professional certifications that would enable them to work in their previous careers. Prior to the war, Nermina had worked as a journalist in a mid-size town in the Herzegovina region. Hana had owned and operated a small sandwich shop in Mostar. Enisa was an accounts manager at a bank in Prijedor. Upon arrival in the United States, Nermina stocked shelves at a discount department store, Hana cleaned houses, and Enisa worked in hotel housekeeping. Nermina and Enisa had studied some English while in school in Bosnia and were able to build on this skill to improve their circumstances by the time we met. Nermina worked as the community outreach coordinator for TCC, and Enisa had moved to the employee insurance claims division of the hotel. Nermina's husband worked in long-distance trucking, and their combined salaries made it possible to raise two sons, now young adults. Enisa no longer needed to provide for Nasiha; however, she supported her aging mother.

Hana continued to clean houses, had added two nights a week as a home health aide, and also served as an on-call floor attendant for the overnight shift (11:00 p.m. to 7 a.m.) at a north side hospital. Hana's and Damir's circumstances were more representative of the majority of Bosnian refugees in Chicago, and their efforts to obtain material stability were inextricably connected to the material and emotional ruptures wrought by the war. Not only did people lose material possessions and social status in their forced migrations; they also lost family. Everyone knew someone who had died during the war, and what family remained struggled to get by and to maintain familial connections and expectations across vast distances. Thus, refugees in Chicago were embedded in what have been described as "transnational social fields," that is, sustained identification with and material connection across state borders.[1] Bosnians' transnational social fields included wage remittances, phone calls, return visits, and gifts used to bridge the divide between Bosnia and Chicago, often drawing on newly available consumer credit to address shortfalls. The combined pressures of family expectations and consumer debt added to the trauma of refugees' displacements and were a heavy weight and constant concern for Hana, and for others. This chapter explores the effects of these stressors, and finds they were often expressed in gendered family social relations and embodied ailments.

MANAGING MIGRATION HARDSHIP WITH DEBT

When Bosnians arrived as refugees in the United States during the mid-1990s, welfare reforms were not the only policy shifts that affected their opportunities and well-being. They entered an increasingly debt-driven economy made possible by newly deregulated financial markets. This ramping up in individual debt load was in direct relationship to the scaling back of social benefits and declines in public investments. As corporations chased capital returns in the globalizing free market, they sought also to evade pressures to reinvest profits locally through taxes, labor, and environmental stewardship. These changes resulted in diminishing wages and benefits in the face of rising costs of living for many Americans who turned to this new credit market in their attempts to buffer the effects of public sector divestment, a phenomenon that Brett Williams likens to debt peonage and labels "debt for sale."[2] Bosnians in Chicago also entered this market in their efforts to realize plans to establish homes in their new city, and to meet the expectations of those who remained in Bosnia.

During this period, refugees were enrolled in courses offered through volags with titles like "how to build a credit history," where they were introduced to American customer and consumer roles.[3] Hana caught on quickly to this form of finance. She was confident with money and felt she had good luck with it, repeating memories about how she frequently won small sums in her hometown's lottery, much to her younger brother's annoyance. Her sandwich shop in Mostar had catered primarily to students from the neighborhood high school, and some from the nearby university, and she had ideas about how she might similarly establish a small business in Chicago. In the late 1990s, she selected a department store credit card as her pathway to establishing a credit history. Once she was approved for a line of credit, she paid it off diligently, in person and in cash, every month.

Hana not only used credit to establish herself and extended family in the United States; she used it to support those who remained in Bosnia. The country's postwar economy was radically altered by the simultaneous ruptures of war, and of pressures to force the socialist economy to privatize and further embrace neoliberal capitalist values.[4] Bosnia relied on International Monetary Fund (IMF) loans from western European and North American countries to begin rebuilding, and this form of credit commanded a significant portion of the small country's budget; in 2000, nearly two-thirds of the state budget went to servicing foreign debt obligations. Further, Sarajevo canton, the capital among ten cantons in the Federation entity, commanded more than one-third of the entity budget.[5] Regions outside of Sarajevo canton received less resources, and rebuilding occurred at a slower pace. Hana's and Damir's migrant earnings helped to fill the gap in places in the north and southwest, like Prijedor and Mostar.[6] In the early aughts, migrant earnings from refugees in Chicago contributed to the significant flow of remittances into Bosnia-Herzegovina, a figure that the World Bank conservatively estimated in 2005 amounted to 1.3 billion dollars (U.S.), and comprised nearly 20 percent of the small country's GDP.[7]

By 2002, Hana was one of many immigrants who had credit cards, some of whom were also applying for home financing. Little did they know that they were entering a housing market comprised of high-risk loans that would "bubble," and then burst, contributing to the Great Recession of 2009, and what Hana would later refer to simply as "the crisis." People in the United States lost more than $16 trillion in wealth as a result of the financial crisis, and much of this wealth was located in housing property value. What were Hana's and Damir's motivations for entering this consumer credit market? In order to answer this question, we need to have some understanding of the meanings of home for Bosnian refugees, and its relationship to the social and economic circumstances in both Bosnia and the United States.

THE SIGNIFICANCE OF HOME / KUĆA AMONG THE BOSNIAN DIASPORA

Kuća is the word for home in Bosnian. Like the English distinction between "home" and "house" it connotes more than a physical space. Based on her 1980s fieldwork in central Bosnia, Tone Bringa describes kuća as both a physical place and a moral space. She found kuća to be based on kin relations that are manifest in practices through which members constitute and express values: the preparation and consumption of food, the construction and decoration of the homespace, the maintenance of social networks through hosting extended family, neighbors, and friends, the instruction of children. Women, men, young people, and elders, all were expected to contribute to the home through their labors and, if they had access, income.[8]

The Bosnian homespace gained particular symbolic significance in the postwar years because refugees had been forced to leave their homes under threat of violence, and many had experienced the damage and/or destruction of their home before their expulsion. As Bringa points out, these home losses carried a distinct layer of suffering. In Bosnia, building a house was often a life-long endeavor that required family members to pool labor and resources, and took ten to twenty years to complete.[9] This was the case with Hana. Her father and mother had built their family home in Mostar, and when Hana left her first husband, her father and brother built a small addition to the house for her to live in with her toddler son.[10] Even if a home was not too damaged in the war, it was likely occupied by strangers in the post-war years. Many refugees responded to this loss through very active engagement with homemaking in Chicago.

When they were not at their jobs, I learned that adult women and men allocated much of their time to purchasing and making furniture and window treatments, preparing food and consuming it with others, hosting friends, neighbors, and family. The home was the primary site for communicating, via phone and Internet, with friends and family living elsewhere; in Bosnia or other former Yugoslav republics, in Germany, Sweden, Canada, Turkey, Australia, the United States, and other parts of the world. It was a place to display objects that referenced particular cultural heritage sites in Bosnia-Herzegovina. Photographs and paintings of *Stari Most* / the Old Bridge in Mostar and the *sebilj* / Ottoman fountain in the Baščaršija section of *Stari Grad* / the Old Quarter in Sarajevo hung on walls, and ornately engraved copper *džezve* / coffee services on serving trays were prominently placed on china-cabinet shelves and living room end-tables. Women also put objects to use; Hana daily used the pressure cooker she had brought from Bosnia to prepare meals for her family, and many women, and some men, prepared Bosnian coffee in džezve, serving it in small porcelain cups / *fildžani*.

Yet for all the activities surrounding the production of home, Balkan migration scholars have paid surprisingly little attention to the topic, instead centering their research on the explicitly political domain of homeland.[11] Here, land and nation remain the primary focus through which we are to understand people's attachments to "the homeland."[12] Men's homeland nostalgia figures in reports on diaspora politicking and in cultural forms such as epic poetry.[13] While this primarily male-centered literature offers a gendered focus on the recognition that land and nation are often configured as female, we are left with little sense of how gender figures within social categories and activities that produce social relations through everyday encounters in the home.[14] The work of feminist anthropologists has shown that even in societies where women are more closely associated with the household, and men with the official domain of politics and economy, the domestic sphere can be a space where women do behind-the-scenes political work, and that the home may sometimes be a space wherein women exercise a great deal of power—in particular over other women and children. Again, Hana's experiences illustrate this phenomenon.

When Hana returned to her family home, she was fleeing not only her husband's physical abuse, but his mother's as well. The couple was nineteen years old when they married, and both of Hana's parents (who were divorced by that time) objected to the marriage. Hana defied their wishes and the young couple moved into her husband's mother's house. But when Hana didn't conform to the sort of housekeeping duties her husband's mother demanded, the woman beat her, and demanded that Hana's husband also beat her. A feminist analysis of gendered status and inequality in the home highlights women's efforts to shape their life course, and is central to understanding the home as a critical social and material space in Bosnians' postwar lives.[15] My focus on the home shows that expectations and choices surrounding household labor, employment in the labor market, and the selection of finance options are intimately connected to how people viewed and evaluated themselves and one another as family members. Thus, as both classic and contemporary social scientists have shown, I demonstrate that individuals' negotiations of the market economy are always also guided by a relational moral economy delineating senses of proper care and provisioning that are linked with notions of kin and belonging.[16]

GOOD SONS AND GOOD DAUGHTERS INVEST MONEY IN FAMILY

The combination of large-scale social and political change, family expectations regarding material well-being, and economic hardship generated some of the earliest Bosnian migration to Chicago in the nineteenth and early twentieth centuries. In his book, *100 years of Bosnians in Chicago*, local archivist Muharem Zulfić presents a 1926 image of Bosnian male laborers repairing the sewage lines and streetscape beneath the newly established "el" commuter train stop at the intersection of Loyola and Sheridan/Broadway in Rogers Park, a neighborhood that seventy years later would become home to

Hana, Damir and and many, many more.[17] The all-male photo of laborers and their employers (in suits) reflects the relationship between labor migration and the local economy at the time. The 1929 financial collapse had not yet occurred, and the city's industrial elite directed large-scale infrastructural expansion projects that relied on cheap migrant labor. It is likely that these men were sent by their families for the express purposes of sending money back to build homes in Bosnia, where the region was reeling from the aftermath of nationalist uprisings against Ottoman occupation, followed by Austro-Hungarian administration, and the destruction wrought by World War I.

By the time Zulfić published his book in 2003, a more fitting image of Bosnian migrants and the local economy may be found in a real estate advertisement from a 2004 issue of the Bosnian publication, *Zambak*.[18] The advertisement features a Bosnian woman Realtor who markets her services to Chicago's Bosnian diaspora, and is only one among hundreds aimed at Chicago's Bosnian refugee-immigrant market over the course of the tremendous 2002–2005 boom in mortgage lending that precipitated the 2009 financial crises. The ad narrates the relationship between the real estate agent and her clients, a Bosnian family, in the languages of intimacy, "until recently only your acquaintances, nowadays your friends," and of business, "thanks to our friendly professionalism." The image, of a man and woman with a daughter and a son sitting together on a sofa beneath framed images of Bosnia, invites the viewer to see Bosnians in heteronormative nuclear family form. But this happy image glosses the familial ruptures imposed by war and refugee life, erasing the multigenerational family, extended family, and the single parent family, all prevalent forms in the refugee cohort.

Take, for example, Fadila's family and home. I'd met Fadila at TCC's senior women's group and when she learned I'd like to interview her she brought a large coffee-table style book to show me. The book was published during the late Yugoslav period and centered especially upon her hometown of Počitelj, its medieval and Ottoman architecture, and its role since the mid-1960s as a significant artist's residence and sanctuary.[19] When I asked Fadila if she'd grown up in Počitelj, she told me that she had, and that she only agreed to marry her husband, whose family was located a two-hour drive north in Konjić, when he consented to relocate to her home, and live with her and her mother. (Fadila had never known her father as he was killed during World War II, when Fadila was only two years old. Her mother did not remarry.) Fadila explained to me that the 1990s wartime bombing of Počitelj devastated the city, but in 1996 UNESCO placed the small Neretva River Valley town on a list of the world's most endangered cultural sites, and she was hopeful that reconstruction would occur. In fact, she told me, her sister had already accessed some of the UNESCO-granted restoration funds and directed this toward reconstructing the family home. I would soon learn that homemaking were central concerns for not only Fadila and her sister, but also for Fadila's Chicago-based family members.

During one of my afternoon visits to her home, Fadila, her nine-year-old granddaughter Lara, and I sat on comfortably worn sofas watching a Mexican telenovela, "Ruby," on the Serbian PINK television network (beamed into their living room via satellite), as Fadila's son-in-law Joso returned home from his job as a sanitation worker. Fadila lowered the volume on the television to greet Joso who had sat down in the entryway to take off his heavy work boots, preparing to head to the shower. When I asked Joso how he was, he replied that he was "tired of working, all the time working, they [nodding toward Fadila and Lara] are always wanting money, always . . . money." Fadila's face flushed as Joso spoke, and she looked at Lara, turned to me and said in a low, quiet voice, "Joso je dobar sin / Joso is a good son." Joso's complaint about his mother-in-law and daughter made openly, in front of me, was characteristic of the ways in which family members joked with and prodded one another. What is interesting here is that Fadila took care to describe him positively to me, and in gender and kin terms: Joso was a "good son" who worked for his family and brought money into the home. Further, Joso also indexed gender and kin in his complaint: his wife's mother, and his daughter were the ones "always wanting money."

Fadila's and Joso's was a multi-generational arrangement, housing Fadila and her husband Arman, their daughter Aida (Joso's wife), and Aida's and Joso's children Enes and Lara. Aida and Joso had managed to purchase the small single-family home in 2002 on the basis of their combined incomes: Joso's from a suburban waste removal company, and Aida from her job as a stock clerk at a nearby discount apparel store. Fadila and Arman received Medicare and a small Social Security check every month that they contributed to the household. In addition, Arman cultivated and tended a modest rose garden in the front of the house, and a vegetable garden in their small backyard. He and Joso made many improvements to the property, such as opening up the second story dormers to make a bedroom and bathroom for Fadila and Arman. Fadila did the bulk of the cooking for the household, and she and Arman took care of the children after school and during the day when school was not in session. Both Fadila and Arman made crafts that were displayed prominently in the home. Arman made scenes of pressed flowers, and wooden stools and serving trays decorated in a wood-burning technique common throughout the Herzegovina region; Fadila embroidered curtains and pillows and made needlework portraits of flowers and idyllic peasant scenes. When I visited Fadila and Arman, Joso and Anita were rarely present.

They were not elderly like their parents and did not possess the English skills and American cultural preferences of their children's generation and thus they were constantly working in low-wage positions. These generational differences intersected with gender differences to show that in addition to a place of nurture, the home was also a site of tension.

While Fadila and Arman were settled in Chicago, her sisters remained in Bosnia, and so did Joso's sister and mother. Everyone had surviving family members who remained in Bosnia, or who had been relocated as refugees to other parts of the world.[20] Given their refugee status, Bosnians living in the United States by and large have not had to contend with the specter of illegality as regards their immigration status, and young children have not been separated from parents by deportation. But families were nonetheless separated and adults of both Joso's and Fadila's generations attempted to span this distance in myriad material ways. They felt a tremendous sense of responsibility to those who remained in Bosnia. Joso's comments about Fadila and Lara "always wanting money" came during a period when the household was struggling to finance a return trip to BiH. Even though they had booked the trip off-season at the end of the summer, when travel costs were lower, the plane tickets were $900 apiece, bringing the amount of air travel alone to $5,400. Family in Bosnia would provide room and board during their stay, but they would need to spend a lot of money on gasoline and car rentals, were expected to bring many gifts with them, to fund and host large meals, and to make purchases at shops, restaurants, and cafes during their stay. They estimated the total cost of their two and a half-week trip at close to $8,500, and expenses needed to be paid for the most part in cash—the small local travel agencies that catered to the diaspora operated on a cash-only basis. Joso in particular would need to bring over significant amounts of cash because he was expected to pay for his mother's health care. The fact that he lived so far away from her made his mother very angry, a sentiment she shared with him frequently in long-distance phone conversations. This was difficult and frustrating for him, as he expressed to me on more than one occasion. He had in fact arranged to sponsor her relocation to the United States, but at the last minute she had backed out and decided to remain in Bosnia. Fadila and Arman might contribute a small amount of their modest Social Security income, and Aida's wages would help, but Joso would finance the bulk of the trip. Joso's family's strategy for the balancing of cash and credit expenses—taking on consumer debt to free up cash for spending and provisioning in Bosnia—was similar to that of Hana's family. The stresses produced through these economic strategies and kin obligations were made material in bodily ailments among senior and adult family members.

Chapter Two

HOUSEHOLDING FOR THE HOMELAND

Hana's motivations for establishing credit and investing in property were not solely aspirational. She was also induced by her obligations to care for family members. Further, her investments were generated by her and Damir's efforts to build a postwar life that remained connected to Bosnia, although they differed on what they thought the breadth and depth of these connections ought to be. I became aware of these differences one afternoon as Hana's teenaged sister, Sara, and I trudged up the stairs, huffing and puffing from the late September humidity. We plopped down our bags of groceries outside the heavy brown door while Sara rummaged through her purse for the key to unlock the apartment. With key in hand, she went to open the door, but, just as she reached for the knob, her eight-year-old nephew Haris opened the door from the inside, "did you get the chocolate?" he asked. "You'll have to wait until we get inside to see! Here, help us carry these bags!" replied Sara, handing off two bags to Haris. The three of us made our way down the hallway to the kitchen where Haris's mother, Hana, stood over the sink, washing the breakfast dishes. Hana turned toward us: "Did you get everything? What about the eggs?" "Yes sestra, geez!" Sara replied, inserting the Bosnian word for sister. The family had recently purchased the modest two-flat building, and by and large viewed it as an improvement from their previous rental: the new apartment was much larger, with three bedrooms rather than one, to better accommodate the six to eight family members that stayed there at any given time. There was no central air conditioning, so the stairwell of the flat tar-roofed building had become a virtual sauna over a succession of unseasonably steamy late summer days. I unpacked two cartons of eggs and placed them in the refrigerator while Sara found the container of Nutella, showing it to Haris before putting it in a cupboard. Hana had promised to make him crepes filled with the hazelnut chocolate spread for dinner since he had done well on his first homework assignment of the year. We were all irritable and tired from the heat, but Hana seemed particularly perturbed. After Sara and Haris left the kitchen, I asked her if anything was wrong. "I had to call her again," she replied. Hana was talking about her husband Damir's mother, Anka. While Hana's and Sara's mother, Vehida, had also come to the United States as a refugee, Damir's parents remained in Bosnia. Both were ailing in their old age, and Damir and Hana were trying to manage the elders' care from their new home in Chicago.

As was the case with Hana, Damir was also in his late twenties when he arrived in the United States, and prior to the war, he had also run a small business: a garage and auto-repair operation he co-owned with his younger brother. In addition to his work at the plastics factory, Damir earned extra income doing mechanical repairs and auto-body finishing at a garage owned by the husband of someone they had met through their volag. They saved scrupulously, but with different goals in mind: Damir saw their savings as an investment in Bosnia, while Hana wanted their earnings to be directed to building a life in the United States. Their mothers, Vehida in the United States, and Anka in Bosnia, loomed large in the couple's discussions and disagreements over money, and the mothers shared Damir's hopes for the family's eventual return to Bosnia. Although Hana's and Damir's end goals differed, they each felt intense pressures to provide for their aging parents, and for their own futures, a pressure that manifested in embodied injury and pain. Their struggles illustrate some of the common dilemmas faced among the diaspora.

Damir's mother, Anka, had remained in Bosnia, where she lived with his father in their family home on the outskirts of Mostar along with a nephew who suffered from mental illness and physical disability. Like many war survivors in Bosnia and in Chicago, Anka had been prescribed anti-depressant medications. According to Damir and Hana, Anka's depression was the result of wartime trauma, and the subsequent migrations of her three adult children: Damir's sister and her husband now lived in Canada, and his younger brother and wife lived across the Adriatic Sea in Italy.

Recently, Anka began resisting taking her medications, and refused to take them unless Damir phoned from the United States and coaxed her to take the pills. These ritualistic conversations occurred daily, lasted for an average of thirty minutes, and were comprised of Anka's lengthy lamentations on the vast distance between Mostar and North America. If Anka did not take the prescribed anti-depressants, she became paranoid and disoriented, and difficult for Damir's father to care for. The phone calls were a significant source of stress for Damir and for Hana, who sometimes made the phone calls in Damir's absence, as she had on the afternoon that Sara and I went on the grocery errand. And it was not only Anka who needed special care. Hana's mother, Vehida, had also become a challenge to deal with.

According to Hana, Vehida had also been prescribed anti-depressants, but took them sporadically, rather than as prescribed. Vehida struggled tremendously with the war and its aftermath and could not seem to find comfort in her survival. Hana's younger brother Nermin had fought and died in the 1992–1993 conflict in Mostar. Hana had shown me photos of Nermin during one of my first visits to her home, but she rarely spoke of him. Vehida, on the other hand, seemed never to have stopped mourning his death, and had a VHS recording of his funeral that she viewed frequently. I learned about the video only after she asked me to watch it with her one day when we were waiting for Hana to return home from cleaning houses. When I later told Hana that her mother had shown me the film, she was livid. She explained to me that she thought her mother's behaviors were very unhealthy, and that Vehida did not want to be happy. When the first waves of return to Bosnia occurred in the late 1990s, Vehida left her husband in the United States and attempted to move back to Mostar, into her sister's home. Yet she found no comfort in the hardships of the postwar city, and months later returned again to the United States, this time moving with her husband to join the large survivor population in St. Louis, Missouri. Amidst all of these changes, Vehida expected Hana and Damir to continue to help support her financially.

All of this stress over concerns for their mothers' well-being was causing strain on Hana's and Damir's relationship: they had been arguing for months. Damir wanted to visit his ailing mother and father in Bosnia for fifteen days during the summer months. Hana wanted to take a vacation somewhere in the United States, like Colorado. Damir had already visited Bosnia without Hana once and was insistent that she accompany him this time (they had gone together once before). Among the reasons she gave him for not wanting to go was her weight. Since leaving Bosnia, she had gained fifty pounds. She wanted to lose weight before returning again but had been unsuccessful thus far; twice she had used diet pills, the second time culminating in an emergency room visit for heart palpitations. After that episode Damir had become increasingly worried and had even implored me to talk to her with the hope that maybe she would listen to me, since she had not heeded his warnings and pleas to stop taking the pills. As a holiday gift, he had paid for a gym membership, which Hana had taken up enthusiastically for two months, combining this with a Weight Watchers diet plan. But work demands encroached on her regimen; cleaning houses five days a week, evening and weekends at the hospital, and daily householding demands left her with little energy for workouts. Not long thereafter, Damir began to experience debilitating migraine headaches, nausea, and sharp abdominal pains, the latter of which were finally diagnosed as gallstones after an emergency room visit. In the midst of all this, they were unable to agree on the pending Bosnia trip.

When I asked Hana about why she didn't want to go, she replied, "I will be broke for two years," referring to the money they would have to spend in order to make the trip. She went on to describe how in Bosnia, "women have to cook, entertain," and since Damir's brother and his wife would travel from Italy to join them, that would only mean more mouths to feed since the wife was "lazy" (that is, she would spend the entire day at her own mother's house, and then show up at Damir's parents' home in time for evening coffee). Thus, the bulk of the labor for shopping, cooking, entertaining, and cleaning up after everyone—at the least seven adults and four children—inevitably would fall to Hana. While Damir said he would help, Hana felt this was not a realistic offer, and that even if he did help some, it would fall to Hana to organize and orchestrate everything. Similarly, if she wanted to go to the Adriatic coast in Croatia for a couple of days, she and Damir would need to pay for everyone else to accompany them. Going without the rest of the family would be seen as rude and stingy, but none of the others had money to pay for such a trip. They would also be expected to host meals at Damir's parents' place, during which neighbors would arrive unannounced to be fed and entertained. According to Hana, friends and family thought that she and Damir had a lot of money, since they lived in America, and that they should spend a lot of money when they were in public: at a store, or in a café.

Like Joso, Fadila, Arman, and Aida, Hana and Damir had managed to purchase a property. They were able to afford the new apartment by renting out the first-floor unit and doing the majority of the maintenance themselves. By 2004 they had refinanced the home, taking a second mortgage to help pay for Vehida's multiple relocations. They also planned to pay in cash for dental work in Bosnia: Hana needed a root canal, crown, and post procedure and in Bosnia the treatments would cost less than half of the United States rate. Perhaps most important to Hana was the purchase of a gravestone to mark her father's burial. He had died of a heart attack at the beginning of the war. Her parents were divorced and Vehida had remarried, and Sara was still in high school—Hana was the only one in her family with the resources necessary to buy the headstone. In addition to the cash freed up from the refinance, Hana and Damir had accrued a significant credit card debt that Hana managed by opening a new account every 6–12 months by searching for zero-interest balance transfer deals. Although they had avoided paying interest on the debt, they were not able to pay it down. Furthermore, the refinance had liquidated a large portion of the equity they had built in their home. In maintaining their obligation to kin who remained in Bosnia—obligations that included portraying an image of American success and wealth for their friends and family in Bosnia—Hana and Damir had taken on a burdensome amount of consumer debt.

SEVAP AND THE TRANSNATIONAL DISTRIBUTION OF CARE

When I met Nasiha, she was 27, and had been married to Edo for one year. Unlike Hana and Damir and Joso and Aida, Nasiha and Edo did not have young children or ailing parents to support. The couple also did not have the significant debt loads that the others had incurred in their efforts to meet expenses and expectations. Yet the problem of how to approach their long-distance ties to Bosnia was a point of disagreement in their home.

Like Hana, Nasiha was reluctant to visit Bosnia. Although Nasiha and Edo—who was from a small village in northern Bosnia—had returned to visit former Yugoslavia once, Nasiha had decided to remain in Croatia while Edo visited Bosnia. These differences arose in part from their wartime experiences. While Nasiha had spent time in the Trnopolje concentration camp during the war, Edo was already outside of the country when the wars started, working as a migrant laborer. His mother died at a young age, and when his father remarried, Edo's father placed him in the care of his maternal grandparents who were quite poor. In fact, it turned out that Edo would be the one to care for them. Given their meager circumstances and their aging bodies, the bulk of household labors fell to Edo, and he left their home for the first time at the age of sixteen to begin working as a migrant laborer. Since then Edo had worked on large scale construction projects overseas before coming to the United States. In the summer of 2005, Nasiha and Edo planned to return to former Yugoslavia again, and this time Edo, Nasiha's mother, her mother's brother, and her grandmother combined forces, urging her to return to their hometown of Prijedor. Her grandmother's best friend, Elma, remained in Bosnia, and struggled to survive there. Elma had no children of her own who could help care for her in her old age, and her sole living relative—a sister—had her own family to care for; Elma had no relatives abroad to send money to her. Nasiha's entire family was close to Elma, and they all contributed to make a donation to her. Nasiha's grandmother also wanted her to personally deliver a scarf she had selected as a gift for Elma. Not only did they want Nasiha to return to Prijedor; they wanted her to visit her father's home in a small village outside of Prijedor.

Given Nasiha's parent's divorce and her father's alcoholism, her father had not remained a part of her life. He died shortly after the war, and his family sent word to Nasiha that he had left a humble piece of property in her name. During a conversation over dinner one night, Nasiha began telling me more about her father and the visit that her husband and family wanted her to make. Although Nasiha's father was from a Bosnian Croat family, his village was home primarily to Bosnian Serbs, and she was uncomfortable with the idea of going anywhere near Prijedor, which fell in the Republika Srpska (RS) entity of Bosnia, where, she exclaimed: "there are no jobs, refugees everywhere . . . someone could kidnap me! It is a crazy place with crazy people who have guns!" to which Edo responded by getting up from his seat on the couch, telling me, "don't worry, not everybody over there is crazy," and, while giving Nasiha a disapproving look, headed for the kitchen, asking me if I wanted a Coke.

But Edo and her mother's family wanted her to claim the land her father had left to her, and they wanted her to bring money to his surviving family members, who were very poor. While Nasiha didn't speak of them in such terms, these acts were demonstrations of the Islamic principle of *sevap* (a Turkish word). Sevap is based on good deeds that demonstrate to God one's efforts to adhere to tenets of the faith and are expected to positively affect one's experiences in the afterlife. Not all acts that constitute sevap are explicitly specified in Qur'anic doctrine, and Bringa describes Bosnian interpretations of sevap that understand it as affecting not only the afterlife, but also having an effect on the worldly present and future.[21] You may earn sevap through prayers, and doing acts of kindness, especially for the benefit of the less fortunate. You may also earn sevap on behalf of others. By contributing to Nasiha's grandma's friend's well-being, as well as to Nasiha's father's kin, her family would be able to perform a religious duty and affirm their belonging in a moral community. These acts would also enable them to share the benefits of their well-being in the United States among those who remained in Bosnia, and to assure them that they were not forgotten among the diaspora. Like Hana, Nasiha agonized over returning to Bosnia to visit, preferring to remain on the Croatian seacoast where her aunt lived.

CONCLUSION

It is rare to think about financial debts owed to credit card companies, banks, and other lending agencies, in intimate terms. The concept of the "free market" presents the illusion that every individual is equal in their dealings with financial institutions and market exchange. In reality, choices regarding money and matters of trade and exchange are always relational and guided by circumstance. Bosnian refugees had to navigate an increasingly debt-driven economy in the United States while also meeting their obligations to family remaining in Bosnia where the post-war economy was greatly dependent on loans from the International Monetary Fund, and on diaspora remittance monies.

For Bosnians displaced by the war, the moral framework of homemaking took on particular significance in the face of massive wartime destruction targeting homes. Money-choices in this context were directed in part by individuals' understandings of the obligations met by "good" daughters and sons, and the expectations that mothers, in particular, held for their adult children. At the same time, the American consumer credit market opened up one avenue for meeting financial obligations to family in Chicago and in Bosnia, but, given their relatively shallow credit history due to the short time period they'd lived in the United States, many Bosnians only qualified to enter the housing market through Adjustable Rate Mortgages (ARMs) or similar high cost loan instruments rather than lower fixed prime rate loans options. As the "bubble" swelled and then burst between 2002 and 2010, debt burdens shifted and intensified, and the effects reverberated in the interpersonal relationships where the needs and desires driving the accrual of financial debt were felt most acutely.

These social and economic injuries may also be seen as manifest in bodily ailments: Hana's heart palpitations, Damir's gallstones, their mothers' socio-emotional travails. While the sojourn to Bosnia offered many opportunities to meet moral obligations through accruing sevap, and to dedicate sevap on behalf of others, the trips created financial and labor burdens for working women. Despite these hardships, in 2005 both Hana and Nasiha hesitantly agreed to join their husbands in return visits to Bosnia. Hana arrived home invigorated from her journey, but when we discussed the visit in-depth, she explained that it was the brief time spent in Italy, with Damir's brother's family, that was most enjoyable. Croatia, she said, was "only good for vacations and schools," while Bosnia was not even good for those things. However, during the trip she and Damir had determined they would relocate to Italy. She explained that Damir's brother's boss would help them with the necessary sponsor paperwork and that as long as they came with money and declared they would open a business that would create jobs for Italians, they would be welcome. They would sell their property in the United States and settle in Italy, where they could drive to Mostar, or go by boat or a short plane ride, and thus be nearer to Damir's parents without having to cope with the challenges of living in postwar Bosnia.

But four years later, in 2009, Hana and Damir remained in their apartment in Chicago. They had lost all of the equity in their home during the financial crisis, and their mortgage rate had tripled in the meantime. Some of Hana's clients had canceled her cleaning service in their efforts to save money: they were also reeling from the crisis. Damir retained his job at the factory, but the company continued to reduce its workforce and speed up production demands, adding overnight shifts, but not adding any worker benefits on top of the new workload. They could not afford to sell their building.

While Nasiha could not bring herself to give money to the family of a father who had done so little for her during her childhood, Edo insisted on giving them money when he and Nasiha made a day trip into Prijedor to visit Elma, and then to her father's village, where his parents and brother's family prepared a meal for them. Upon their return to Chicago, both Edo and Nasiha's grandmother urged her to sustain the relationship with her father's family by periodically sending them care-packages of goods from Chicago. Since they were fluent in English and had American certifications, did not have a mortgage or dependent children and senior relatives, Nasiha and Edo were able to weather the financial crisis relatively unscathed. Fadila, Arman,

Joso, and Anita continued to live together in the small home in their efforts to economize by pooling income and household labors.

The men and elder women in Hana's and Nasiha's families viewed Bosnia as a space that represented their longing for a different time and a different situation. These desires were sometimes born out of a nostalgia for the past that was; for their mother's and grandmother's generations, Yugoslavia was a relatively stable state, where one could find employment, build a home, and receive a good pension. And there was also an imagined past, in which the difficulties during that period were minimized in relation to the present challenges. For their male counterparts, returning to Bosnia represented a future with the possibility to perform a duty, to care for the elder generation, and perhaps to cultivate land. Both Damir and Edo wanted to retain land in Bosnia and spoke of eventually retiring there. For the elders and the men, Bosnia represented a reprieve from the hardships of refugee life in America. Hana's and Nasiha's views of Bosnia were quite different. The two women saw Bosnia as a space that fostered unpredictable vulnerability, exploitative labor, and even hostility. They cared for Bosnia, but they found their elders' and husbands' views on Bosnia lacked sensibility and pragmatic purpose.

The above patterns of desire and obligation between adult children and their parents, and between spouses, was something I witnessed over and again, and they generated a consumer debt burden that I suggest is best understood as the product of a transnational social field created by the challenges of maintaining relationships in the face of fewer social supports in both Chicago and in Bosnia. The hardworking endeavors of their adult children were a constant topic among women like Fadila, as were the seemingly endless demands aging parents made for attention and money among women like Hana. What appeared to be competing demands evaluated in terms of gender and generation became most apparent around the issue of investments in the home / kuća, both in the United States, and in Bosnia-Herzegovina. Such investments constituted relations among people as well as places and were intensified by access to financing through credit card and mortgage debt in fragile and uncertain social and economic circumstances. These phenomena demonstrate home to be a lively and unpredictable site of exchange and obligation, the burdens of which cannot be expressed to the credit card companies and banks that are the debt holders, but rather are shouldered by the most intimate of relationships.

NOTES

1. I use "transnational" in this discussion rather than other terminology such as "transborder" (Stephen, Lynn. *Transborder Lives: Indigenous Oaxacans in Mexico,*

California, and Oregon. Durham, NC: Duke University Press, 2007) or "translocal" (Halilovich, Places of Pain) because transnational conceptualizations of these ongoing cross-state relations emphasize the particular historical and structural relations between states that largely circumscribe the frameworks through which people pursue such connections. See Fouron and Glick Schiller for a discussion of transnational social fields Fouron, Georges and Nina Glick Schiller. "All in The Family: Gender, Transnational Migration, and the Nation-State." *Identities* 7(4): 539–582, 2001. See Stef Jansen for a discussion of Bosnian male refugees' coping strategies with status loss while in Australia ("Misplaced Masculinities: Status Loss and the Location of Gendered Subjectivities Among 'Non-Transnational' Bosnian Refugees." *Anthropological Theory* 8(2): 181–200, 2007). See Bonfiglioli, "Gendering Social Citizenship" for a discussion of relying on family networks during economic precarity in the SFRY, Bonfiglioli, Chiara. "Gendering Social Citizenship: Textile Workers in Post-Yugoslav States," *The Europeanisation of Citizenship in the Successor States of the Former Yugoslavia*, Working Paper 2013/30. Edinburgh: University of Edinburgh School of Law, 2013; see Le Normand for reliance on migration strategies during SFRY economic precarity, Le Normand, Brigette. "The Gastarbaiteri as a Transnational Yugoslav Working Class," in *Inequality and Discontent in Yugoslav Socialism*, Archer, Rory, Igor Duda and Paul Stubbs, Eds. New York: Routledge, 2016.

2. Williams, Brett. *Debt for Sale: A Social History of the Credit Trap*. Philadelphia, PA: University of Pennsylvania Press, 2004.

3. Mallon, Mary T. "Development Amidst a Fragmented Community." M.A. thesis, Graduate Program in Intercultural Studies, *Wheaton College*, 1997.

4. Jansen, Stef. "The Privatization of Home and Hope: Return, Reforms, and the Foreign Intervention in Bosnia-Herzegovina." *Dialectical Anthropology* 30: 177–199, 2006.

5. International Crisis Group. "Bosnia's Precarious Economy: Still Not Open For Business." Balkans Report No.115, August 7, 2001.

6. At the time, Prijedor was one among fifteen municipalities located in the RS entity.

7. In 2000, 1/3 of the state budget funded state institutions and ministries while 2/3 was used to service foreign debt. "Bosnia's Precarious Economy: Still Not Open For Business," International Commission on the Balkans Report No. 115: Sarajevo/Brussels. August 7, 2001: 2.

8. Bringa, Tone. *Being Muslim the Bosnian Way*. Princeton, NJ: Princeton University Press, 1995.

9. Bringa, *Being Muslim the Bosnian Way*.

10. In her 1980s ethnography of a central Bosnian village, Tone Bringa provides the following definition, "Kuća is the name both for the house as a building and for the household: the one represents the other and is at the same time both a moral unity and a unity of interaction in the village (1995: 85). According to Bringa, women are seen to embody this moral quality. She further specifies that in village settings, kuća included only those people who "ate from the same pot" (Bringa, *Being Muslim*, 42).

11. See Jansen for exception (Jansen, Stef. "Troubled Locations: Return, the Life Course, and Transformations of 'Home' in Bosnia-Herzegovina," *Focaal: Journal of Global and Historical Anthropology* 49: 15–30, 2007).

12. Haris Halilovich's *Places of Pain* (2013) is an exception to this. Halilovich's study of the postwar diaspora takes the concept of *zavičaj*—emotional and intimate local community—as a primary analytic for understanding refugees' ongoing attachments to Bosnia. Yet kuća, and the material and social activities that constitute and sustain it, remains largely absent from this discussion.

13. Hokenos, *Homeland Calling*; Winland, *Between Desire*; Sugarman, Jane. "Imagining the Homeland: Poetry, Songs, and the Discourses of Albanian Nationalism." *Ethnomusicology* 43/3 (Fall 1999), 419–458.

14. See Jansen's Misplaced Masculinities for exception.

15. See "Toward a Unified Analysis of Gender and Kinship," in *Gender and Kinship: Essays Toward a Unified Analysis*, Jane Fishburne Collier and Sylvia Junko Yanagisako, Eds. Stanford, CA: Stanford University Press, 1987: 15–50. for examples of senior women's authority in the domestic realm. See Stack for women's women's household-based economic networks and strategizing in the context of labor market segmentation and exclusion, Stack, Carol. *All Our Kin*. New York: Basic Books, 1974.

16. See for example: Wilson, Ara. *The Intimate Economies of Bangkok: Tomboys, Tycoons, and Avon Ladies in the Global City*. Berkeley, CA: University of California Press, 2004; Thompson, E. P. *The Making of the English Working Class*. Toronto: Penguin Books, 1991.

17. Zulfić, Muharem. *100 godina Bosnjaka u Cikagu*. Dzemijetul Hajrije: Chicago, IL, 2003. p. 72. Zulfić emigrated to the United States in 1954. See also Agić, Senad. Immigration and Assimilation: *The Bosnian Muslim Experience in Chicago*. Lima: Wyndham Hall Press, 2004.

18. Zambak. No. 78. Chicago, October 2004.

19. See for example, "Počitelj, the Pearl of Herzegovina," published 11.26.2016 by photojournalist Jim Marshall for Balkanvibe. accssed 5.21.2018 https://www.balkanvibe.com/story/Pocitelj-the-Pearl-of-Herzegovina/256

20. Transnational family forms have often been understood as a structural effect of globalizing processes that shape people's economic opportunities. In this vein, Lynn Stephen chronicles the contexts in which Mixtec and Zapotec migrants from Oaxaca to the United States as largely defined by both Mexican and United States racialized political economies that discriminate against indigenous Mexicans and shunt them into employment in low wage agricultural, domestic, and day labor sectors of the U.S. economy. Stephen argues that migrants' economic strategies in this context result in "transborder" family forms due to the myriad social borders people must traverse, such as racial and linguistic barriers, in addition to political state borders. Some ethnographers have been especially attentive to how children's lives vary when they have a parent who is not present for extended periods of time due to labor migration. Rhacel Parreñas and Pei Chia Lan, for example, look at state-run training programs in the Philippines and Indonesia that recruit women to labor abroad in care work such as domestic service, child care, elder care, or nursing, and document mothers' uses

of cell phones and other new technologies to remain connected to their children who remain in the custody of extended family and friends during their mother's absence.

Unlike these women, the parents migrating to the United States from Mexico, Central America, and South America have had to contend with an increasingly hostile labor migration policy environment, the impact of which can be seen on family forms wherein spouses, children, and migrant parents are often separated for more than a decade without the possibility of return visits (Gomberg-Muñoz 2017). Even as the U.S. economy demands cheap labor provided by migrants who have few alternatives, the state simultaneously places restrictive citizenship statuses enforced through punitive measures that make crossing the U.S.–Mexico border an incredibly risky and dangerous undertaking. Patricia Zavella describes these families as living in a "divided home" that is wrought with tensions over such separations, and, in a deeply sensitive account that builds on Cecelia Menjivar's earlier work, Leisy Abrego delineates how children in particular find it difficult to grasp the structural forces that circumscribe their Salvadoran parents' mobility, and sometimes respond with blame and resentment at parents'—mothers' in particular—absences.

21. Bringa, *Being Muslim*, 161.

Chapter Three

Ajla in Stolac

One hot morning in the small Bosnian town of Stolac, I waited, along with four other people, outside an abandoned municipal building for the next bus to Sarajevo. A mother tried to get her young boy to stop jumping on top of a bench by tempting him with a soda, an effort his sister reinforced by performatively showing that she was properly seated and sipping a soda. I struck up a conversation with a woman who looked to be in her early twenties by asking her where she was headed: our final stop in Sarajevo? Or would she disembark on one of the stops on our way? She was on her way to Konjic. She wore a pair of skinny jeans, a button-down blue and white checked blouse, black sneakers, and stood several yards away from the bench, smoking a cigarette. She asked me where I was from, and what I was doing in Stolac. After telling her that I was a teacher from Chicago, and was in Stolac to learn about relationships between migrants and their family and friends who remained, she told me that I was lucky to be an American woman with a U.S. passport: I could come and go as I pleased; I could cross the Bosnia/Croatia border with ease and move about the entirety of European Schengen Zone without even applying for a visa for the duration of my trip.[1] "Bosnian women cannot do that: you should tell your students that," she said, then turned slightly, and resumed smoking her cigarette, signaling the end to our conversation.[2]

The young women I met during my visit to Bosnia wanted mobility. They yearned for the possibility to leave Bosnia—to travel freely throughout Europe, and to visit the United States and Canada, places where many of their family and friends had been resettled as refugees. They didn't necessarily want to leave Bosnia permanently, rather they wanted to visit family, the possibility to obtain more stable employment, and to experience other parts of the world. The young woman at the bus stop wasn't the only one to remind me of my American privilege; people repeatedly told me that I was lucky to have

American mobility. Yet those for whom the possibility of travel outside of Bosnia remained remote found ways to signal their aspirations through their display of objects that represented their transnational ties to, and knowledge of, the United States. This was the case with Ajla.

Ajla was my friend Edin's cousin and became my primary guide when I traveled to the Herzegovina region of western Bosnia in order to learn more about the transnational relationships maintained among Bosnians in Chicago and their families who remained in Bosnia. Edin's family was originally from Stolac, a small, historic, hill town outside of Mostar.[3] The people of Stolac had suffered tremendously during the war, when the Croatian-led HVO militia attacked non-Croats, seeking to establish a separate Croatian mono-ethnic state in the Herzegovina.[4] In 1993, the HVO forced the entire Muslim population of Stolac to leave, and looted and destroyed their homes and neighborhoods. The militia detained Bosnian Muslim men in concentration camps, and deported women and children to areas under control of the VRS.[5] By the time I arrived in the region in summer 2009, the majority of municipal operations and services were segregated by ethnicity, often with Bosnian Catholics receiving superior services. (During my time in Stolac, people use the terms "Catholic," "Christian" [meaning Orthodox], and "Muslim"; I rarely heard people use "Croat" "Serb" or "Bošnjak.") The two largest ethnic groups, Bosnian Catholics and Bosnian Muslims, were assigned to different medical facilities in the town, and Bosnian Croat children entered the schools' front doors while Bosnian Muslim children entered the back door. Catholic kids attended school in the morning; Muslim kids attended in the afternoon.[6]

Edin was a preteen when he fled Stolac along with his siblings and parents, Memo and Fatima, and the family eventually relocated as refugees to Chicago. Their home in Stolac had been destroyed, but they maintained a modest apartment for family visits, and they helped to support Memo's sister Safija, Safija's husband Faruk, and their young adult daughter, Ajla. When I first met Ajla, she pulled up to the corner near Edin's family apartment in a dark blue Fiat to drive us down to the nearest city, Mostar, at the bottom of the canyon. I could hear the pop music emanating from the car's speakers as the car approached, and I opened the passenger side door to the sound of Lady Gaga's "Poker Face" playful refrain on bisexuality.

"Do you like Gaga?" asked Ajla. "Sure," I replied, settling into my seat and closing the car door. Ajla's straight dark brown hair fell to her shoulders. She wore skinny blue jeans and a turquoise cotton tank top with lavender leather flats; the latter, I would learn, were a gift from her aunt in Sweden. "Do you think she's gay?" Ajla asked. I knew that Gaga (Stefani Germanotta) was openly bisexual and advocated for LGBTQ rights. "I think she likes women, and men?" I replied. A broad smile crossed Ajla's face "Yes, that's what I heard too!"⁷ Ajla had the energy and curiosity of people in their early twenties. After telling me that I didn't "look like a professor," Ajla launched into questions she seemed to have been saving up: "I've been to France, but never to the United States. I really want to see the blue grasses! The horses and the blue grasses! Is it true that it's really blue? In some of the pictures I've seen, it looks kinda blue, but in others, not so much." I had not come prepared to discuss Kentucky blue grass. I thought of the only time I had been to Kentucky, for a church youth work project. It was the 1980s and we drove in two large passenger vans from Chicago to an Appalachian coal town in hard-bitten Hazard County to do service work with Habitat for Humanity. All I could recall from that trip was the poverty people were coping with and that the drinking water was so contaminated by coal production most everyone drank cola instead. I decided not to burst Ajla's Kentucky blue grass bubble, "I've only been to Kentucky once, and I didn't see that part of it," I replied. I asked her about her studies. Edin had told me she was a student at the University of Mostar, which was our first stop this morning. She explained that she was studying to become a civil engineer because she wanted to play a part in forwarding the region's postwar redevelopment. I remarked how cool I thought it was that she wanted to do that sort of work. We continued the remaining twenty minutes descending the mountain with Lady Gaga playing in the background, our hair blowing in the hot Mediterranean wind.

When we arrived at the university, Ajla told me she wouldn't be long, but wanted to collect her work from an exam she'd recently taken. I walked over to a little outdoor kiosk to purchase a soft drink while Ajla went inside, then sat at one of the picnic tables on the lawn and waited for her return. After some time had passed, Ajla emerged from the engineering building, followed by two older adults who looked to be in their thirties. The two adults took a seat at a different table while Ajla approached me and asked if I could wait a little bit longer for her; her classmates had asked her to go over their exams with them. I said sure and watched as Ajla sat with her classmates and pored through architectural blueprints and engineering equations and numerical formula. On our drive back up to Stolac, she told me the classmates had asked her to explain where they had gone wrong in composing their answers to some of the problems. "You got them all correct?" I asked. "Not all. But most!" she replied. I learned that civil engineering was something of a tradition in Ajla's family.

Although many of Stolac's residents had returned to the small town once the war officially ended and the violence had subsided, they made-do under quite changed and challenging circumstances.⁸ This was the case for Ajla's family. When they returned to Stolac, they found their home badly damaged by the war. It was habitable, but there were a lot of repairs to undertake. Faruk and Safija both held civil engineering degrees from the University of Sarajevo and had been employed in their field prior to the war, but now there were no jobs. They tried to run a small cafe/store, but Faruk was overusing alcohol as a way of coping with the violence, displacement, and downward mobility caused by the war, and they were forced to close the cafe. In the meantime, Safija began to suffer from a severely degenerative auto-immune disease. The disease negatively impacts blood circulation to such a degree that people who suffer from it develop topical sores and deformed limbs.

When I first met Safija she took care to show me a portrait of her with Faruk and friends during their college years. It was difficult to recognize the young woman standing in bell bottoms and turtleneck, shoulder length hair framing her laughing smile captured by the photographer, in the woman who sat before me now. Safija had lost much of her hair, including her eyebrows. What hair she had was pinned up in tiny ringlets on the sides of her head. Her left foot and ankle were thickly bandaged, and her hands had become so deformed that it was difficult for her to hold a cup, or a pen. These symptoms meant she needed 24-hour care and assistance, and Safija's sister, Sara, and Ajla together became her primary caregivers. Ajla had applied to the University of Sarajevo, a two-and-a-half-hour drive away in the capital, where she dreamed of following in her parents' footsteps to study civil engineering. Ajla was admitted to the university but declined to attend at the request of her parents. Although Faruk was currently sober, he could not be counted on to consistently tend to Safija. They asked Ajla to remain in Stolac and attend university in Mostar, rather than in Sarajevo. So, Ajla stayed in Stolac.

Edin's parents sent money from the United States when they could, to assist with Safija's care. The money from Memo and Fatima helped to alleviate some of the vulnerability brought about by these hardships, a point that Ajla took great care to illustrate to me. For example, she told me the little navy Fiat car was from her mother who had purchased the car with funds from Memo's family, along with money from the meager pension she received. Safija, Ajla explained, needed Ajla to drive her to doctors' appointments, and, if necessary, to the hospital. The best regional hospital and doctors were located in Mostar, and although buses ran daily, their schedules were rather unpredictable, and generally took closer to an hour or more (rather than the more typical forty-minute car ride) because of stops along the way.[9] Relying on such transit could mean the difference between life and death for someone in Safija's fragile condition. But there was another layer to Safija's car gift: it was also a compensatory gift for Ajla's sacrifice of her Sarajevo dream. The car enabled Ajla to commute to the university in Mostar on a more flexible and dependable schedule than the bus transit offered. The car also enlarged her social world; she could come and go as she pleased, as well as extend rides to friends.

Through the purchase of the Fiat, Safija made tangible and visible the care, work, and sacrifice the extended family contributed to her well-being. These relational properties of the car are what Appadurai describes as "the social life of things" and enabled Safija to demonstrate the thoughtful investment of her brother's family's wages, transforming these into a useful object that provided mobility to Ajla and others, like me. The car also marked the status of the family: it was an economy model, not flashy, but clearly new.[10] In addition to extending Ajla's social world, the car investment objectified and reaffirmed multiple family relationships in Ajla's and Edin's families: the sibling tie between Safija and Memo; the parent-child tie between Safija and Ajla; and the new tie established with me that intensified the transnational connection between Memo's and Safija's families and their households. This reaffirmation relied on kinship identities established through reciprocal giving that also included hosting me in Edin's family's postwar apartment and helping me to navigate the social landscape of Stolac and Mostar.

Social relations in the region were tense at the time. I had arrived in the midst of a government stalemate that arose following the 2008 elections the previous fall. The city council in Mostar was unable to pass a budget or elect a mayor, and had stopped paying city workers: teachers, municipal workers, and construction workers and staff at publicly owned companies had not been paid since March. The city's governance structure mirrored the Dayton-imposed ethnic formula, and the two primary ethno-nationalist aligned political groups, the HDZ and the SDA, exploited ethnic tensions to forward their own goals.[11] This created a fraught social landscape for many in Ajla's generation, and for those who were younger, many of whom were born after the war. Ajla's approach to this was to maintain relations with Catholic and Muslim peers. There were not a multitude of opportunities for inter-ethnic socializing, but Ajla introduced me to one that involved cafes and the street.

There were a number of outdoor cafes throughout the region that catered to Ajla's generation by selling soft drinks and beer and playing American pop music. Stolac had a few such establishments, referred to as "kafić," often clustered along the same street, and Ajla and I went to several of these during the evenings. One evening we were sitting at a kafić that was owned by one of Ajla's friend's brothers, drinking cedavita (water with a vitamin C packet) when a young man at a different kafić across the street said Ajla's name and waved at her.[12] "Tino!" she exclaimed, waving back, "he's a funny guy," she said to me, "I know him from before, from school." Tino was walking across the street toward us. He came and stood near Ajla's chair and the two of them chatted for a bit. He invited us to a party later that week. As he walked away, I asked, "Did you want him to join us? He could have sat down." "He is Catholic . . . that kafić is where the Catholics go," she replied. "So he didn't want to sit down?" I asked. Ajla paused, then said, "He could sit, but some people might say things. He doesn't care, and I don't care; we are friends with everyone. But some people are stupid." I had originally assumed that Ajla took me to this kafić instead of the one across the street because she knew the owner. But it was also because our kafić was known as a Muslim space, and the other kafić was Catholic-owned. It occurred to me that I had observed a number of these street visits over the previous weeks. I thought it had just been friends happening upon one another, but then, why didn't they just choose one of the kafić and sit there together? The visitor always returned to their original seat after they'd conducted the social encounter.

These street-kafić social visits can be understood as a form of what Azra Hromadžić defines as a tradition of "trans-ethnic" social practices in the region.[13] In these sorts of encounters, ethnic difference is not ignored or glossed over, nor is ethnic difference celebrated or politicized. Rather it is acknowledged and then minimized through social exchange. Ajla didn't have much to say to me about the political situation in Mostar, other than that she was fed up with it. Ajla preferred to talk about love.

On one of my first evenings in Stolac, she took me to walk along the Bregava River, a tributary to the Neretva. In addition to Ajla and me, this stroll along the popular promenade included mostly senior men and women, walking slowly, in couples, with their hands clasped behind their backs. "Do you have a boyfriend?" Ajla inquired after we'd been walking quietly for several minutes. "No one serious right now," I replied. "What about you?" "I want to show you something," Ajla said. We walked on a bit farther, and Ajla showed me where, if you took several steps off the path and to the right, there was a bench sheltered by several large trees. The bench was not visible from the path. We sat down. "Two weeks ago, I kissed him here," Ajla said, her eyes bright with the thought of the kiss. "Oh yeah, really? This is a nice spot for a kiss," I said. "Who is he?" She went on to say that he was a cousin of a friend, and to offer more details, including that there was another woman, an ex-girlfriend who was upset by the new romance. Apparently, Ajla's love interest had become "depressed . . . I don't really believe in magic, but I think she [the ex] put some magic on him that is causing this depression," Ajla said. Further complicating the matter was the fact that he was older, and Faruk and Safija were not enthusiastic about their dating. Ajla continued on with her newfound love for the duration of my visit, and, I would learn later on from Edin, she continued her studies.

CONCLUSION

More than a decade after the political confrontations in Bosnia had officially ended, postwar reconstruction proved challenging in the context of myriad layers of governance that at times worked at cross-purposes. This was the case in the Mostar metro region where school classrooms were divided by ethnicity and local governance was at a stalemate. Despite these structural challenges, many young people remained hopeful about Bosnia's future and drew on transnational family relations to bolster their wellbeing in the postwar state.

Ajla's hopes and dreams for her future were deeply connected to her hopes for the future of her city. She aspired to rebuild the infrastructure, but also to foster cross-generational and cross-ethnic social ties as illustrated in her post-exam meeting and her street-kafić social visits. In the context of Mostar's fraught political economic context and her parents' injuries, Ajla's family was especially reliant upon her, and her ability to put to use Memo's Chicago family's monetary investment in her car. This gift from her mother helped Ajla achieve some autonomy even while she put aside her Sarajevo dreams to care for her parents.

POSTSCRIPT

Back in Chicago, in spring 2011, I received terrible news about Ajla. Edin phoned, his voice noticeably quiet, "Ana, Ajla is dead. She died." Ajla's death was a devastating loss to the family. She was just twenty-five years old. She died at home, due to unknown causes. Faruk and Safija observed the Islamic principle against fragmenting the integrity of a dead body and declined to autopsy Ajla's body. I had duplicate photos made of my visits with Ajla and her family and friends in Stolac and put them in a small handheld photo album. I placed the album inside a picture book of horses in Kentucky blue grasses, and sent the package with Edin, so he could give it to Safija and Faruk. Like the young woman waiting for the bus, Ajla craved mobility. She envisioned a larger world for herself than what postwar Mostar had to offer. Although she never had the opportunity to study in Sarajevo, or to visit Edin's family in Chicago, Ajla was embedded in transnational material social relations that shaped her too-short life. Her memory lives on in the family and friends who loved her.

NOTES

Parts of this chapter are based on material which was previously published in Croegaert, Ana. "Cars, Coffee, and 'The Crisis': Balkan Migration in Precarious

Times," in *Everyday Life in the Balkans*, David W. Montgomery, Ed. Bloomington: Indiana University Press, 2018.

1. As a U.S. passport holder, I was able to travel to Bosnia without a visa because my stay would be less than ninety days.
2. This changed after my visit. In 2010, Bosnian citizens could travel throughout the Schengen Zone without a visa as long as their stay was less than ninety days. At the time of this writing, this is projected to change again in 2021, when Bosnian citizens will be required to possess a valid European visa in order to travel in the Schengen Zone (ETIAS visa, European Travel Information and Authorization System, valid for three years). These visas are increasingly costly.
3. Stolac is built on the Bregava river bank, in the Herzegovina-Neretva Canton, surrounded by mountains Hrgud and Vidovo Polje. The current town dates to middle ages, and portions of the settlement have been under UNESCO protection since 1980. Medieval necropolis with life-size engraved gravestones called stećci are maintained throughout the region. The area is home to numerous waterfalls and gardens, and the oldest pool in BiH, built in neo-Ottoman style during the Hapsburg period.
4. Bosnian Croats held a numerical majority in some parts of Mostar and the Herzegovina region prior to the war, and their numbers increased proportional to Bosnian Muslims after the war, as a result of HVO and Croatian militias violence against Muslims.
5. See Kolind 2007, pp. 123–140. According to the 1991 census, the municipality of Stolac totaled 18,681 people; classified as 43.4 percent Muslim; 33.1 Croat; 21 percent Serb, and the town totaled 5,530 people; classified as 62 percent Muslim; 20 percent Serb and 11.8 percent Croat. During the Dayton Peace Agreement in 1995, a new settlement called Berkovići was established across the border, in the RS entity where former residents identified as Serb now live (Kolind, Torsten. "In Search of 'Decent People': Resistance to the Ethnicization of Everyday Life among the Muslims of Stolac," in *The New Bosnian Mosaic: Identities, Memories, and Moral Claims in a Post-War Society*, edited by Xavier Bougarel, Elissa Helms, Ger Duizings, 123–140. Burlington: Ashgate, 2007).
6. For an in-depth study of Mostar's segregated school system see Hromadžić 2015 (Hromadžić, Azra. *Citizens of an Empty Nation: Youth and State-making in Postwar Bosnia and Herzegovina*. University of Pennsylvania Press, 2015).
7. Ajla and I communicated through a combination of her partial English skills, and my partial Bosnian skills. I reproduce our exchanges here in English.
8. At the time, the official rate of unemployment in 2009 in BiH was 25.7 percent, as compared with 9 percent in Croatia and 10 percent in the United States; five years later, the unemployment rate in BiH was virtually unchanged. These numbers were much more extreme when it came to youth unemployment; among this age group (15–24) the unemployment rate was 48.7 percent in 2009. Statistical Yearbook 2010. *Federation of Bosnia and Herzegovina, Federal Office of Statistics*. Sarajevo, BiH: Zelenih beretki 26, 71000 Sarajevo http://www.fzs.ba/Godisnjak2010k.pdf

Statistical Yearbook 2015. *Federation of Bosnia and Herzegovina, Federal Office of Statistics*. Sarajevo, BiH: Zelenih beretki 26, 71000 Sarajevo http://www.fzs.ba/SG2015.pdf

For Youth Unemployment, see http://data.worldbank.org/indicator/SL.UEM.1524.ZS?page=1(2009) http://data.worldbank.org/indicator/SL.UEM.1524.ZS (2011–2015). In 2015, the youth unemployment rate in the United States was 14 percent. Croatia's was much higher, at 45.9 percent, but this is still ten percentage points lower than Bosnia's. Obtaining accurate labor, wage, and income statistics is a challenge. The unemployment rate is based on the number of persons in the labor force (ages 15–64) who are registered as job seekers with local employment service agencies, and thus does not capture unregistered job seekers. Further, these reports do not capture activities in the informal economy.

9. On the days I took the bus into Mostar, I consistently found that the stops, and even the routes changed.

10. According to my conversations with people in Mostar, twenty years earlier it would have been unusual, but not unheard of, for women to own and drive cars in Mostar—an activity associated primarily with men. Indeed, I was told by a male friend from Mostar that I "drive like a man," which he meant as a compliment (!). But women drivers were becoming increasingly common; during my stay I saw young women driving electric scooters, and a woman-owned food delivery operation, "MakDonald Jela's Pita," run out of a station wagon.

11. Bosnia's postwar governance structure emphasizes ethno-political affiliations by dividing the country into two "entities," a rotating tri-ethnic presidency, and myriad ethnic-designated appointments at cantonal and municipal levels. This structure was imposed in the U.S.-brokered peace agreement, included "oversight" of a European High Commissioner, and has significantly stalled the effective governance necessary for reconstruction. Bosnians who are not members of the three majority ethnic groups, such as Bosnian Roma and Jews, have filed discrimination claims with the state based on their exclusion from ethnically designated positions.

12. Young women at kafić drank sweet drinks like cola or cedavita, while men more often drank beer.

13. Hromadžić, "Discourses of Trans-ethnic Narod."

Chapter Four

Shifting Time in the Social Life of Bosnian Coffee

Amina's name came up several times when I asked people for recommendations as to who else I should be in touch with to understand Bosnian refugees' experiences in Chicago. Amina herself, however, had not come to Chicago as a refugee. She was among a handful of Bosnian professionals who had drawn on international connections to leave the country just prior to the war, either through family sponsorship or via work visas. When Chicago began receiving wartime refugee cohorts, Amina found employment with local volags and social service agencies that sought her Bosnian language and culture expertise. After a number of email exchanges, we had arranged for my visit to her home. I entered the large lobby of the high-rise building where Amina lived, walked across a sparkling tile floor past the sectional seating area, and approached the doorman who called Amina. Once she gave the okay for me to visit her apartment, I walked over to the elevator and rode it up multiple stories to Amina's floor. I located her apartment, knocked, and Amina opened the door, inviting me inside. I asked her if I should take off my boots, and she replied, no, most Bosnians would insist that I do, but that she did not mind if I kept my boots on. I decided I would take them off anyway and handed her the small plant I brought as a gift before bending down to remove my boots, quickly turning my right sock in an effort to conceal a small hole that had appeared near my big toe.

The apartment was small and beautifully decorated. I followed Amina over to deep dark orange couches nestled in a corner of the room, directly in front of a set of large windows that now looked out into the dark evening but would show the lake in the morning light. I sat with my back to the windows, facing the kitchen that adjoined the living and dining area vis a vis a bar-level countertop. The room was lined with bookshelves containing titles in Bosnian and in English, and Amina had pulled titles she thought might be of particular interest to me and set them atop the coffee table in front of the sitting area. I remarked upon her thoughtfulness and started to look through one of the books. Amina offered to make us a coffee. I said I would love a coffee and continued to read while Amina went to the kitchen and opened a package of Starbucks coffee pods, popping two, one after the other, into an instant espresso machine. When the machine finished processing the coffees, she brought two small espresso cups over and placed one on the coffee table in front of me, and the other near her seat.

As I visited with Amina, I learned that she had enjoyed many of the best comforts that Yugoslavia had to offer. She came from a highly educated family, and she selected traditionally feminine areas of study: advanced study in Slavic languages and literature. Like many women of her generation, she built a career out of her studies and traveled as a SFRY education emissary to teach Slavic languages and culture through the Yugoslav embassy in places as diverse as China, Algeria, and Ghana. She was a champion of Yugoslav languages in Chicago as evidenced in her involvement in English as a Second Language curriculum in some of the Chicago Public Schools with the highest numbers of Bosnian students. She had contributed numerous articles in Bosnian and in English to Chicago area Bosnian language publications, and to newsletters intended for social workers and teachers working with Bosnian refugees.

Amina believed in the assimilation model of immigration, wherein the goal is to teach immigrants American norms that by the second or third generation will be fully adopted by the immigrant cohort, leaving them thoroughly Americanized and recognized as such. She framed her involvement in Bosnian refugee life in Chicago with this assimilationist lens and over the past few years she had developed a set of opinions about the challenges faced by refugees that she shared with me. She drew a distinction between her prewar migration experience and those of people who arrived later as refugees explaining that she had a sibling already situated in Chicago years before the war, thereby providing a foundation for Amina's migration. In addition to arriving with strong professional credentials, Amina arrived fluent in English, which further smoothed her transition to American living. Finally, she had lost her property in Bosnia, and lost some of her social standing by emigrating to the United States, but she did not lose family in the wars, and she saw this as a critical difference between her circumstances and the circumstances of those who were forced from their homes during the war.

When I asked her what she thought of Bosnians' work and employment circumstances she emphatically declared that "Bosnians are very hard workers," and then went on to say, "but, you know, we have a problem, a cultural problem of 'nema problema,' do you know what that is?" "It's like when you seem upset by something people think you ought not to be upset by, right?

Like, they want you not to worry, right? Like saying 'take it easy,' or 'no worries'?" I offered. Amina nodded, and replied, "sort of" but then went on to say that "Bosnians are too easy about time," and offered an example, "Bosnians are always late for meetings: if they tell you they'll be there at five o'clock, this means six o'clock, and if they have invited you, and tell you to arrive at five o'clock, it means they will be ready for you at six o'clock." According to Amina, if you were to say, "hey, where were you at five? Or, why didn't we begin at five?" a typical response would be *nema problema,* which translates literally as "no problem." Amina's critique of Bosnian refugees' relatively relaxed approach to time highlights the significance of people's senses of time and space to organizing their social worlds.[1] While Amina looked unfavorably upon this laid-back sensibility, her perspective contrasted markedly with many of the other refugees I met. The women in the seniors' group at TCC, and Selma, one of the most successful small cafe owners in the community, embraced a slower approach to time that they associated with Bosnia, and emphasized through the production of a particular kind of coffee service, what Bosnians refer to as *prava kafa / the real coffee*. Coffee consumption emerged as a key focus because people insisted that I pay attention to it. In this chapter, I explore coffee practices among the Bosnian refugee diaspora and ask: what can the social life of a cup of coffee tell us about refugees' postwar lives in Chicago?

PRAVA KAFA / THE REAL COFFEE

Amina's coffee was unlike the coffee I'd grown accustomed to drinking at TCC, and during my other home visits, the coffee known as *"prava kafa"*: "the real coffee." Prava kafa, or Bosnian coffee, sometimes glossed as "Turkish coffee," is a traditional coffee service that spread throughout the Balkan Peninsula and across parts of the middle east and north Africa during the Ottoman period. The various coffee practices that developed over time in these regions share some qualities: this type of coffee emphasizes service, sociality, and the investment of time. Yet these practices also delineate distinct regional histories. For example, the traditional Bosnian coffee carafe, known as a *džezva (pl. džezve),* is made by artisans using hammering techniques to embellish the copper carafes with locally derived motifs, and, while Turkish style coffee often incorporates sugar during the brewing process, and sometimes spices as do Ethiopian and Syrian processes, Bosnian coffee does not use spice, and never uses sugar in the brewing, rather offering a sugar cube with the coffee that the drinker can dip in the beverage according to their individual preference.

To prepare Bosnian coffee, you need:	The following is a typical brewing process for making Bosnian coffee:
<ul><li>heat source, preferably open flame (but electric is ok)</li><li>water</li><li>džezva (may use special copper džezva, but enamel or stainless steel are more common)</li><li>extremely finely ground coffee (traditionally with a cylindrical handmill)</li><li>fildžani, small porcelain cups</li><li>two or more people to drink together</li><li>somewhere to sit</li><li>*optional:* sugar cubes, lokum ("Turkish delight," a candy gel made with sugar and starch)</li></ul>	While you bring a kettle of water to boil, place ground coffee in a džezva. Since džezve come in different sizes, a reliable measure is to tilt the džezva clockwise at an angle and place enough coffee to meet the center of the inner base of the carafe. Once the water has boiled, let it sit for a moment (until there are no bubbles) and pour hot water into džezva until it is half-full, stir the coffee, and place džezva over the heat source. As soon as the liquid begins to bubble and climb toward the džezva's lip, remove the džezva (turn off heat). Pour a little bit of the leftover hot water on top of the coffee to help the grinds settle. Serve the coffee to guest(s) in fildžani, placing a sugar cube on the saucer next to the cups. If there is any leftover coffee in the džezva, place it on the table so that cups may be refilled.

There are a number of variations on these steps, for example, some brewers insist that you must settle the grinds with cold water, rather than warm, and people have different methods for measuring the coffee portions, but these are the basic steps.[2]

Bosnian coffee is integral to hosting practices, and the process of brewing and serving Bosnian coffee is labor-intensive; the emphasis is on the brewer who must remain at the heat source during the entire brewing process to prevent the coffee from boiling and burning. The brewer is almost always also the server, who in turn emphasizes her service skills by being attentive to her guest's preferences and making adjustments accordingly: "do you like foam, or no foam?" "sugar?" "would you like another cup?" When Bosnian coffee is offered in the home, the brewer is almost always a woman, but there were exceptions to this. Nasiha for example, never made Bosnian coffee for me, but her husband Edo prepared it for her and me to drink together on several occasions.

Bosnian coffee also relies on distinct equipment, in particular, the džezva and fildžani, as well as handmills used for grinding the coffee beans. During the nineteenth and early twentieth centuries, these objects were often gifted during marriage and handed down among family members, and thus were among the treasured items people sought to bring with them when they fled

Bosnia during the war.³ But many people were unable to bring them, or the items were stolen along their journey, and arrived in the United States without them. Thus, if people were able to bring these valued objects with them to Chicago, they made a point of using them, or at least displaying them. Vehida illustrated this point for me early on when she showed me the handmill she had managed to bring with her from Bosnia and used it to grind the beans for our coffee, although she easily could have used Hana's electric grinder and coffee machine instead. With me, and sometimes Hana, as her captive audience, Vehida used the slow performance of Bosnian coffee making and service to create a social space in which she was in control and could share some details of her life prior to the war.

Both coffees, American and Bosnian, or "regular" and "the real," were also available at TCC. There was an automatic drip coffeemaker in the staff room that seemed to never be empty. But for the senior women's group on Fridays, Ajša, the group leader, would prepare Bosnian coffee. Since there was no stove at the center, Ajša bought a hot plate for TCC, and used it to heat the water and make the coffee. This was a less than ideal setup that yielded rather lukewarm results, but the women nevertheless appreciated Ajša's efforts, thanking her as she moved slowly around the rectangular table, filling the small fildžani and offering sugar and some small cookie, often a nutella-filled wafer, or a graham-cracker-like biscuit. I had also learned that if I entered TCC with a coffee in a to-go cup, I should be prepared to be reprimanded: several women staffers and members of the senior group had scolded me for this, telling me that coffee should be taken while seated, not in transit, and ought to be sipped, not gulped. I had witnessed Vehida similarly admonish Hana and Sara for bringing to-go coffees into the home. The consumption of Bosnian coffee, then, was seen to help make a particular kind of body. Unlike the thriving American coffee-to-go industry that marketed the beverage's stimulant properties to appeal to people's efforts to get a body fueled for work or for school, Bosnian coffee was seen to make bodies social, restful, and satisfied.

SERVING UP AND DRINKING-IN THE NATION

The shelves, deli counter, freezers, refrigerators, and produce bins at Devon Market burst with myriad color, texture, shape, and scent. It's the kind of bustling neighborhood store where you have to wind your way around store clerks kneeling beside boxes of newly arrived produce as they attempt to restock shelves in their efforts to keep up with competitive shoppers from the multi-story senior housing complex down the block. Grandmas and grandpas, aunties and uncles pluck rice and beans from the shelves; poke and point at flank steak and ground meat at the deli counter; smell, shake, and tap onion, melons, and cabbage; browse rows of wine bottles; and inspect the packaged cookies and candies. In their quest to prepare the weekend meal, host their neighbor, and provision neighborhood kids, they seem intent on emptying the shelves just as quickly as the store clerk can fill them. Devon Market was also among the most popular places to shop for the finely ground coffee used to make Bosnian coffee.

The market was owned by a Greek immigrant family and it was one of many stores specializing in imports for immigrant groups on a two-and-a-half-mile stretch of Devon Avenue bounded on the west by the Skokie Canal. The store's offerings from the former Yugoslavia included chocolates, cookies and sweets, pickled peppers and *ajvar* (a condiment made from red peppers and eggplant, typically eaten with the sausage *ćevapi/ćevapčići)*, and coffee. For a country of only 4.6 million people, and a diaspora population of between one and two million, the number of different coffee brands produced in postwar Bosnia-Herzegovina was striking. The brand-names and packaging on these products tell a story of the region's history.

Gendered images of idealized home-life adorned the colorful caffeinated packages: a typical Bosnian-style house, a hostess wearing a crown, and variations on the *džezva*. I found that the two most popular brands people had in the homes, and also at TCC, to be one called simply, "Bosnia," and another called "Aroma," described as "Turkish style." The *Bosnia* coffee package came in a rectangular box that shows a traditional Bosnian Muslim home (square and with a roof made of four-triangle panels whose tips meet in the center, like regional mosque architecture) and is roasted, ground, and packaged in Visoko, central Bosnia. The "Turkish Style" *Aroma* coffee came in a white and turquoise aluminum can and was roasted and packaged in Chicago. These coffees could be found in the "ethnic" food section at Devon Market, and the *Aroma* coffee was stocked in both the "ethnic" aisle, as well as in the general, unmarked, coffee and tea section several aisles over, along with *Folgers* and *Maxwell House*. This shifting aspect of the Aroma "Turkish Style" brand allowed it to belong in the marked category of "ethnic," as well as in the unmarked category of "American," and indexed the social history of coffee in the Balkans.

The Ottoman Empire brought the coffee beverage to the Balkan Peninsula during the Empire's 400-year administration from the mid-fifteenth to mid-nineteenth centuries. Coffee cultivated in colonies in Northeast Africa and in the Arabian Peninsula was used across the Empire's metropoles in practices primarily involving men. Historian Ralph Hattox writes that Sufi Muslims

Figure 4.1. Devon Market Coffee Shelves. October 2006. Photo by Ana Croegaert.

used the beverage to help reduce the need for sleep and to stimulate the energy required for *dhikr* rituals (religious praise ceremonies).[4] But the extension of coffee drinking beyond religious ritual occurred through the institution of the "coffeehouse," a place where men could go to socialize outside of the hospitality codes of the household while remaining within social norms of the "proper." In the multi-faith empire, Muslim men were discouraged from socializing in taverns that served alcohol. But while various local ulema (Muslim religious scholars, versed in Shari'ah, the Islamic code of conduct) debated the proper application of Qur'anic doctrine to coffee drinking, coffee ultimately was declared a legal substance, whereas alcohol remained officially prohibited. Thus, initially, coffee drinking practices in the Balkans were connected to urban spaces and restricted primarily to social uses among educated and cosmopolitan groups of Muslim men.[5]

For some among Chicago's Bosnians, the association of Bosnian coffee with Islam is also made, as depicted in Isak Berbić's cover photo on the 2004 October / Ramadan issue of *Zambak*, a Chicago-based Bosnian language diaspora publication.

The džezva service here is in the hammered copper style distinctive to Southern Bosnia, and serves as backdrop to baklava, an archetypal Middle Eastern sweet. The Zambak cover, and the packages on the market shelves, offer a view to this coffee's multiple meanings. First, they reference Bosnian coffee's transnational foodways through the intersection of Islam and Empire. Second, they are emblematic of the new post-SFRY Bosnian state. The *Bosnia* image of the house, pictured on a postage stamp, and the association

Figure 4.2. *Zambak* Magazine Ramadan 2004 cover shot with džezva and fildžan. Photo courtesy of Isak Berbić.

of Bosnian coffee with the magazine title, "Zambak" symbolize this new national identity. "Zambak" is the Turkish word for "lily" and references the fleur-de-lis emblem on the flag of the Republic of Bosnia-Herzegovina (1992–1997).[6] The fleur-de-lis represents the medieval kingdom of Bosnia that existed prior to Ottoman administration and associated religious conversions and migrations. These references elide the SFRY era, and weave together a complex set of allusions to pre-Ottoman Bosnia, Ottoman Bosnia, and post-Yugoslav Bosnia and Herzegovina that simultaneously posit Bosnian coffee as a national, transnational, and pan-ethnic food. This approach to coffee is akin to what Richard Wilk described as the creation of "real Belizean food" in his comparison of dinner visits in pre- and post-independence Belize. Wilk argues that the creation of "local" cuisine helped to diminish status differences among Belizeans, and to authorize Belizean national identity. In the case of diverse Bosnian refugees, these coffee products offered sensory connection to and a disaporan affiliation with pre- and post-1991 Bosnia-Herzegovina.[7]

Finally, although coffee practices in the Balkans originally signaled explicitly Islamic, urban cultural practices, their cultivation during the Ottoman-era meant that a greater number of people could take part in the practice, and this resulted in the development of coffee drinking as integral to hospitality and home life. When the domestic sphere incorporated coffee brewing and consumption, women of all nationalities, in city and in village, became central to the process. Thus, in addition to being a marker of ethnic and religious difference, adaptations of "Turkish coffee" service has served for many Bosnians as a symbol through which ethnicity is recognized and traversed.[8] This is particularly so among women, whose uses of coffee home-visits in Bosnia have facilitated the recognition of death, marriage and household formation, hardship, and religious holidays among Muslim, Catholic, and Orthodox households.[9] When women entered the labor force during the SFRY's industrialization and urbanization push in the 1950s–1980s, they brought the tradition of the coffee visit with them, preparing and drinking Bosnian coffee together during work breaks. While I participated in many coffee visits in people's homes, I focus here on immigrants' uses of *prava kafa* outside of the home. I argue that because Bosnian coffee symbolizes the aforementioned Southeast European sociocultural, political, and historical elements and is associated with both domestic space and public space, Bosnian coffee provided women refugees a familiar set of social activities through which they could channel their evaluations of living in the United States, after war, and after Yugoslav socialism.

MAKING SENSE OF POST-MIGRATION LIFE OVER BOSNIAN COFFEE

On an exceptionally frigid Friday in February, I approached the Center, wondering how many women—if any at all—would be present for the seniors' group. The cold temperatures and slippery sidewalks made venturing out of doors a treacherous undertaking since many walkways had not been effectively cleared of the most recent snowfall and its icy aftermath. When I entered the activities room, I was surprised to find that most of the seats were taken. Nasiha was there, along with five of the regular participants, and two occasional attendees. The women chatted with one another across the rectangular table, and Ajša was passing out fildžani. I greeted the women and took a seat next to Esma. Her husband had recently died of cancer, and this was her first visit to the group following his death. She appeared to me to look a bit weary around her eyes, but she was smiling in conversation with Zumreta, who was known for her jokes and for her efforts to find a wife for her adult son.

Ajša confirmed how many women wanted a coffee, and then walked over to a shelf where the hot plate sat. It was a double-burner hot plate, so she could heat the water on one side while heating the other burner for when the water was ready to brew the coffee. She pulled out a large enamel džezva and set to work measuring in the grounds, adding the heated water to the grounds, stirring, and then placing the džezva on the electric burner. Ifeta, one of the occasional participants, had brought a package of mini nutella wafers that she passed around the table. Ajša brought the džezva over and walked around, slowly filling the small cups in front of the women near Nasiha's half of the table and remarked that she would make more for the remaining five at the other end of the table. Soon, we were all sipping fildžani full of dark coffee.

I came to think of these Friday afternoon senior group meetings as similar to what Schwartzman describes as a particular kind of sense-making social form. Schwartzman examined meetings at a Chicago mental health center and found that the explicit function of the meeting as an important arena for organizational or group decision-making was *not*, in fact, the most important role of the meeting in organizational or group culture. According to Schwartzman, the more significant aspects of the meetings were not items spelled out in the agenda, but rather that meetings provided continuity by reproducing a social form (the meeting) through which groups exercised power by validating and making sense of problems, identities, projects, and activities. Central to her analysis were participants' gestures, bodily movements, uses of objects, facial expressions, and speech that did not pertain directly to the meeting topic.[10]

Ajša's incorporation of džezva, fildžani, and the practice of making Bosnian coffee during these meetings was not an official part of the meeting agenda, but rather introduced the familiar practice to mark the opening of the meeting—a gathering of women of varied class, ethno-religious and regional origins, and political backgrounds. As we saw in chapter 1, tensions around these differences occasionally arose, and people sometimes projected war-time experiences onto post-war social interactions.[11] In this context, the shared familiar coffee elements were critical to establishing a collective Yugo-Bosnian space through which senior women diagnosed their postwar, post-migration lives. This group experience was distinct from the refugee-ethnic coherence framework TCC staff were pressured to project to funders and external audiences such as those who had attended the *Necessary Targets* play. In the senior women's group, the shared conversation topics emphasized gender and generational similarities more so than refugee status and ethnic affiliations.

As was typical, the day's official meeting discussion topic, heart disease and diabetes, for which several of them were being treated, was quickly addressed and the women moved on to discuss the problems of their adult children, namely how tired and overworked they were. This was a recurring topic and seemed to be both a point of pride as well as a point of concern among the senior women. Zumreta, for example, told of how hard her son was working in construction (non-union) and emphasized that this hard work ethic would make him a good husband. But there was also a history of heart disease and early heart attacks in the family, and she worried that the work was too strenuous, and also feared that he put too much pressure on himself to work as many days and projects as possible. Ajša, Nasiha, and I acknowledged Zumreta's concerns, and another woman, Ifeta, suggested Zumreta encourage her son to look for a different job.

Ifeta was in her early fifties, younger than the more senior women, but older than their children. Technically, she wasn't age-qualified for the seniors' group, but she was friends with Ajša and Fadila, and occasionally attended the meetings if she did not have work. She came today because she wanted to tell us about her new job. She was very excited because her hourly wage would increase, and she would be required to work fewer hours. I had interviewed Ifeta previously and knew that she had decades of experience in food services. In the SFRY she had worked for fifteen years as a cafeteria cook preparing meals for workers at a shoe factory that employed hundreds of workers. After arriving in Chicago, she had worked first on the salad line at a hotel kitchen, and more recently at a nursing home kitchen. She was glad to be able to quit the nursing home because she was always scheduled to work overtime, but since she was technically employed by a placement agency that the nursing home contracted with to fill their labor needs, the home was not obligated to compensate her with overtime pay. She estimated that she regularly clocked in fifty or sixty hours of work per week at the same hourly rate of ten dollars.

Ifeta's anticipation of improved conditions at her new job, with another long-term care facility in an adjacent suburb, led her to recount the challenges of work in the United States. She described how, after she paid for her commute, her monthly health insurance premium that covered her, her husband, and her two teenaged daughters, she only had money left for rent and food. "I want to return there, where it is better, where you have a job, a pension, and a more relaxed life." Ifeta went on to say that the "only" major difference between America and Bosnia was time: "There [in SFRY Bosnia] you could work for eight hours and have a good life, here [United States] you must work nonstop to have a good life—to vacation, spend time with your family." As Ifeta spoke, some of the other women chimed in about the precarious circumstances of their sons and daughters, several of whom did not have full time work, or were subsisting on public aid or social security. Ifeta was only able to avoid public assistance because she, like Fadila, had access to the income of other employed adults living in her household. Zumreta, perhaps galvanized by Ifeta's unfavorable comparison of the United States with

Bosnia / SFRY, extended the discussion by offering a colorful, visceral adage. She set up the following exchange between a doctor and a patient: The patient awakens to find the doctor standing over his hospital bed. The doctor gives the patient a choice before providing an account of the patient's ailment and prescribed treatment: would the patient prefer to hear the good news first? Or the bad news? The patient requests the bad news first. The doctor replies that, unfortunately, he had to cut off the patient's gangrenous legs in order to prevent the spread of infection. And the good news? Now that the patient had neither legs nor feet, the patient no longer needed his shoes; the good news is that the patient can make money by selling the shoes. Zumreta ended the story with the statement: "Money is everything in America."

In this narrative, America figures as the doctor and Bosnian refugee-immigrants as the patient, and money trumps physical injury. While Zumreta's was among the more obvious interpretations of their recent migration as a form of uneven exchange, it resonated among the women around the table. For these women, the most visible symbol of difference between living in SFRY Bosnia and in present-day America were the tired, overworked bodies of people like Zumreta's son, and like Ifeta. Ifeta's experiences and Zumreta's insertion of the mini narrative about dismemberment and money further emphasized and extended this distinction by connecting time, work, and money. In Yugoslavia, people had enough. They had work, but they were not overworked. They had the means to care for their bodies and keep them whole. They did not have to experience injury in order to make money so they could buy health insurance. They had enough time; they didn't have to buy it by working overtime in a low-wage job.

The senior coffee meetings also created a space where people from mixed families could signal their belonging within a majority Bosnian Muslim group. The most obvious aspect of this group belonging was made visible by demonstrating one's familiarity with the real coffee by maintaining the social norms associated with the practice. For example, knowing that you don't place your sugar cube in the coffee, but rather dip the cube to soak up some coffee and then suck the cube. Or, by offering an opinion on the best grounds to use for the coffee. But women also used the meetings to implement strategies to demonstrate their belonging among the group.

Nasiha, for example, explained to me that even though her mother and her maternal grandparents were Muslim, because her father was Bosnian Croat, and because her mother was single, she was met with skepticism when she began showing up to TCC community events. She consistently showed up at events, and began helping with senior programming at TCC, often bringing her grandmother with her. She felt her persistence had paid off, and that over time her refugee peers had come to view her with trust. And one afternoon

Fadila shared a story with the group that when Croatian nationalist forces entered her town, and her Muslim neighbors prepared to leave, she told them to bring their valuables to her home. Since her daughter's husband was Croatian, and his family were friends, she was certain they would be protected. Instead, when the armed militia arrived, they forcibly expelled Fadila and her entire family, along with her son-in-law, and set about destroying and looting their belongings, including her neighbors' television and other possessions. By sharing this story with the mixed senior group, Fadila presented herself, and her Croatian son-in-law, as allied with the others in the refugee diaspora.

Ajša's decision to include Bosnian coffee thereby distinguished the meeting place from other TCC programming (where Bosnian coffee was not served), and over the prava kafa, women created a space where individuals could bring problems to the table and have them identified, affirmed (or not), and interpreted by a group of their peers. Regardless of their differences, they were all familiar with the "real coffee," and could draw on this practice to minimize their differences and emphasize their shared experiences of displacement. In deviating from the day's official meeting topic of heart disease and diabetes, the women moved the discussion from a medicalized discourse on bodily health to one that centered bodily weariness and interpreted this as the result of an economic system driven by overwork and a lack of social welfare. In this space over cups of Bosnian coffee, Zumreta's and Ifeta's comments provided both validation and evaluation of their displacement, felt most acutely in the ramping up of time work demands in return for an ever elusive "good life."

WHO HAS TIME FOR ĆEJF?

Bosnian Yugoslav refugees felt the pressures of the different sense of an American time: deliberately hurried rather than unhurried. Notably, in conversations about Bosnian coffee people emphasized that coffee was for resting, for when you wanted to take a break in contrast with an American emphasis on coffee as a beverage needed for activity and for work. This American sensibility of caffeinated time is aptly illustrated in the Dunkin' advertising slogan, "America runs on Dunkin.'"[12] The Dunkin' ad tells this story visually with four blocks: the first contains the continental United States, the second a running unisex action figure with what appears to be a coffee cup for legs, the third with the word "on" and the final block containing the "DD" logo. While middle- and working-class laborers gulped their American "yuppie coffees" as they passed by TCC on their way to work, Bosnian refugees brought a form of slow coffee drinking to Chicago. Bosnian coffee proved to be such a significant social form among the refugee diaspora that I created an interview guide centered on the practice.[13] Nasiha and Dženi helped by conducting interviews with the senior generation about their memories and stories of Bosnian coffee, while I documented the interviews. A common theme in these interviews was the concept of *ćejf*, as for example it emerged in Dženi's interview with Rasima (in her late seventies at the time):

> *Dzeni*: And do you remember the whole ritual? You said at the beginning that it was mainly old folks and men who drank coffee. Do you make one pot of coffee and then they are sitting and sipping like that for an hour, two, and talking? Do you remember that? Can you bring it to life for us?
>
> *Rasima*: You call it *cejf*, you know. Like, pleasure. Some drink their coffee for an hour, two, sitting, and a little [sipping], and especially if they're smoking. . . . And so, if they have time, they're sitting, sitting over that coffee, sip a little bit. . . .

For many, Bosnian coffee conjures sensory experiences that involve slowing time and shifting space. People describe this coffee as "about time . . . there was some special magic (*čar*)" offered another woman. Nasiha's aunt Tidža reported that one took coffee "when you get tired and coffee hits the spot . . . to get some rest." People also emphasize the pleasure of drinking coffee; "we knew how to relish (*ćejfit*) it" and contrasted this to the practice of drinking coffee to-go, or in transit when people "just gulp it down . . . you don't relish [the experience] (*ne ćejfis*)." This focus on embodied sensations linked to time and space add another layer to the meaning of Bosnian coffee and emphasize its significance to marking structural changes in time and space.

In this sense, it is helpful to think of Bosnian coffee as a mnemonic device, as a practice whose elements emphasize memory and distinctions of time among the diaspora. As with the senior women's group, much of the talk over Bosnian coffee marked time: before the war and after the war, as well as place: here and there, and also people: those who left and those who remain. Anthropological studies of consumption show that people's social uses of foods establish consumption norms that maintain social boundaries. Through food, people create cultural contrast, cultural mixing, and cultural change. Ethnographic explorations of consumption in formerly communist Europe for example, highlight the links among commodity-use and discourses of temporality and place, and document people's strategic uses of commodities and products to generate meaning by linking personal histories to state histories, often proposing counter-narratives to new (and old) hegemonic forms.[14]

As Rasima's exchange with Dženita suggests, Bosnian immigrants also identified differences in acts of consumption through the concept of "ćejf."

Amra introduced me to "ćejf," which often involves drinking coffee slowly, perhaps while smoking a cigarette. These were in fact the activities in which Amra was engaged when I happened upon her on a Saturday afternoon at the community center. In addition to Friday afternoons with the seniors, I also attended Amra's Saturday morning Bosnian language lesson for kids. After class, I remained behind to talk with some of the kids as they waited for parents or their older siblings to pick them up. Once the kids were gone, I looked for Amra and found her smoking a cigarette near the alley-exit door. A coffee (American) sat on her desk near the exit. She laughingly accused me of "interrupting [my] ćejf," explaining that she was savoring the quiet before returning home to the apartment she shared with her husband and preteen son.

There is no direct English translation for ćejf, and whenever I asked for one, speakers offered up replies with the disclaimer that the translation did not adequately convey the meaning of ćejf. Significantly, ćejf (v. ćejfiti) involves senses of time: slowing time; transcending time; to "enjoy life without hurrying."[15] And, like the origins of coffee in the Balkans, ćejf is a concept that draws on the region's Ottoman history: the Bosnian ćejf is derived from the Turkish word "keyif." But perhaps equally important, ćejf is a pleasure principle that emphasizes sensory experiences and depends on what some described as "atmosphere." Snežana Žabić, a multilingual Yugoslav Chicago-based writer, translates ćejfiti as "to relish." As a pleasure principle, ćejf is an expression of very individual and particular desires, but it is most often achieved in the peripheral presence of others, such as in public spaces, or community spaces like the Center. Nasiha described it as

> along the lines of a guilty pleasure that relaxes you and gives you a lot of pleasure, without the guilt! It is about enjoyment for one's own benefit. Also, it is used as an excuse when there is no rational reason why you would do something. It is often used in the context of somebody interrupting you and you replying, "do not spoil my ćejf,"

as Amra had in fact accused me of doing. Nasiha and Edo elaborated further when I asked them about it, explaining that ćejf is the ability to experience, with pleasure, sights, sounds, smells, foods, "everyday pleasures [it's] not about fantasy, but about reality." People repeatedly remarked upon their sense that those who remained in Bosnia-Herzegovina had more than enough time to experience ćejf, "they spend all their time sitting in cafes," as Amra put it, while the refugee diaspora in the United States had too much work to have time for ćejf.[16]

Thus, even as the senior women, along with Amra and others, offered critiques of hurried American time, like Amina, they also offered narratives that alternatively critiqued "Bosnian time," and exploited Bosnian time sensibilities in the sale of slow coffee to both Balkan and American customers. In the case of the latter, a female entrepreneur drew upon Bosnian/Turkish coffee service and its association with ćejf, fusing these with gourmet locavore and slow food principles to attract and sustain her client base. These activities relate to a more implicit set of critiques of the work speed-ups and the celebration of consumer taste-cachets of neoliberal capitalism and are articulated through modes of comportment, consumption, and conduct.

Selma's Café: Slow Coffee & Commodifying Ćejf

While ćejf emphasizes the small pleasures of everyday life, it also specifies individual taste, a distinction that is roundly and notoriously exploited in the market segmentation that accompanies capitalist consumption.[17] Ćejf thus lends itself to commodification, in addition to critique. Selma's Café (owned and operated by Selma) provides an example of the commodification of ćejf through the strategic combination of Bosnian coffee which she marketed as "Turkish coffee" and pan-Balkan cuisine, framed by references to American trends in "slow food" and "locavore" food cultures.

Selma is Muslim, from a coastal town in Montenegro, and arrived in the United States in 2000, when Montenegro was still, along with Serbia, officially part of the Federated Republic of Yugoslavia.[18] In Montenegro, she had more than fifteen years of experience managing a large grocery store with a staff of twenty. When I met her in 2006 in Chicago, Selma operated out of a small storefront flanked on one side by a hair salon and on the other, a tax accountant. Selma is friendly and had developed a strong network that included family members, her Bosnian boyfriend, and Maria, who owned the salon next door and had emigrated from Mexico, whom she could rely on to help her run the business. When Selma had to make trips back to Montenegro to check on her ailing mother and her brother, who was slowly dying from cirrhosis, she left the cafe in the care of her sister Rada, and of Maria and Maria's teenage son José to manage it in her absence. Her daughter and boyfriend helped with restocking the kitchen and preparing the menu.

I quickly learned that Selma prides herself on making meals that she describes as "fresh and traditional," and, upon discovering that I was an anthropologist interested in migration and food practices, Selma made a point of telling me that all her meats were purchased from the same local halal butcher, and she insisted on taking me back to the kitchen on every visit to show me what she had in the refrigerator and what she was making for the day's menu. Selma's short menu centers on an assortment of pan-Balkan foods.

The spot was frequented by sets of regular customers. Migrant male contract construction workers from Central America, Mexico, Poland, and the Balkans stopped by to pick up *pita*, a traditional Bosnian pie made of wafer-thin pastry dough stuffed with ground meat, potatoes, and onion (this version

Specialties

*Pita/Burek Rolled dough stuffed with your choice of cheese, spinach & cheese, beef & potatoes & onions, onions & potatoes,..$6

*Homemade Eastern European Bread..............................$2

Salads

Cabbage Salad (diced white and purple cabbage with oil and vinegar)...$3
Mediterranean Salad (diced tomatoes, cucumbers, and green peppers)...$3
Greek Salad (Mediterranean Salad with feta cheese on top)...$4

Drinks

Tea, Coffee, or Soft Drinks............$1.50
Turkish Coffee.........................$2

Sweets

For carryout needs you can call us in advance or just stop in!

Figure 4.3. "Selma's" Restaurant Menu.

is called *burek*) or spinach, cheese, and onion, rolled into tubes, and wound into a pinwheel for their midday meal; neighborhood American couples in their forties and fifties often came for dinner; an older man who grew up in Greece and emigrated in his twenties orders the "Turkish" coffee; and faculty and graduate student "foodies" from nearby universities enjoy "the Yugoslav setting," as one self-described academic foodie characterized his experience to me. At the time, Chicago boasted a growing "locavore" movement comprised of restaurateurs and organic farmers who partner to cater to "modern gourmets" interested in eating locally grown produce, and locally raised beef, lamb, pork, and poultry.[19] Participants viewed this as a way to support organic farming practices, invigorate local markets, and decrease their "carbon footprint" because consuming locally means food transport routes are reduced, and thus fewer fossil fuels are used.[20] The locavore movement was one of several new food-related consumer social movements of which the western European-based "Slow Food" movement is perhaps the most well-known. True to its campaign title, the Slow Food movement is about promoting the slow production, preparation, and consumption of food in deliberate opposition to the rushed processes that support the fast food industry.[21] Thus, like ćejf, the slow food movement centers on rearranging and slowing time, in part, by focusing on lingering in the sensory pleasures of food cultivation, preparation, and consumption. Selma tapped into such taste aesthetics when she stressed that her foods were "healthy" and tasty because they were produced locally and handled with care in her kitchen.

By emphasizing her role in preparation and service, Selma also reiterated the significance of the confluence of gender and status in these consumption practices. When she emerges from behind the curtain that separates her small kitchen from the cozy dining area comprised of five table and chair sets, Selma issues steady encouragement to her customers to savor the foods she places in front of them, "like a mother," one American customer suggested. Coffee here again provides the most elaborate and dramatic medium through which to communicate the slowing of time and the affirmation of status.

Selma served American coffee that she prepared with an automatic drip machine stationed on the kitchen's back counter; labeled on the menu simply: "coffee." Selma also served "Turkish coffee." The American coffee costs less than the Turkish coffee, because, as Selma explained, it doesn't require as much work. Selma's "Turkish coffee" is brewed following the same steps as Ajša's Bosnian coffee. Selma uses the finely ground Bosnia and Aroma coffee brands, and serves the coffee in copper džezve, similar to the one pictured on the Zambak cover.

In using the "Turkish coffee" moniker, and arranging a pastiche of Balkan dishes around it, Selma's space incorporates not only Yugoslav, but also Ottoman cultural references. Her ability to connect these elements with American, western European food niches supports a diverse clientele, and brings to mind Bourdieu's discussion of taste preferences in food as a feature of "distinction," as a marker of cultural capital wherein it is not solely people's incomes, but their cultivations of certain consumption dispositions that creates the "taste distinctions" that constitute and solidify class belonging.[22] Indeed, amidst the cornucopia of "choice" available in America, Selma had chosen well. Her café was one of the few remaining from a number of Bosnian-themed cafes that had opened and closed in Chicago by 2006. Her success can be attributed to the combination of her prior experience in management and food services in Yugoslav Montenegro, her site selection and friendly relations with her small-business neighbors, and her mixture of Balkan fast and slow-food items with the commodification of ćejf that appealed to myriad consumers: Balkan émigrés, day labor immigrant construction workers, and American "slow food" enthusiasts and Yugo-nostalgics.

CONCLUSION

So, what can the social life of a cup of coffee tell us about refugees' postwar lives in Chicago? Bosnian slow coffee highlights the altered time dimensions and tensions felt in post-war migrants' lives by providing a frame for creating diverse spaces centered on hosting, conversation, and consumption. First, Bosnian coffee products and coffee objects helped to affirm a national identity that also indexed the multi-ethnic and multi-faith regional Ottoman social histories. Second, the Bosnian coffee products lining Chicago store shelves, home cupboards, and counters provided the links among memory and nostalgia upon which women at TCC constructed counter-narratives to evaluate the present and convey care and solidarity that favorably contrasted their lives under Yugoslav socialism with the degraded social world wrought by American neoliberal capitalism.[23] Finally, Bosnian coffee provided the means to challenge consumer fast food norms through the coarticulation of ćejf taste cachet and slow food aesthetics of pleasure. In this way, women refugees used the preparation and consumption of Bosnian coffee to restore a sense of sociality and belonging that were denied during the dehumanizing attacks they experienced as Bosnian Muslims during the 1990s political violence.

NOTES

Parts of this chapter are based on material which was previously published in Croegaert, Ana. "Cars, Coffee, and 'The Crisis': Balkan Migration in Precarious Times," in *Everyday Life in the Balkans*, David W. Montgomery, Ed. Bloomington: Indiana University Press, 2018.

1. The relationship between time and space is a longstanding concern in analyses of the radical alterations modernity and capitalism wrought on people's everyday social lives (see e.g., Durkheim, Emile. *The Division of Labour in Society.* Trans. W. D. Halls, New York: Free Press, 1997; *The Elementary Forms of Religious Life*: Newly Translated by Karen E. Fields; Thompson, E. P. *The Making of the English Working Class*. Toronto: Penguin Books, 1991; Harvey, David. *The Condition of Postmodernity: An Enquiry into the Origins of Cultural Change*. Cambridge, MA: Blackwell, 1990).

2. These variations in materials and methods also occur across regions. For example, traditional Turkish carafes are made from similar materials, but with different

motifs, and are called *cezve* or *ibrik* (this word is used interchangeably with *džezva* in Bosnia and in other parts of the Balkans). Turkish style also uses small cups, but with handles. Ethiopian style uses a cup without handles, like *fildžani*, called *finjal*, while the brewing carafe, called *jebena*, is made from clay and has a long neck and handle similar to a pitcher. Turkish coffee tends to incorporate sugar in the brewing process, and Turkish, Ethiopian, and other related styles often add a spice such as cardamom. People also gave me different reasons for certain steps, for example, some people held that you must keep a container of coffee water available on the stove at all times, retaining a bit of the original coffee brew. When a guest arrives, you are always prepared, and always working from a previously prepared source, akin to a yeast starter for breads or a fermented starter for kombucha.

3. Kinship among Bosnians was often reckoned bilaterally during the nineteenth to twentieth centuries (Bringa, *Being Muslim*: 144). This can be seen from the reciprocal gift-giving practice that often occurred between the bridegroom's and bride's families during the first few months of marriage. In this practice, the bridegroom's parents would bring gifts / *dar* to the bride's household and present them in a public display / *pohod*. These included individual gifts of clothes or fabric, cigarettes, coffee for close family members such as parents and grandparents, as well as prepared sweet and savory food dishes and fruit juices to share during the gift-presentation. The bride's parents were expected then to reciprocate within a few weeks or months (depending on how much time it takes to gather the resources needed to assemble a comparable presentation), this time in a public gift-presentation at the bridegroom's parents' household. This gift exchange was meant to emphasize affinal relationships—those ties established between the two extended families by the marriage. In addition to the pohod, the bride's parents were expected to provide furniture and kitchenware (*oprema*), and decorative linens (*ruho*). These were gifts from her family, to her, not to her in-laws. Džezva and fildžani sets might be included in this gift. Bringa describes how coffee service delineated status hierarchies, particularly in patrilocal households where a daughter-in-law / *snaha* was subordinate to her mother-in-law / *sverka*.

4. Hattox likens the dhikr to the Christian Eucharist because the coffee drinking among such Sufi orders was conducted by consuming the drink by ladle from a communal bowl, thus signifying brotherhood among those present (Hattox, Ralph. *Coffee and Coffeehouses: The Origins of a Social Beverage in the Medieval Near East*). Seattle: University of Washington Press, 1985. Among Muslims in Bosnia, Macedonia, and Kosovo, these rites are called "zikir" (Bringa, *Being Muslim*: 220–224).

5. During the nineteenth and into the early twentieth centuries, educated and cosmopolitan women would also have socialized in urban coffee houses in cities like Istanbul and Sarajevo.

6. This flag was replaced by the UN High Representative with one designed by a non-Bosnian (Carlos Westendorp). This externally imposed flag does not include any historical references to Bosnian symbology.

7. Wilk, 1999. This sensory diasporan link is vividly rendered in Aida Šehović's annual public art installation *ŠTO TE NEMA?/Why are you not here?* (See conclusion.)

8. I propose this use of coffee is similar to the "trans-ethnic" belonging Hromadzic theorizes based on her fieldwork in post-war (Hromadžić Discourses of Trans-ethnic

Belonging," and Citizens of an Empty Nation). While Hromadzic builds her theory based on observations of speech choices, I suggest we may usefully employ the term to theorize the language of food. There were exceptions to coffee as symbol through which to connect; for example, several people told me that during the war one's pronunciation of "coffee" in Bosnian—kava or kafa—was used to indicate, or to try and ascertain, someone's ethnic and political affiliations.

9. I witnessed these kinds of interactions in Chicago as well. Such everyday exchanges across lines of difference belong to a set of conventions that, although obscured in recent scholarship focused on the violent dissolution of the Yugoslav state, have a sustained presence in the Balkans, and, I argue, among the diaspora. See Helms, Elissa. "The Gender of Coffee: Women and Reconciliation Initiatives in Post-War Bosnia and Herzegovina." *Focaal: Journal of Global and Historical Anthropology*, 75(Summer): 17–32, 2010; Sorabji, Cornelia. "Bosnian neighborhoods revisited: Tolerance, commitment and komšiluk in Sarajevo, in *On the Margins of Religion*, Ed. Joao de Pina Cabral and Frances Pine, 97–112. Oxford: Berghahn Books, 2003; Bringa, *Being Muslim*.

10. Schwartzman, Helen B. "The Significance of Meetings in an American Mental Health Center." *American Ethnologist* 14(2): 271–294, 1987. See also Weick, K. E. *Sensemaking in Organizations*. Thousand Oaks, CA: Sage Publications, 1995.

11. In addition to ethno-religious and regional variations, members of the Chicago Bosnian diaspora had also supported different political platforms and politicians during the war. A primary difference was in people's affinities for the two Bosnian Muslim members of Bosnia's tri-ethnic presidency in 1990: Alija Izetbegović and Fikret Abdić. Izetbegović represented the Bosniak nationalist position of Bosnia for Bosnian Muslims, with other Bosnians being classified as protected minorities (mirroring the SFRY arrangement) and was anchored in the southeast Sarajevo-based political enclave. Fikret Abdić took an opposition stance toward Izetbegović and his SDA party during the wars. In the decades preceding the wars, Abdić had constructed a client-based "fiefdom" in the northwest corner of Bosnia, around Bihać, a very poor region of the country. Abdić was instrumental in establishing an agricultural conglomerate, Agrokomerc, that employed 13,000 people at its height. But in the 1980s, the company crashed in an economic scandal, bringing great economic loss and uncertainty to residents, many of whom maintained their faith in Abdić and saw him as a local "Big Man" who was invested in developing their region. Abdić and his sympathizers established the "Autonomous Province of Western Bosnia" (APZB) that operated in concert with Bosnian Serb VRS and Bosnian Croatian militias between 1993–1995. Abdić was convicted of war crimes and spent a decade in prison before being elected the mayor of Velika Kladuša, in 2016.

12. The "America Runs On Dunkin'" tagline was introduced in 2006 and is still in use at the time of this writing. Donuts in fact constitute a very small element in Dunkin's annual sales; the bulk of their revenue comes from their coffee sales.

13. See www.dzezvacoffee.com for interview guide.

14. For example, Berdahl describes how Ossis (East Germans) in a border village in post-unification Germany reclaimed and valorized GDR products like Trabi cars and worker smocks as they became increasingly aware of Wessis' (West Germans') devaluation of East German work and values (Berdhal, Daphne. *Where the World*

Ended: Reunification and Identity in the German Borderland. Berkeley, CA: University of California Press, 1999. 160). In a complex rendering of another German post-Wende context, Buechler and Buechler describe how small-scale artisanal bakers in the GDR found articulation with both communist and capitalist production systems. Even though their very operations provided a daily challenge to state forms of production, because their product, artisanal breads, was central to German cultural identity, they were permitted to continue private production during the communist era and were not viewed as a threat to the state. Although these small-scale bakeries decreased under post-Wende capitalism, many Ossis preferred the Ossi-rolls in contrast to the new industrial Wessi bread imports (Buechler, Hans, and Judith-Maria Buechler. "The Bakers of Bernburg and the Logics of Communism and Capitalism." *American Ethnologist* 26(4): 799–821, 1999). East German commodity-"[N]Ostalgie" practices and the Bernberg bakers' relation to their craft and product are not unlike those of Yurchak's Soviet-era subjects, who indirectly critique state authority and western-style capitalism by deftly applying socialist principles to western objects: beer cans, cigarette packs, plastic bags. By considering such products as "semi-empty," the "last Soviet generation" constructed an "imaginary west" by infusing western objects with different meanings-building different forms of social life, derived from alternative biographies (Yurchak, Alexei. *Everything Was Forever, Until It Was No More*. Princeton, NJ: Princeton University Press, 2006, 159, 203–204).

15. Alexander, Ronelle. *Bosnian, Croatian, Serbian, a Grammar: With Sociolinguistic Commentary*. Madison: University of Wisconsin Press, 2006, 407.

16. This comparison pointed to people's profound senses of conflict over having left family and friends in BiH and being subsequently straddled with the burden of expectations that they become wealthy capitalists in America and distribute these new riches in BiH.

17. As with any pleasure principle, ćejf can be indulged too far, a phenomenon signaled in a 1974 Bijelo Dugme song about a scoundrel who has lost his land, sweetheart, and money, but uses ćejf as a disclaimer, telling us, "pa sta bio mi ćejf / so what, it was my ćejf." Goran Bregović lyrics (1974) Album *kad bi bio bjelo dugme / if I were a white button*. Yugoton. Thanks to Snežana Žabić for translation.

18. Montenegro declared independence in 2006, based on referendum results.

19. Wilk, Richard. "From Wild Weeds to Artisanal Cheese," in *Fast Food/Slow Food: The Cultural Economy of the Global Food System*. Richard Wilk, Ed. 13–30. Lanham, MD: Altamira, 2006, 14.

20. But see Banwell et al. for critique. Banwell, Cathy, Jane Dixon, Sarah Hinde, and Heather McIntyre. "Fast and Slow Food in the Fast Lane: Automobility and the Australian Diet," in *Fast Food/Slow Food: The Cultural Economy of the Global Food System*. Richard Wilk, Ed. 219–240. Lanham, MD: AltaMira, 2006.

21. Petrini (2001) but see Wilk (2006) for analysis of Slow Food reliance on Industrial Food products.

22. Bourdieu, Pierre. *Distinction: A Social Critique of the Judgement of Taste*. Richard Nice, trans. Cambridge, MA: Harvard University Press, 1984, 77.

23. See Berdahl, *Where the World Ended*, for similar analysis based on post-Wende Germany.

Chapter Five

American Balkanism and the Optics of Violence

On a warm September Friday in 2004, I sat with Danijela as we waited for her mother, Mia, to join us at a north-side cafe near the women's homes. Nasiha had introduced me to Danijela, who had arranged for me to talk with Mia about her experiences with making a life in Chicago. Mia had also brought along her two friends, Jasmila and Tajma. The women were in their late forties and arrived dressed in their work clothes: dark slacks, soft sweaters and blouses, and modest heels. Their hairstyles ranged from short to long, red, blonde and black, curly to straight; Jasmila's was the longest and she wore it gathered in a low ponytail at the nape of her neck, while Mia and Tajma wore theirs cropped above their shoulders and loose. They greeted one another with happy exclamations and walked over to browse the snacks in the display case next to the counter. We ordered our beverages and situated ourselves at one of the corner tables.

The three older women asked me about my project while we sipped our drinks. After explaining my interests in learning more about what it was like for them to find work and housing and a social life in the city, they eased into speaking frankly about their refugee-immigrant experiences. The women had met on the job, in hotel housekeeping. All of them had professional degrees from the SFRY and had developed their English skills enough to enable them to cultivate social networks and advance to more favorable work situations. Tajma found a job as an elementary school teacher's aide, and Jasmila and Mia had both been promoted within the hotel. They joked together about their early days at the hotel, and Jasmila, tall and reserved, relayed a common narrative of worksite disappointment:

> One day I came to work and my boss told me we had a special project today. I got so excited! I thought, this is very good—we have been cleaning, cleaning, and

I am so bad at that [Mia and Tajma laughed and nodded their heads, exclaiming what a bad housekeeper Jasmila was, how slow she was] but now we will have a "project" like in school! I had studied foreign languages and literature, specializing in Arabic and Turkish, and I thought maybe we would make something, a presentation or something! I was so disappointed when I found out "the project" was to learn a different cleaning method!

We all laughed at this, and as we continued on my questions prompted the women to query one another. Remembering together, they traded stories back and forth in an exchange that invoked encounters with their employers' and co-workers' (mis)understandings of their homeland and the wars that brought them to Chicago. They each expressed amusement and frustration at Americans' general lack of knowledge about Yugoslavia, and Bosnia, which Jasmila summed up by saying: "They think we are just animals in a jungle [making aping motions] running around killing each other" [pantomimes wielding an axe or sword]. The other women laughed nervously, chiming in, "Yes, that is so true!" Exchanging tentative glances, they lowered their eyes and voices: "We never talked about this before," said Tajma. That the characterization of Bosnians as animalistic and violent was both a familiar and a taboo subject among such close friends suggested this was a sensitive topic.

Mia gently moved the conversation forward by saying that she was happy Danijela was doing well in America. Danijela was ten years old when she arrived in Chicago along with her mom and brother. She had completed high school and was now enrolled in classes at a community college while also working part time as an administrative assistant at a small design firm. Tajma and Jasmila chimed in, remarking on "how smart [Danijela was] and what a good daughter!" This led to each of the women discussing their relationships to family members, those in Chicago as well as those in Bosnia and elsewhere. Tajma told me about arriving in Chicago with her husband, whom she divorced several years later. When I said that it must have been difficult, going through the war, refugee life, and then a divorce, she replied,

> We divorced because my husband became very frustrated by not being able to provide for us in the same way that he had in Bosnia, before the war. And we fought. Constantly. It was hard for our kids. Many of my husband's family also came to Chicago, but they didn't help, [they] always took his side. And all of my family, other than my children, are back in Bosnia. So, I decided to divorce him.

Tajma got quiet, although it seemed to me that she had more to say. After a pause, Mia said, "yes, but you are [all] good now," and the other women nodded their heads in agreement. Tajma felt that since there was no family advocate available to her, divorce was the best option. We conversed for a while longer before parting ways, but I wondered if there was more to Tajma's divorce than she had shared that evening.

When I saw Danijela the following week, I asked her about Tajma's divorce and whether or not Danijela thought that Tajma's and her husband's disputes ever became physical. Danijela replied that she also had thought of that when Tajma was talking about the divorce, and that after I had left that evening, Tajma brought up the divorce again, emphasizing that it was difficult for her to talk about it because it had been very contentious, and hinted that physical abuse was part of her divorce petition.

What was it like to pursue a divorce in a foreign country, when your husband's family is against you and your own family is far way? What is it like to arrive in a foreign country and find that many of the locals assume that where you are from is a violent place and by extension, you also are presumed to be violent? This chapter describes some of the perceptions about Bosnia and Bosnians in Chicago by exploring various depictions of the Bosnian wars in relation to spaces where war refugees addressed some of the challenges of their post-war experiences. I approach these spaces as "publics" that are "self-organized through discourse."[1] The circulation of texts, images, lyrics, speech and other embodied practices establish the discourse—the representational frameworks—through which publics emerge. In this way, publics produce a sense of belonging among individuals. I argue that the circulation of stereotypes in international reports, Chicago-based cultural performances, and American newsmedia focused on the Bosnian wars constituted a dominant public centered on oversimplified characterizations of Bosnians as prone to violence, and Bosnian men as especially violent against women. This discourse of violence informed Bosnian refugee women's opinions and decisions about trusting social service agencies and the police, and thus, the circulation of these gender-based stereotypes generated a Bosnian counterpublic concerned with negative American perceptions of them and characterized by efforts to project a positive and cohesive "community" presence in the city.[2] The women's cafe conversation is part of this Bosnian counterpublic, as is Tajma's account of her divorce. Thus, while organized by discourse, these publics are not merely textual and symbolic, but in the context of refugees' immigrant status had adverse material outcomes that placed the burden of addressing domestic violence on already-strained families, and on women in particular.

Although I do not address particular coverage of Bosnian war crimes cases heard at the International Criminal Tribunal for the former Yugoslavia (ICTY) and the International Court of Justice (ICJ), which were widely televised, sometimes receiving live coverage, these international courts form a significant backdrop to the publics described in this chapter. Genocide charges made by Bosnia-Herzegovina's government against the governments of Serbia and Montenegro and against individual military personnel have proceeded through multiple courts since 1992, with the most notorious "events" being the abuses and killings that took place in July 1995 in the Srebrenica United Nations–declared "safe haven." Despite well-established evidence documenting the Serbian state's coordination with the Bosnian Serb Army (VRS) and local militias to assault the Bosnian Muslim population, including evidence that these attacks overwhelmingly targeted civilians, genocide denial continued to be promoted by some Serbian government officials and leadership, Serbian media, among the Serbian diaspora (see chapter 6 and the conclusion, "Gathering Grounds: A Reflection").

Central to the efforts of those who would deny that such atrocities occurred and that they constitute genocide is the claim that the thousands of Bosnian Muslim men who the VRS killed were armed soldiers rather than civilians. This claim has been disproven over and again and denies the significance of factors such as Serbia's appropriation of the JNA (SFRY Army) military apparatus, the international arms embargo against the ARBiH, and the VRS strategy of rounding up Bosnian Muslim communities and cutting them off from food, fuel, and medical supplies, particularly during the winter. Some civilians starved to death, and many of those killed at Srebrenica were emaciated, disabled, pubescent, and elderly—hardly capable of posing a credible threat to the heavily armed VRS.

The first ICTY genocide conviction was in 2001, appealed and upheld—although revised—in 2004. Beginning in 2006, the ICJ began a year of public hearings regarding Bosnia-Herzegovina's charge against Serbia and Montenegro for the genocide in Bosnia, before issuing its judgement finding of genocide in February 2007. Many Bosnian refugees in the diaspora followed the ICTY and ICJ hearings closely and were aware of the defense's efforts to portray Bosnian Muslim men in particular as violent combatants. Thus, for many survivors there was much at stake in how their male family and friends were depicted in media that discussed the war. My discussion in this chapter addresses war depictions that appeared between 2004–2008, during roughly the same timeframe as the 2004–2007 genocide deliberations in the international courts.

THE BALKANIST FRAME

The word "Balkan" is a Turkish place-name for a mountain range in Bulgaria, and dates to the early period of Ottoman administration in the fifteenth century.[3] In the nineteenth century, the word was codified as a geographical term for a region: the Balkan Peninsula.⁴ By the early twentieth century, the geographic designation became a metaphor: the noun became a verb. The metaphor is a negative one, associated with the effects of the break-up of the Ottoman Empire into small, comparatively weak and dependent nation-states.⁵ Nowadays the term "balkanize" still carries with it this meaning and an undeniably negative valence. Maria Todorova identifies this shift in balkanization as part of a set of approaches to knowing the Balkans and its inhabitants that she calls "Balkanism."⁶ Todorova draws on a diverse archive to demonstrate that Balkanist framings are often particular to certain genre, journalistic and "quasi-journalistic" forms, in which she includes travelogues, political essays, and "academic journalism"; significantly, these genre all have popular audiences. Balkanism is similar to Orientalism in that both discourses emerged in the context of imperial and colonial, followed by national, modernization projects, and among those who were concerned with defining what constituted being "modern" and the related concept of "civilized." In this context, challenges of development in the region in conjunction with the romantic nationalist bent in political opposition to external rule "created a situation in which the Balkans began to serve as a symbol for the aggressive, intolerant, barbarian, semi-developed, semi-civilized, and semi-oriental."⁷ Over the course of the twentieth and twenty-first centuries there were upticks in Balkanist publications following political conflicts and wars, a trend that is reflected after the 1990s wars.⁸

In April 2005, months after my cafe visit with Danijela, Mia, Jasmila, and Tajma, a new publication illustrated the pervasive pejorative application of Balkanism to the region. *The International Commission on the Balkans* report, "The Balkans in Europe's Future" was written by 19 delegates brought together by western foundations and think-tanks in the early aughts to identify challenges in the region, and to recommend policies to mitigate these issues. The report was the third of such documents; the first was issued at the onset of World War I, "Causes and Conduct of the Balkan Wars of 1912 and 1913," the second, "Unfinished Peace," was published in 1996, directly after the 1990s wars in Bosnia and in Croatia. These types of reports are widely read and disseminated among what is commonly referred to as the "international community," of people whose work contributes to international agencies such as the Red Cross, the United Nations, USAID, and the World Bank.⁹ Among these agencies are employees and volunteers who write, recommend, and implement refugee policies to advance their ostensible agenda to establish peace and support development across the world. For example, the second commissioner's introduction describes his commission's mandate as "[to] achieve peace, a durable one, to pave the way to democracy, prosperity, well-being and a humane society."¹⁰ The commissioner and former Prime

Minister of Belgium, Leo Tindemans, goes on to further clarify the context for this democratizing project: "[to] help transform the proverbially chaotic, bloody and unpredictable Balkans of the past into a stable, peaceful and dependable Southeastern Europe of the future."[11] This portrayal of the region as disordered, violent, and in need of taming and cultivation—from "Balkan" to "Southeastern Europe"—is emblematic of Balkanism.

Giuliano Amato, the chairman at the helm of the third report, presents their commission's charge as "to present results which will stir the debate on the future of the region and to ultimately develop a vision for the integration of the countries of Southeast Europe into the European Union."[12] Following a reference to western European Union member states' "enlargement fatigue," in reference to the EU's incorporation of member states from the formerly communist countries, Amato issues a cautionary warning that is also premised on Balkanist orientations,

> [I]n the absence of headline-grabbing violence, many European politicians and civil servants hold on to the hope that the status quo is working just fine. However, if the reform and transition process fails, the Western Balkans will become even more of an isolated ghetto, and loom as a threat to stability and peace.[13]

Here again, the region, even when there is no active armed conflict, is portrayed as a specter of poverty and violence with the power to explode European unification. These sentiments were not solely textual; they emerged in my conversations with aid workers and "internationals" who had worked with Bosnians in Chicago.

For example, when I interviewed John, a local university administrator who had also volunteered with one of the larger volags in the city to help resettle Bosnian refugee arrivals, he offered me this sweeping generalization, "You know, Bosnians, more than any other Balkan people, will be incredibly friendly to you, and if you burn them, [they are also] incredibly vindictive." At the time I was at the beginning stages of my fieldwork, and John was sharing with me all the things he thought I "should know" before I began identifying potential Bosnian interview subjects. It is noteworthy that in addition to its obvious Balkanist framing and lack of nuance, his warning situated Bosnians as the utmost exemplars of these negative traits, and further, illustrated he lacked an understanding of migration and refugee resettlement as social processes through which norms of exchange and reciprocity are established and negotiated, often in the context of inequality. In an effort to better understand some of the dominant public discourse about Bosnian refugees in Chicago, I read English-language newsmedia and attended a number of film and theater productions that portrayed the Bosnian Wars, but did not include Bosnians in the production process, and were not intended for Bosnian audiences.

BALKAN CARICATURES:
VIOLENT MEN AND VICTIMIZED WOMEN

A key word search of "refugee" in newspaper articles from the *Chicago Reader* and the *Chicago Tribune* between 2003–2005 shows a recurring focus on film, theater, literature, or art installations that related to Bosnia and/or to Bosnians, all centering on the 1990s wars.[14] During this time I attended eight arts events in the city that depicted the wars. The following section focuses on two, a film and an outdoor theater performance, to illustrate the prevalence of gender-based violence as a central theme in artistic productions about Bosnia.

The Dan Ryan Expressway is the gritty section of Interstate 94 that cuts through the interior of Chicago's urban landscape and is always packed with cars and trucks: exhausted drivers in exhaust-emitting vehicles. This artery of exchange is a primary thoroughfare through which goods enter and leave the city. Chicago-born screenwriter director Michael Ojeda's film *Lana's Rain* introduces the viewer to Chicago through an image of this densely populated roadway. Ojeda choreographs the viewer's perspective with an eye/I-camera shot that goes from dark to light when a faceless man hurls open the back of the truck revealing Lana, the film's protagonist. Here, Lana is both a passenger, and, like the freight in the back of other countless trucks traversing the Dan Ryan, Lana is cargo. According to the film's narrative, Lana is human trafficked into the country by her own brother, Darko.

I attended the *Lana's Rain* debut in 2004 at the old Music Box Theatre, a fixture in the city's Lakeview neighborhood, and an anchor for recent gentrification along the Southport strip. Lakeview's northern boundary abuts Uptown but is more closely associated with the upscale neighborhood immediately south: Lincoln Park. The film's narrative is centered on Lana. She is raped repeatedly during the Bosnian wars, then trafficked and pimped by Darko from the hills of Herzegovina to the urban grid of Chicago. The war rape and the sibling violence rely on gender stereotypes of violent men and victimized women. In the promotional materials for the film we see Lana, fair, beautiful, wounded, and holding a lighter. Her brother Darko is dark,

Figure 5.1. *Lana's Rain* Ticket Stub.

swarthy, leatherclad, and sporting an eyepatch. They are separated by the words "Stinging Authenticity!" that apparently most accurately summarize this antagonistic rendering of the sexes.

After surviving multiple scenes of violence and abuse at the hands of her former rapists who have pursued her across the Atlantic, Lana emerges triumphant. She kills the evil rapists and in the final scene we see her standing outside of a municipal building, smiling and holding a valuable emblem of U.S. citizenship: a social security card. In the film's subtext we can detect a fantasy of American liberation of the Bosnian woman, embodied in Lana. Her country, her past, all of the horrors from which she is released, is depicted in the film by violent male symbols—a premise that comports to what Leila Ahmed describes as "colonial feminism," and makes use of the abstract victim "Muslimwoman" figure whom Abu-Lughod argues animates U.S. governmental and popular discourse on U.S. war and occupation in Muslim-majority Middle-eastern countries.

Undoubtedly, the presence of thousands of Bosnian refugees in the city could have inspired Ojeda to write the screenplay, although Lana's migration story more closely resembles those of women who may have passed through Bosnia in their westward migrations, but were originally from other eastern and southeastern European countries.[15] While there were many undocumented Europeans in the city, they were primarily from Poland and Ukraine, countries whose immigrant presence in Chicago far outnumbered those who arrived as refugees from the Bosnian Wars. Bosnian women were also less likely to be trafficked than Eastern European women; for example, the first human trafficking prosecution in the state of Illinois dealt with a Chicago-based Russian immigrant who had trafficked several women from Latvia and forced them to work in strip clubs.[16] Of course, *Lana's Rain* is a fictional film, not a documentary. The filmmakers are not responsible for facts like the actual number of Bosnian women who are trafficked to the United States, and they are aiming for dramatic effect. But the narrative's symbolic elements rely on persistent gender stereotypes about Balkan male violence against women. All of Lana's conflict is embodied in men's abuse of her sex, from the rapists to her brother's exploitation of her for sex work upon arrival in Chicago. Further, while "Lana" is a common Bosnian female name across ethnic groups, "Darko," from the root *dar / gift*, is most identified as a Serbian name. The filmmakers likely are not working with these elements in an explicit or overt sense; in fact, they discuss their project and goals in market terms. According to film agent David Sikich:

> Lana's Rain is a different situation [from typical film distribution]: One print, one city. We're doing this really grass roots. There is such a substantial East European presence in Chicago—Bosnians, Albanians, Croatians, Serbians,

Bulgarians, Ukrainians—so our challenge right now is to prove that there is an audience for this film. If we can generate big numbers our first weekend, it could really help us get a DVD deal.[17]

Sikich is correct in noting that Chicago has a substantial "East European presence." In addition to being home to one of the largest Polish-descent populations outside of Poland, the city has a long history of migration from Eastern and the Balkans/Southeast Europe. The theater was fairly full the night of the film screening and included many heritage viewers from these regions. But judging by the languages being spoken, and the tone of the question-and-answer session that followed the screening, the majority of these viewers were primarily second and third generation Poles, Bulgarians, Serbs, and Croats. None of the recently arrived Bosnians I had come to know were in attendance, and when I asked people several days later if they had heard about the film, none of them had. Not surprisingly, they did not seem interested in the film either; they did not need reminding of the wartime horrors and its aftermath. The actual "market" for this film about Bosnia and Bosnians was English-speaking and not the Bosnian refugee diaspora. This rendering of gender-based violence appealed to American audiences, even if second-generation American, and not necessarily to those whose lives provided the grist for the script.

In the summer that followed the *Lana's Rain* screening, I attended an outdoor performance in Chicago's latest lakefront public park. Millennium Park sits atop what was formerly Illinois Central rail yards, and by the time it opened the park was massively over-budget and had become a flashpoint for conflicts over municipal funds. In an effort to soften some of the resentment over taxpayer funding for a large portion of the $475 million project, the city's park district ushered in the park's public debut with a series of ticketed events, free, but with limited admission. Among these was a performance of the Polish alternative theater group Teatr Biuro Podróży's original production, *Carmen Funebre / Funeral March*. On a clear July evening I queued in a line along East Monroe Drive, hoping to get a ticket. My friend and I were among the final few to receive tickets, while at least 30 people behind us were turned away. The sun was beginning to set, and we were directed into the park where a makeshift outdoor theater-in-the-round had been constructed by lining the performance area with folding chairs several rows deep on all four sides. The theater area made use of low man-made hills to host those of us who were not early enough to get chairs, so we climbed the inclines to get a view of the show.

The performance program described *Carmen Funebre* as having been "inspired by the war in Bosnia, and other ethnic conflicts," and the performance began with an unseen actor reading W. H. Auden's 1939 poem, "Refugee

Blues," written to draw attention to the plight of Jewish refugees fleeing Nazi Germany.[18] Teatr Biuro Podróży uses stilt walking to emphasize scale in its outdoor performances, and in this instance, used dramatic sound and lighting to create a choreography of chaos and a sense of fear among the audience. The cast included five soldiers, two warlords, one grim reaper (all male figures), and five civilian victims (two women and three men). Bright spotlights beamed from the arms of masked warlords draped in long dark capes, as they roamed to-and-fro on stilts to ferret out select actor-victims planted next to unsuspecting audience members in the chairs closest to the main performance space. Once they had chased their five captives into the center of the space, the towering warlords moved to policing the perimeter while soldiers emerged and encircled the victims. The soldiers separated the men from the two women, moving one of the women into something like a cattle pen, then made a circle around the other female victim and used a rope to pen her, fling her about, all the while drunkenly spitting red wine at her while the sound of sirens and explosives blared over the outdoor speakers. The men's wine-soaked mouths and the woman's torn red dress signaled the bloody rape we witnessed.

Figure 5.2. Teatr Biuro Podrozy *Carmen Funebre*.

Shaken throughout the performance, I watched and listened for other audience responses. People seemed disoriented, perhaps the troupe's intent as a way to get the audience to identify with the victims' horror. In fact, when I later researched the troupe's body of work, their website described the production as one in which the troupe

> uses means which can attract the attention of the experienced spectator as well as the accidental passer-by. Stilts, fire, searchlights, spectacular sets, and chilling music threaten the audience while evoking both fear and compassion. Although there are few words in the performance, the images are clear and powerful.[19]

While there was a program note in our playbill that referenced the Bosnian wars as the "inspiration" for the production, this setting didn't seem to register for many among the audience. I overheard confused remarks: "Okay . . . what was that all about?" and relief: "Glad that's over," once the performance ended. So, the audience was successfully disoriented and frightened—the perspective of the victim—but their apprehensions of the story were also confused. These responses were in keeping with many of the remarks I'd encountered among Americans regarding the Bosnian wars; people often didn't know much about the conflict, nor the history of the region. In this case, it wasn't even clear that the theatergoers understood the performance to be based on recent events.

This performance narrative was staged by an internationally acclaimed avant-garde Polish theater troupe against the backdrop of Chicago's museums, elite hotels, and corporate headquarters, and sponsored by the Consulate General of the Republic of Poland, the Polish Cultural Institute, the Chicago Park District, the Mayor's Office of Special Events, and the Polish National Alliance of North America. The filmmakers, while appearing sympathetic to the plight of women like Lana's character was meant to portray, seemed oblivious to the fact that thousands of actual refugees of the Bosnian wars were living in nearby Uptown and Rogers Park. The performance venues were located in spaces that were ongoing sites of neighborhood development and debates over gentrification and inequality in the city, and thus show curators must have deemed the theme of war and sexual violence about Bosnia and Bosnians as palatable to the desired audiences for these arts-and-culture events. By appealing to Eastern and Southeast European heritage audiences, the play and film provided both identification with and distance from the region's problems, the latter especially by situating the Bosnians Wars as emblematic of the ultimate Balkan tragedy. The productions' Balkanist framing ultimately by-passed the actual challenges of living as a refugee of that war, in Chicago. As Tajma's divorce story suggested, addressing domestic violence in the context of post-war refugee-immigrant life was among these challenges.

VIOLENCE HITS HOME

Tajma's generation was the first in the former Yugoslavia to participate in and benefit from a shift in state policy and social institutions toward the recognition of domestic violence as a problem to be addressed both at the individual and the social level.[20] Even so, domestic violence in Bosnia remains a taboo topic for public and mixed-sex social settings, as it does in many parts of the world, including in the United States. As Elissa Helms has shown in the case of postwar Bosnia, strategies for dealing with domestic violence were further complicated by the difficulty of addressing "their men" because local men in power were looked at as both victims and heroes of the war, and were often valorized as heroes who had fought to defend "their women."[21] Many men and women suffered tremendous injury and trauma as a result of the wars. But women's injuries were largely associated with rape campaigns and carried the stigma of sexual assault, while men's injuries were associated with fighting during the conflict. (While women also engaged in combat, men were the primary fighters. And while women were the primary victims of sexual violence, men also suffered sexual assault.) This led to a dynamic whereby women, family members, and friends often emphasized external factors when attributing cause for and seeking redress from domestic violence situations involving men. Although women's NGOs in Bosnia were successful in getting the legislature to pass stronger laws against domestic violence in the early aughts, service providers reported that these post-conflict circumstances remained a challenge to getting people to seek help from outside the family domain.[22] A similar set of filters can be seen in Tajma's situation in Chicago, where men's refugee status and experiences with downward mobility, and the pressures to project a cohesive "Bosnian community" identity to outsiders contributed additional layers of difficulty.

In Tajma's view, her husband's status as a non-English-speaking immigrant in Chicago unable to find employment comparable to that which he had held prior to the war in Bosnia was a central source of the conflict between them and of his violent expressions of emotion. Tajma's willingness to empathize with her husband's vulnerabilities is understandable, and men's postwar trauma compounded by their immigrant status was often used to account for situations of domestic violence. In fact, most of the refugee women I had come to know interpreted these behaviors as products of wartime traumas and economic hardships of immigration. However widely acknowledged these issues were within the immigrant population, people preferred to draw on family and friends to address such problems, rather than involve police or social workers. Thus, this was not a situation defined by denial; people agreed that family violence indeed constituted a social problem. But their evaluation of this trouble and how best to address it was filtered both through efforts to establish community cohesion, and through awareness of the American stereotype of Balkan violence.[23] Although domestic violence was not discussed in public, or even in mixed-sex settings, it was discussed in Bosnian women's networks.

This point was made especially clear on a gloomy gray, rainy Friday afternoon in early November, when I entered TCC to find a number of the senior women talking in raised voices. The women were seated as usual around rectangular folding tables and I pulled out a chair to join them. They were routinely a talkative bunch, but today I could hear their voices on the street before I even entered the center. I sat next to Nasiha and tried to figure out what had gotten the women so riled. They were heatedly discussing something that involved Meliha, a woman who worked at a nearby agency that provided family support services for primarily Muslim immigrants, including those from Bosnia.

Their story unfolded as follows: several days earlier, Meliha had received a call from an elderly Bosnian woman saying she was afraid of her husband because he was yelling at her while wielding a knife in their apartment. The woman also said that the husband was suffering from anxiety related to war trauma. Meliha told the woman to call the police. The police arrived at the apartment where the husband was still holding the knife and yelling. He did not respond to the police's commands, in English, to drop the knife. The police then shot the man, and he died the next day. He was seventy-one years old. There were several things that upset the TCC women about this tragedy. First, Ajša explained, the local news media had reported inaccurately that the woman had called TCC instead of the agency Meliha was employed by, thus people, both outsiders and those "in the community," might think that someone at TCC played a part in the man's death. Second, Esma blamed Meliha for what she felt was faulty advice. In her view, Meliha should have sent someone "from the community" to help the scared wife, or at least to be there when the police arrived so that the elder couple would have had someone to translate between them and the police. Another woman, Hajra, agreed with Esma, and extended this argument, saying that while the woman and her husband were in need of assistance, the police should not have been involved because it would be frightening for both of these seniors given that they had fled a war where, instead of protecting civilians, armed militia men had in fact perpetrated grave violence against civilians. Women preferred to work through kin and social networks to cope with matters of domestic violence. The women's heated discussion was not my first encounter with this preference; I was personally introduced to this strategy one month prior to the story recounted above.

Edita, whom I had come to know through TCC, had invited me to visit her home where she lived with her husband Amer, their teenage son Refik, one of their daughters, Šemsa and Šemsa's husband Mirsad, and their son Kenan. This was not my first visit to Edita's and we chatted inside for a bit with the television playing in the background. After some time had passed, Edita told me that she wanted to show me something outside while Amer took a rest before he walked to the grammar school nearby to pick up Kenan. Edita led me around their backyard and showed me the squash they'd recently harvested from their small vegetable garden. As we walked around the small yard, Edita updated me about her other children: she was worried that Refik was caught up with the wrong crowd. He had broken up with his girlfriend, of whom Edita had been a fan, and had taken to staying out late at night even on school nights. When Edita and Amer tried to rein him in, he would get defensive and leave the house again. Their other daughter, Lejla, and her husband Tarik lived with their two teenage daughters a fifty-minute bus ride away.

When she began telling me about Lejla, Edita lowered her voice and told me they were "having big problems" with Lejla's husband, Tarik. When I asked Edita what kind of problems, she told me that Tarik and Lejla had been fighting a lot as of late, and that Tarik had been hitting Lejla. Alarmed, I asked how they were dealing with this, and said that it sounded like Lejla needed help. Edita said that Lejla had been calling their home to tell them about the abuse, prompting Amer to go to Lejla's and Tarik's apartment on one of these occasions and pin Tarik against the wall. Edita pantomimed this act for me, pushing her right forearm against her throat, and saying that Amer told Tarik that this was the last time: if Tarik ever hit Lejla again, Amer and Edita would come and collect Lejla and the girls and take them away. Lejla had her own job and she could stay in her parents' and sister's home until she found a place for herself and her daughters. I then asked Edita what Tarik and Lejla were fighting about, and why she thought they were fighting, because it seemed this was a relatively new development in their relationship.

By way of explanation, Edita began by telling me that Tarik came from Eastern Bosnia, where he had fought with the ARBiH resistance for two years during the war. For nearly one year, Lejla did not hear anything from Tarik, and she took her eldest daughter and fled to Croatia with her parents, Refik, Šemsa, and Mirsad. Communication among and between active military zones and the rest of former Yugoslavia was unreliable, and they didn't know if Tarik was even alive. Two years after they all arrived in the United States, they received word from Tarik: he was alive and would be able to join them in Chicago. The family joyfully reunited, but not long after, Tarik began drinking excessively and fighting with Lejla. Edita said they argued about work and money. Similar to Tajma, Edita's explanation for Lejla's and Tarik's conflicts centered on Tarik's difficulty in finding and keeping stable employment, and thus meeting his and his extended family's expectations for helping provide for Lejla and their daughters. Edita also directed me to Tarik's wartime experiences when discussing Lejla's situation, as had the senior women in their description of the elder man's violent behavior before he was shot by the police. These stories illustrate the pull women felt to acknowledge the effects of war, displacement, and subsequent status-loss on men in their migrant cohort. At the same time, the domestic violence talk was relegated to Bosnian women-only social spaces, in Warner's words the women would have "regarded with hostility or with a sense of indecorousness" such talk if discussed in settings dominated by a discourse of Balkan male violence.

While the senior women preferred to address domestic violence through family and friend networks, and avoided engagement with broader American publics, the younger generation had a different orientation. Some of these young people felt a responsibility to engage these publics as a way to have a say in educating outsiders about Bosnian experiences. Yet in their efforts to communicate Bosnian refugee experiences, they also found themselves confronted with the specter of war and male violence.

"THE BOSNIAN COMMUNITY" AND PUBLIC FACE

Three years later, Nasiha and another young woman named Elmina expressed concerns about public portrayals of violent Bosnian men. They were especially worried about the potential adverse effects these images might have on 1.5 and second-generation Bosnians, as well as on the public face of "the Bosnian community."[24] Elmina and I met when she was a college student and running an after-school arts program for Bosnian kids in Rogers Park. The *Chicago Tribune* had recently published a piece about Bosnians in the United States in which Elmina was pictured and quoted, and I wanted to know what she thought about the story. In fact, the article was one of two that were written by a national reporter for the *New York Times* and had run in both the *Times* and the *Tribune* in the spring of 2007. In February the first article reported on a mass shooting in Salt Lake City. An eighteen-year-old Bosnian refugee had shot and killed five people in a shopping mall, before police shot and killed him.[25] Elmina, along with several other Chicago-based "Bosnian youth," had been interviewed for a related piece that ran in both papers approximately two months after the Utah shooting. While this lengthy piece of national coverage aimed to educate readers about the Utah eighteen-year-old's and Elmina's generation of Bosnian immigrants in America, the article's title, "Bosnians in America: A Two-Sided Saga," and structure suggest an editorial eye informed by Balkanist approaches to depicting Bosnians' experiences.

The "two-sided saga" is depicted visually through the juxtaposition of two highly gendered images of Bosnians in Chicago.[26] The images are stacked, one above the other, and are given significant space in the feature-length article. The top image is of "Adis," and the caption reads: "Adis, 20, dropped out of high school. His father was killed in the Bosnian war, and his mother holds two jobs." The reporter notes that Adis preferred not to give his last name "because of legal troubles." The photo shows only Adis's profile, and he is sitting across from another young man at a popular Bosnian north side cafe/bar. Both men appear to be watching a television that is not included in the image. Adis is dressed in the uniform of young men in the city at the time: oversized white tee and blue jeans, with white sneakers. A woman's name, "Selma," is tattooed on the left side of his neck, and he has a stud earing, and a closely cropped buzz cut. His feet are propped up on the barstool next to him, and he's taking a drag on a cigarette.

Directly beneath the photo of Adis is one of Elmina. Elmina's photo caption reads "Elmina Kulasic, 21, wearing stripes, a former war prisoner, teaches Bosnian music and dance." Elmina is laughing, and surrounded by seven kids, all facing one another, although we see only the faces of the girls. The two boys have their backs to us, and unlike the girls who are standing and laughing, the boys are seated. The depiction of Adis portrays him as an asocial urban youth, a fatherless son raised by a hardworking single mother. Alternatively, Elmina is the picture of sociality and no reference is made to her family life. Elmina offered this reflection on the interview process and finished piece:

> I am a little critical, but I feel like the war story should not be shoved down our throats whenever something is written about Bosnia . . . there is no reason for the progress [immigrant integration "progress"] to be connected explicitly to the war. No one asks us about our lives prior to the war . . . I just mean that Bosnians are like all the other immigrants before us: trying to make a living in the US—they are coping with their past, but as they are coping, they are embracing the future. The New York Times article touches the integration part but it is overshadowed with our war stories. I think that is why my story fits in 'cuz I am a concentration camp survivor and there is a parallel between me and the Utah boy in terms of war experiences. I am the "normal" one.

Elmina expressed frustration at the reporters' insistence on taking the war as a starting point for their story about Bosnians in the United States. The reporting does little to connect refugees' experiences to broader trends in the U.S. economy that significantly shaped refugee employment prospects. And while the story draws out some individual differences among refugees, they are illustrated solely through gendered contrasts, a point Elmina makes when she interprets the selection of her narrative as providing intentional contrast to that of her male peers. Elmina's story is held out as the "good" side of the Bosnian immigrant "two-sided saga." Two young men are also profiled in the story, but their war experiences differed from those of Elmina and the Utah teenager, both of whom were detained in concentration camps during the war. It is Elmina who provides the foil for the Utah shooter, as well as for Adis.

Several months later, Elmina, Nasiha, and I attended a planning meeting for a new Bosnian cultural and community organization. We were meeting as the ad-hoc board of this new association, along with the local imam, Harun, a forty-year-old Bosnian professional and community advocate, and a non-Bosnian female representative from a local pan-Islamic organization. As we discussed programming objectives, the issue of how best to address social problems arose. All three of the Bosnian young adults had extensive experience working with Bosnian youth and families in the city, and they raised concerns about high school graduation rates, substance abuse, and domestic violence among the people with whom they worked.[27] The story of the senior man's death at the hands of the police emerged again. Nasiha reminded us of this tragedy, stating, "We have to be very careful," in dealing with "family issues," and that we would need to be clear about what sort of advice and referrals we are qualified to give. We decided that our center would not be equipped to directly address domestic violence cases but that we would offer programming that might prevent such problems: same-sex support groups for adult men and women with themes such as "health," "empowerment," and activities such as chess, co-ed youth programming, and multi-generational programs that would connect youth with elders. If people called with a direct need, we would have a list of volunteer trained translators and certified social workers and first responders to which we could confidently refer people. The reminder of the man's death here indexed a continued concern with how "the community" was represented to outsiders, as well as with how well outsiders would care for and understand Bosnian immigrants in the city. As the next chapter shows, these concerns did not dissipate in the years to come, rather they took on increased urgency in the context of debates over how the wartime atrocities should be remembered among survivors and outsiders.

CONCLUSION

Simultaneous to high-stakes international court cases regarding the genocide against Bosnian Muslims during the 1990s political confrontations a series of popular media and performances depicting the wars were produced in

Chicago. This dominant public centered on figures of violent men and female victims and drew on a Balkanist discourse that Maria Todorova and others have argued belong to a set of literary and performance devices that arose from concerns with defining and measuring what constituted "modern," "civilized," and companion tropes of "backward," "uncivilized," in the context of developing nineteenth and twentieth centuries' nationalisms. The circulation of images of Bosnian Muslim men as potentially—or actively—violent in the context of genocide deniers who defended Serbia's attacks on Bosnia by claiming, falsely, that the VRS war crimes constituted pre-emptive strikes against a powerful Muslim enemy-within and the lack of closure for the families of the thousands of Muslim men killed in massacres in Prijedor, Srebrenica, and elsewhere fostered a public sphere in which Bosnian women refugees in Chicago engaged in a counterpublic when discussing problems of domestic conflict. In this counterpublic violence at home, in intimate relationships, was attributed to the aftermath of wartime violence, displacement, and status-loss. While women provided these structural explanations for domestic violence, they often sought to address the problem at the family level rather than engage state or community institutions. This approach meant that the consequences of domestic conflict were absorbed by families that were already beleaguered by the radical ruptures of war and displacement, and whose socio-political world was shaped by ongoing challenges to the documented massacres of thousands of Bosnian Muslim men at the direction of the Serbia-led JNA, the VRS, and local militias. Bosnian women of Nasiha's and Elmina's generation were actively involved in efforts to memorialize those who had been killed, the subject of chapter 6.

NOTES

1. I am drawing on Michael Warner's re-formulation of "the public sphere" as consisting in fact of a number of publics, plural: "The way *the* public functions in the public sphere—as *the people*—is only possible because it is really *a* public of discourse. It is self-creating and self-organized, and herein lies its power as well as its elusive strangeness" (Warner, Michael. *Publics and Counterpublics*. New York: Zone Books, 2002: 51–52. Italics in the original). My approach to discourse is inspired by Vološinov's historical formulation of discourse as a series of rejoinders and ongoing conversations through time and across space (Vološinov, V. N. *Marxism and the Philosophy of Language*. Translated by Ladislav Matejka and I. R. Titunik, New York: Seminar Press, [1929] 1973).

2. According to Warner, "In the sense of the term that I am advocating here, such publics are indeed *counterpublics*, and in a stronger sense than simply comprising subalterns with a reform program. A counterpublic maintains at some level, con-

scious or not, an awareness of its subordinate status. The cultural horizon against which it marks itself off is not just a general or wider public, but a dominant one. And the conflict extends not just to ideas or policy questions, but to the speech genres and modes of address that constitute the public and to the hierarchy among media. The discourse that constitutes it is not merely a different or alternative idiom, but one that in other contexts would be regarded with hostility or with a sense of indecorousness. . . . Friction against the dominant public forces the poetic-expressive character of counterpublic discourse to become salient to consciousness" (Warner 2002: 86. Italics in the original).

3. I am drawing here on Gregory Bateson's concept of "frame" as the boundaries surrounding a piece of text or speech that readers or hearers use to interpret what is written or said (Bateson, Gregory. *Steps to an Ecology of Mind*. New York: Ballantine Books, 1972; see also Goffman, Erving. *Frame Analysis: An Essay on the Organization of Experience*. New York: Harper and Row, 1974).

4. According to Todorova the Balkans includes present-day Greece, Bulgaria, Albania, parts of Western Turkey, and all of former Yugoslavia, except Slovenia (see her chapter, "Nomen" for in-depth historiography of "Balkan" as a geographical designation) (Todorova, Maria. *Imagining the Balkans*. Oxford: Oxford University Press, 2009). See also Ballinger for discussion of anthropological approaches to Southeastern Europe as a "culture area" (Ballinger, Pamela. "Definitional Dilemmas: Southeastern Europe as 'Culture Area'?" *Balkanologie* 3(2): 73–91, December 1999).

5. As Victor Friedman has pointed out, rather than an indication of difference and fission, among linguists, a "balkanism" refers to *shared* features of the variety of languages spoken in the region that is the Balkans (Friedman, Victor. "Observing the Observers: Language, Ethnicity, and Power in the 1994 Macedonian Census and Beyond," in *Toward Comprehensive Peace in Southeast Europe: Conflict Prevention in the South Balkans*, Report of the South Balkans Working Group of the Council on Foreign Relations Center for Preventative Action. New York City: The Twentieth Century Fund Press, 1996).

6. In her historiography of the Balkan region Todorova built on postcolonial theorist Edward Said's formulation of "Orientalism," whereby he argued for a discursive approach to understanding the vast production of knowledge and institutional frameworks western European colonial agents generated that was devoted to the histories of colonial territories and their societies. Said traced the coincident rise of western specializations in "the Orient" with the colonial project and showed how the two phenomena were mutually reinforcing. From the outset, Todorova made it clear that although she shared Said's discursive approach, her formulation of "Balkanism" was distinct from Orientalism. While there are numerous public and private institutes, archives and museums devoted to "the Orient," there is no equivalent institutional apparatus devoted to "the Balkans." For Todorova, the absence of a large institutionalized structure designated to Balkanism is a key difference from Orientalism. Todorova further argues that the groundwork for Balkanism was established during Byzantine and Ottoman administration of the region, imperial frameworks that were distinct from those of western European colonial imperialism. See also Bakić-Hayden and Hayden 1992 for an early critical discussion of Orientalism as a

conceptual framework in historicizing power and inequality in the Balkans. Todorova's book, and the debates associated with it, have generated a substantial body of scholarship since its first publication in 1997. See Fleming for a review of the earlier work (Fleming, K. E. "Orientalism, the Balkans, and Balkan Historiography," *The American Historical Review* 105(4): 1218–1233, 2000). See Longinović 2005 for a critical analysis of internal Balkanism within Serbian literature (Longinović, Tomislav. *Vampires Like Us: Writing Down "The Serbs."* Belgrade: Belgrade Circle Journal, Belgrade Displaced Series, 2005). Rasza and Lindstrom for a discussion of Balkanism during Franjo Tudjman's presidency in Croatia (Rasza, Maple and Nicole Lindstrom. "Balkan is Beautiful: Balkanism in the Political Discourse of Tudjman's Croatia. *East European Politics and Societies* 18(4): 628–650, 2004) and Helms for an excellent discussion of the conceptual usefulness of Balkanism in relation to gender in Muslim-majority parts of post-war Bosnia (Helms, Elissa. "East and West Kiss: Gender, Orientalism and Balkanism in Muslim-Majority Bosnia-Herzegovina." *Slavic Review* 67(1): 88–119, Spring 2008).

7. Helms ibid, p. 194. For an overview of Islam in the Balkans see Butorović, Amila. "Islam in the Balkans." *Oxford Bibliographies Online*. New York: Oxford University Press, 2009.

8. Todorova, *Balkanism*; Fleming, "Orientalism, the Balkans, and Balkan Historiography."

9. These institutions are dominated by fully industrialized "first world" capitalist states.

10. International Commission on the Balkans, 2005: 3. The Commission was convened with the support of the Robert Bosch Stiftung Foundation, King Baudouin Foundation, German Marshall Fund of the United States, and the Charles Stewart Mott Foundation, and its nineteen members include representatives from countries, outside of the Balkan Peninsula, as well as those considered at various times to belong to it: Turkey, Romania, Macedonia, Bosnia and Herzegovina, Albania, Croatia, Slovenia, Serbia and Montenegro, Greece, and Bulgaria.

These agencies have also received criticism for forwarding a global capitalist agenda, an issue I do not address here.

11. Ibid., p. 3.
12. Ibid., p. 4.
13. Ibid.
14. I used the boolean search terms <Bosnian> AND <Refugee> AND <Chicago>.
15. Sex commerce in Bosnia flourished during and after the wars when international UNPROFOR troops provided a large consumer market. Bosnia was also used as a human trafficking transit route during this period.
16. In 2002, Alex Mishulovich was sentenced to nine years in prison ("Human Trafficking in Illinois Fact Sheet").
17. Metz, Nina. "Lana has week to prove itself." *Chicago Tribune*: Chicago, 2004.
18. "Refugee Blues—WH Auden," PoemHunter.com, last accessed February 14, 2020, https://www.poemhunter.com/best-poems/wh-auden/refugee-blues/
19. "carmen funebre," tbp, last accessed February 14, 2020, http://www.tbp.org.pl/carmen-funebre.html

20. Helms 2013: 184.
21. Helms, *Innocence and Victimhood*: 155.
22. Helms ibid., see especially pp. 115, 155, and 184. See Bonfiglioli ("Gendering Social Citizenship") and Nikolić-Ristanović on increased reports of domestic violence following the wartime militarization and lack of postwar employment (Nikolić-Rištanović, Vesna. *Women, Violence, and War: Wartime Victimization of Refugees in the Balkans*. Budapest: Central European University Press, 2000).
23. Kimberle Crenshaw's foundational text on intersectional theory is helpful in understanding the diverse social factors that shaped Bosnian refugee women's experiences in the United States. Crenshaw draws primarily on the experiences of Black women with both sexist and racist structural inequality in the United States to advance the call for analyses that bring together different avenues of inequality through the metaphor of an intersection. According to Crenshaw political projects that fail to incorporate intersectional analysis are bound to fail: "Aiming to bring together the different aspects of an otherwise divided sensibility, an intersectional analysis argues that racial and sexual subordination are mutually reinforcing, that Black women are commonly marginalized by a politics of race alone or gender alone, and that a political response to each form of subordination must at the same time be a political response to both" (Crenshaw, Kimberle. "Mapping the Margins: Intersectionality, Identity Politics, and Violence against Women of Color," *Stanford Law Review* 43(6): 1241–1299, 1991: 1283).
24. This is a nod to Erving Goffman's concept of "face-work," although I used the term here not in the sense of individual impression-management in the context of micro-interactions, but rather extend the term to the level of social power and structural inequality that a discursive approach entails.
25. There was no clear motivation reported for Talović's shooting. His parents and acquaintances described him as antisocial and a loner (Johnson, Kirk. "Anti-Bosnian Backlash Feared in Utah." *New York Times*. New York City, February 15, 2007: 6, 18).
26. Clemetson, Lynette. "Bosnians in America: A Two-Sided Saga." *The New York Times*. New York City, April 29, 2007: 14.
27. While these concerns were raised, no one presented any statistical evidence that Bosnian refugee-immigrants experienced these social problems at rates that diverged significantly from that of the general population, and I have not found reliable statistics relating to rates among Bosnians in Chicago for this time period. That said, people did identify these as concerns. Both my own research with refugees in Chicago, and Barbara Franz' research with Bosnian refugees in New York City found multiple accounts from Bosnians, and from social service providers who worked with them, of husbands who experienced status loss and sometimes became abusive toward family members. In many accounts, men who found themselves in these circumstances also became the targets of physical and verbal abuse from family members (Franz, Barbara. *Uprooted and Unwanted: Bosnian Refugees in Austria and the United States*. College Station: Texas A&M University Press, 2005).

Chapter Six

A Trade in Stories

In October 2000, women refugees, volag staff and volunteers, and others gathered in the Berger Fieldhouse, a twentieth century lakefront mansion that was turned into a Chicago Park District facility during the 1980s. Dan Žena Izbeglica / Refugee Women's Day was advertised as an event open to the public that would feature the "real-life stories of women who survived the war in Bosnia. *Their* experiences will change *your* life forever" (emphases added). Who were the "you" sought as an audience here? And how would the women's refugee experiences change the lives of this "you"? A participant's review of the event offered one answer to these questions; Venice Johnson wrote that she was appointed to read aloud the refugee women's stories and described the impact of this exercise:

> No one can fully understand or know such pain unless he or she has lived it, but I learned one valuable thing that I will carry with me forever; I connected to these women and their stories. Their pain and their joy has been imparted to me. They are my sisters. I began to understand that we are all a part of a universal family.[1]

While Johnson acknowledges the differences in experiences between herself and the refugee women whose stories she narrated that day, she also uses the idiom of kinship to minimize these distinctions and to describe how she was affected by the women's stories. This event took place before I began the fieldwork for this project, and I do not know how the women's stories were curated, how they were composed, how they were translated, nor how Johnson was selected to read them. I discovered the event a few years later, in the March 2001 issue of a local Bosnian publication, *Nova Žena / New Woman* that had published Johnson's review. Catholic Charities of the

Figure 6.1. "Women of Bosnia Tell Their Story" Announcement.

Archdiocese of Chicago Refugee Resettlement Program funded the publication and associated programming by sponsoring the group that produced both the magazine and the Refugee Women's Day event: the Women's Support Group.[2] According to the editorial page, the Women's Support Group "was born out of the need for mental health services for refugee women.... [T]he support group empowers women by publishing stories of refugee women; their testimonies about trauma suffered during the war, flight from their native country, separation and loss of family members, and experiences during the resettlement process."[3] The support group and magazine were established by a couple of women professionals who were originally from Yugoslavia, but had emigrated to Chicago prior to the war.

The magazine and Refugee Women's Day belong to a human rights movement devoted to highlighting certain features of women's lives in refugee experiences. A key platform of this movement is to compel a re-interpretation of the United Nations definition of refugee to include gender as a qualifying "group" membership-claim based on women's vulnerabilities to domestic violence, state-sanctioned violence against women, and rape. Feminists trained in the western liberal tradition that centers notions of individual human rights as embodied in a universal human subject lead this movement, and they were key actors developing policies designed for international liberal institutions such as the UNHCR and Catholic Charities, as well as for rapidly proliferating non-governmental organizations. While the movement to incorporate gender in refugee classifications began in the late 1970s, culminating in the UN General Assembly's 1979 adoption of the Convention for the Elimination of All Forms of Discrimination against Women (CEDAW), its effects could be seen more clearly in the 1990s and the early aughts. This was the period when NGOs dedicated to "women's empowerment" could be found throughout parts of the world where liberal democracies sought to increase their influence in the geo-political reconfigurations brought about by the end of the Cold War. Women's NGOs also expanded in the United States; I worked in the development office of one such NGO devoted to "women's empowerment" through literacy programs in Chicago and found that many of the philanthropic associations which funded the NGO also designated empowerment among their program priorities.

As with the American characters in Eve Ensler's play, the Refugee Women's Day event was premised on a liberal feminist understanding of narrating trauma as essential to bringing forth a transformational healing. In human rights discourse, narrating abusive experiences is also presumed to be essential to achieving justice. These language ideologies are perhaps most clearly illustrated by the concept of "giving voice," wherein those whose opinions are marginalized in dominant publics are liberated by powerful allies who have greater access to these publics. In this sense, J. S. and Melissa can be viewed as "giving voice" to the women refugees, vis á vis the American women's relationship to the Red Cross and Melissa's access to global media outlets. In a similar vein, Venice Johnson and the Refugee Women's Support Group can be seen as "giving voice" to the Bosnian refugee women in Chicago by providing a connection to Catholic Charities and access to the Berger Park Cultural Center. I argue that the widespread acceptance and prevalence of this type of refugee narrative among human rights NGOs indicates that such stories could function at times as a type of currency. At the same time, Bosnian women's approaches to these narratives were varied and contested. Their experiences reveal some of the shortcomings of the human rights discourse, including the ways such discourse was enlisted for transnational political campaigns.

GIVING VOICE TO SREBRENICA SURVIVORS IN DALEY PLAZA

On a sunny July morning in Chicago, 2005, Fadila and I met at TCC and boarded a yellow school bus along with forty survivors of the Bosnian Wars.

We were on our way to Daley Plaza in the city's Loop to memorialize the Srebrenica genocide, ten years earlier.[4] It was going to be a hot day, and we'd be on our feet for a while. Fadila wore comfortable walking sandals, simple cotton khaki slacks, and a white cotton blouse. Her cropped haircut offered some relief from the heat, and sunglasses shielded her eyes from the summer sun's glare. Once on the bus, several men whom we did not know passed out strips of wide green ribbon meant to symbolize the survivors' and the dead's Muslim identities. Along with the ribbons, we were given white t-shirts with large green lettering in five lines of text: DON'T FORGET SREBRENICA 1995–2005 CHICAGO. Fadila decided not to tie the ribbon around her arm or head as some of the other passengers had done. After placing the ribbon in her tan leather shoulder bag, she pulled the large t-shirt over her head, covering her blouse. I followed her lead, stowing my ribbon and donning my t-shirt. During the bumpy ride south on scenic Lake Shore Drive, the bus passed beaches full of families and summer youth campers, and parks packed with active soccer and volleyball tournaments. We drove past sailboats gliding, and yachts bobbing on the waters of Lake Michigan, and even little paddle-boats out on the manmade lake at Lincoln Park Zoo. A few people remarked on the scenes of pleasure. But for the most part, the thirty-minute drive was a journey of silence.

The bus exited on Randolph and approached the Daley Center, home to the city's mayoral and aldermanic offices. I followed Fadila as we disembarked and joined other people at the foot of Picasso's steel sculpture, where we assembled ourselves behind rows of chairs outlining the front of a stage. Here we were given white placards with black lettering to hold during the demonstration: "Stop Genocide" "Never Forget" "Let's Not Repeat" "Peace." We knew we were attending a memorial to commemorate the men's lives lost in the 1995 massacres in Srebrenica, but beyond the t-shirts, arm bands, and signs, we did not receive any more information about what to expect. We did learn that these materials were provided by a group, Association of Survivors of the Srebrenica Genocide / *Udruženje Srebreničana*, based in St. Louis, a city that is home to the largest concentration of Srebrenica survivors in the United States.

Uncertain of what would come next, Fadila and I observed the plaza-gatherers. In addition to our group's "never again" and "peace" statements, some demonstrators held handmade signs that declared the Srebrenica massacre the largest genocide in Europe since the WWII Holocaust, and several that included emblems and language that were clearly political, including the Bosnian national flag with the medieval kingdom's fleur-de-lis that was rejected by the EU in 1996, and a sign that accused "Četniks" of perpetrating the Srebrenica massacres. Historically, četnik is the term for Serb militia who fought against Yugoslav communists during the Second World war.⁵ In this instance, the term likely referred to the self-declared "četnik" brigades, many of which were led by Serb ethno-nationalist Vojislav Šešelj. While these references were likely lost on many of the Americans present, they would have been legible to Chicago's large Yugoslav diasporas.⁶ Amidst this cacophony of placard-messages, I was particularly intrigued by a sign that portrayed a terrorism timeline. The timeline began with Srebrenica 7-11-1995, moved to 9-11-2001 denoting attacks in New York, then to 3-11-2004 for the Madrid train bombings, and ended with the 7-7-2005 London subway bombings that had taken place only days before the Srebrenica memorial.

While Al-Qaeda operatives or sympathizers claimed responsibility for the civilian bombings in New York, Madrid, and London, justifying the terrorist acts with extremist Islamist ideology, the Srebrenica massacre was carried out by means of the still-existing Yugoslav state (Serbia and Montenegro), headquartered in Serbia. The Bosnian Serb Army (VRS) under the direction of commander Ratko Mladić, who himself reported directly to Radovan Karadžić, proclaimed leader of the so-called Bosnian Serb Republic, and ultimately to Slobodan Milosević, then president of Serbia. Most significantly, the massacres specifically targeted Bosnian Muslim men and included teenagers and the elderly.

The terror-timeline sign placed Srebrenica's Muslim victims of the Yugoslav regime's state-sponsored terror campaigns in the company of the many victims—Muslim and non-Muslim—of terrorist acts perpetrated by Muslim-identified men in Western Europe and the United States. I wondered if this effort at translating Bosnian Muslims' victimhood for an American audience would be understood. The growing crowd included office workers who had wandered over to see what was going on, and Bosnians I recognized along with other people who signaled their Muslim identities through skull caps or headscarves.

On the stage in front of us, 14 male and female teenagers clad in black were assembling into a line separated by gender: seven males, and seven females. The somber line of black-clad teenagers and the memorial signs reminding us to "Never Forget" inserted a stark break in the sunny summer day, as a large, ridiculous "Farmer's Market" banner depicting a medley of colorful fruits and vegetables hung over their heads at the top of the stage. The teenagers and signs only set the stage: the most dramatic aspect of the memorial was yet to come.

The program was meant to begin around noon in the hopes of gaining increased visibility by catching the Loop's lunch break crowd. I hung back with Fadila and some of the other senior women as we listened to a set of statements read by representatives from a number of NGOs with transnational human rights agendas, including: The American Jewish Committee (AJC), The Council of Islamic Organizations of Greater Chicago (CIOGC), and Human Rights Watch. In addition to the presence of these NGOs, there were numerous references to human rights invoked over the course of the speeches.

Following the NGO speeches, a young woman, also dressed in black, ascended the stage and approached the microphone. In her amplified voice, she identified herself as a refugee from the Srebrenica region who had lost family in the war. She went on to narrate her childhood memories of surviving the war. She was between the ages of six and nine during the wars, and she detailed the shelling of her home, fleeing and hiding in mountain caves, and related the utter fear and helplessness she felt as a child witness to war while observing her mother's struggles to care for children while their father fought with the resistance. She ended the story by focusing on her survival, illustrated with the metaphor of a phoenix rising from the ashes. Once she had completed her story, an older man took the podium and interpreted the young woman's survival as a sign of the collective suffering and strength of the Bosnian Muslim people. Then he asked the men and women in the audience to stand, and to separate from one another.

I looked over at Fadila, and after a bit of murmured agreement with the others in our group, we moved over to where women were gathering. Once we had separated, we were told to get down on our knees and kiss the ground. As we did this, a recording of machine-gunfire blasted above our heads through the loudspeakers on stage. Fadila looked shocked. I was shocked. We were taken completely by surprise by this staged re-enactment. People in the crowd seemed upset and began standing up as the man at the microphone explained that the sex-separation mimicked the gendered structure of violence during

Figure 6.2. Daley Plaza Srebrenica Memorial 2005. Photo by Ana Croegaert.

the Srebrenica massacre, when men were separated from women and children, who were then bussed out of the encampment.

During this embodied reenactment an older woman wearing a headscarf and clothing in the rural style fainted, and women crowded around, holding her, fanning her, Ajša intervened and gestured to the women to move back and give the woman space, while sprinkling cold bottled water on the woman's face. We learned that the woman had lost her teenaged son in Srebrenica. Fadila and Ajša were very upset, exclaiming, "Why would they [the organizers] do this?? Are they crazy??!" followed by a series of statements about how thoughtless it was to provoke emotions about such horrible experiences, and particularly in the noonday heat. In fact, many of my elder women companions were shocked by and critical of the dramatic public reenactment, commenting that they had been through enough (as war survivors) and worried that the reenactment would stir up bad memories and feelings, and possibly bring harm to survivors, like the woman who had fainted.

We were all tired and emotionally exhausted by the day's events and Fadila, Ajša, and I along with several others from TCC decided to walk over to the subway and take the red line home rather than wait for the school bus to return. We rode home listening to the sounds of the subway car. We did not speak.

The Srebrenica genocide represents enormous suffering for the families and friends of those who were killed in a series of organized mass executions carried out by the VRS over the course of ten days. Following the 2004 ICTY finding of genocide at Srebrenica, the case was now before the ICJ where hearings would begin in 2006. The case involved the massacres in Srebrenica but arose from the 1992–1993 mass displacements and detainments, executions, and rapes of non-Serbs in parts of northern, central, and eastern Bosnia. Following these events, the government of Bosnia-Herzegovina filed suit against Serbia, accusing the Milošević regime of genocide for its participation in the atrocities by providing critical infrastructural support and guidance to the VRS and affiliated militia. These earlier massacres and displacements led the United Nations to declare certain areas within these regions as "safe havens" for civilians to seek shelter under the protection of United Nations Protection Force (UNPROFOR) security forces. Srebrenica was one such safe haven, but in July 1995, the small 28th division of the Army of the Republic of Bosnia-Herzegovina (ARBiH) defending the area was overpowered by the VRS.[7] Nearly thirty thousand Bosnian Muslim men, women, and children had fled the terror in surrounding areas to seek refuge in the Srebrenica safe haven, where a Dutch battalion of the UNPROFOR was stationed at Potočari, a few miles outside of Srebrenica.

Under Mladić's direction, VRS troops overwhelmed the 350 Dutchbat soldiers, who requested and were denied air support. The VRS took dozens of Dutchbat soldiers as hostages and proceeded to perpetrate extreme acts of violence against Bosnian men, women, and children, who were already emaciated and disoriented from years of violence, displacements, and food deprivation as a result of the VRS cutting electricity, water, and blocking humanitarian aid. Mladić ordered women and children to be separated from men and adolescent boys, telling the captives that the women and children would be taken to VRS-held territory outside of Srebrenica, and that the men would be exchanged for prisoners of war held by the ARBiH. This was a lie; the prisoner exchange never happened, and at least 8,372 men, adolescent boys, and some women were killed and bulldozed into mass graves throughout the area. Aerial photos show this, and also show that the VRS dug up the remains in a number of these graves between August and November 1995, moving them to secondary graves in efforts to make it even more difficult to identify remains. Forensic evidence corroborates the aerial footage, with partial remains of individual bodies found to be distributed across multiple sites.

Despite the multitude of forensic evidence, documented correspondence between the Milosević regime in Serbia and Bosnian Serb leadership, and survivor accounts, as well as a number of criminal indictments, the massacres were contested and denied by some Serbs in powerful positions who had enshrined the war criminals in the public infrastructure of the Serb-dominated RS entity of Bosnia, erecting monuments, displaying portraiture, and naming buildings and streets after them. Some war criminals themselves occupied municipal positions in parts of the entity. In 2005, it was widely known that highly placed people in Serbia were helping both Karadžić and Mladić evade trial at the ICTY.[8]

In the face of continued denial of responsibility for the genocide against Bosnian Muslims, the stakes for characterizing Srebrenica as a genocide remained high for survivors. The Daley Plaza event was one of the hundreds of memorials that take place among the globally dispersed diaspora and in Bosnia every July 11—the day Srebrenica fell to the VRS.[9] Just days before the Chicago memorial, the U.S. Congress and the Missouri state legislature passed a resolution recognizing Srebrenica as a genocide, and the city of St. Louis issued a proclamation that officially declared July 11 as Srebrenica Remembrance Day.[10] These memorial events thus have multiple intended audiences, including: survivors, other countries in the former SFRY, globally powerful governments such as the United States, and transnational human rights organizations.

While everyone present at Daley Plaza that day certainly would have agreed that the Srebrenica massacres were horrifying events that ought never to be repeated, the multiple institutions, affiliations, perspectives, and people present for the memorial illustrate a range of classifications for these massacres: genocide, terrorism, human rights violations, war. The more explicitly political references would have been understood solely by most of the Bosnians present, but for the rest of those gathered in the plaza, the most prominent story was the young woman's narrative of victimization, followed by the unexpected and dramatic re-enactment of gendered separation amidst the sounds of warfare—a scene openly critiqued by the senior women.

BOSNIAN WOMEN ON CAPITOL HILL: A CELEBRATION OF INTERNATIONAL WOMAN'S DAY

Several years later, I headed to Washington D.C. to meet up with Nasiha. Elmina, the young woman featured in the "two-sided saga" news story (chapter 5), was now living in D.C., and at 23 years old was the first and sole lobbyist on Capitol Hill employed by the Advisory Council for Bosnia and Herzegovina (ACBH). Her primary work involved educating and galvanizing U.S. congressional members to support constitutional reforms in Bosnia and to maintain support for a unified Bosnia as guaranteed in the 1995 Peace Accords.[11] This work was deeply personal to Elmina, and she had invited Nasiha and I to join her for an event celebrating the lives and work of Bosnian women, including their efforts to memorialize male family members who had died during the war.

Elmina was born in Kozarac, a small town not far from Prijedor, and located in the now Serb-dominated "Entity" of Bosnia. Like Nasiha, Elmina and family members were detained in the Trnopolje concentration camp before making to it Croatia, then Germany, then the United States as refugees. Elmina channeled her wartime experiences of compounded humiliations, violations, and displacements into a passion for working to maintain a unified Bosnia that would not be divided between the Serb Republic and Federation entities enshrined by the Dayton Accords.[12] Standing at barely five feet tall, with slender limbs and a tousled mop of wavy brown hair, Elmina was often mistaken for a teenager. (In the NYT profile, the photo caption identified her by her shirt pattern so as to distinguish her from the kids with whom she was pictured.) While her build is slight, Elmina possesses a sturdy disposition. She had landed the job on Capitol Hill after completing her B.A. in Political Science and Women's Studies, and an internship in then-Senator (IL) Barack Obama's and Senator (IL) Dick Durban's Chicago district offices. She had invited us to join her in D.C. for an event she scheduled for International Women's Day (March 8), a socialist-era state holiday established to especially recognize and celebrate women's participation in the labor force.[13] We met in Elmina's tiny apartment and then took the subway to her modest office which consisted of a desk, a chair, and some file cabinets in a room that she shared with other small advocacy groups. From her office, we walked over to the Capitol building where Elmina had reserved a room for the event. We entered the regal Capitol Visitor Center, our heels clicking through the marble corridors, following Elmina into a room with plush deep green carpet. As Nasiha and I took seats, Elmina greeted the two prominent female speakers she had invited: Munira Beba Hadžić, the leader of a women's NGO, BosFam, based in Tuzla, and Congresswoman Eddie Bernice Johnson (D-TX), the chair of the Congressional Caucus on Bosnia.

Elmina had learned about BosFam while researching what support services were available to women survivors in Bosnia. BosFam is a woman-operated NGO within the Federation border in eastern Bosnia. A brochure describes the NGO's work:

> BosFam was founded in 1994 as a center for refugee women to gather, knit, and talk during the war. BosFam continues this tradition of community-building while providing women with income-generating handicraft projects. It operates on the principles of humaneness, impartiality, independence, and volunteer work.

This fusion of tradition, culture, and women's crafts as paid employment is phrased more succinctly on the front page of their brochure: "Bosnian Tradition: beauty and work." Bosfam receives funding and promotional support from two international non-profit organizations, and each had sent representatives to the Capitol Hill event. The Heinrich Boll Foundation North America is a German-based INGO (International Non-Governmental Organization), and the US-based The Advocacy Project (DC-based, field office in Kampala, Uganda) which aims to provide "a *voice for the voiceless*" and to "help[s] marginalized communities to *tell their story, claim their rights* and produce social change" (my italics).

As do volags like TCC, BosFam belongs to the global non-profit corporate form, in this case to the massive complex of international organizations funded by western democracies that aim to cultivate democracy by investing in "civil society," or non-governmental institutions. As the NGO form became more longstanding over the course of several decades, it has become apparent that NGOs are not the cure-all their proponents had envisioned. Not surprisingly, some of this disappointment stems from the realization that there is no universal NGO form; rather NGO forms vary widely depending on socio-historical relations of power. Development scholars have noted the ways in which such models effectively accelerate the "withering away of the state" by enlarging the domains in which foreign investment may occur,

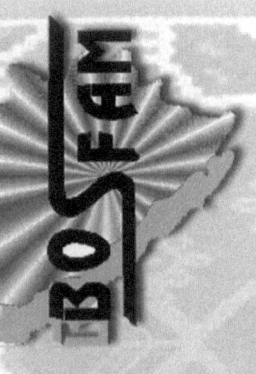

BOSFAM

Udruženje Bosanska familija
Association Bosnian Family
удружене босанска фамилија
Udruga Bosanska obitelj

Bosfam

1. **INFORMISANJE I EDUKACIJA**
2. **PRUŽANJE NEFORMALNE PSIHO-SOCIJALNE POMOĆI**
   - Klub prijateljstva i solidarnosti,
   - Pomoć ženama čiji su članovi porodice nestali u ratu
   - Pomoć starim, usamljenim osobama
3. **RADNO ANGAŽOVANJE ŽENA**
   - Program tkanja ćilima (tradicionalnih-bosanskih i moderno dizajniranih)
   - Program moderne ručno rađene odjeće
   - Organizovanje kurseva za različite vrste ručnog rada
   - BAZARI u Bosfam-u
4. **CILIM SJEĆANJA NA ŽRTVE GENOCIDA U SREBRENICI** - tradicijom protiv zaborava
5. **POMOĆ DJECI U SREBRENICI**

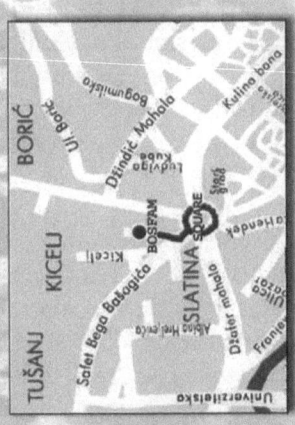

Ul. Stjepana Matijevića 11 (u blizini Skvera)
75 000 Tuzla, Bosna i Hercegovina
Tel./Fax: +387 35 257 534
GSM: +387 61 732 027

Web: www.bosfam.ba
E-mail: bosfam.tz@bih.net.ba

GALERIJA JE OTVORENA SVAKI DAN (osim nedjelje) od 9-18 sati.
Postoji mogućnost posjete Galeriji nedjeljom uz najavu.

BOSFAM

BOSANSKA TRADICIJA
ljepota i rad

VIZIJA BOSFAM-a
Želimo bili dovoljno jaka NVO da kroz informisanje, edukaciju i ekonomsko osnaživanje podržimo žene kako bi one bile osposobljene da same odlučuju o sebi i svojoj porodici, da budu informisane, da uče, da zarađuju, da prevazidu traume

Bosfam's projects

1. **INFORMATION AND EDUCATION**
2. **PSYCHO-SOCIAL AID**
   - Gatherings of friendship and solidarity.
   - Helping women with missing family members.
   - Helping elderly population and lonely persons.
3. **WOMEN'S WEAVING & KNITTING**
   - Carpet production (traditional Bosnian or modern designs)
   - Clothing production (wool and cotton)
   - Organizing showcases for different kinds of handicrafts
   - BAZAR'S IN BOSFAM
4. **THE CARPET OF REMEMBRANCE ON SREBRENICA GENOCIDE VICTIMS** "Tradition against oblivion"
5. **SUPPORT SCHOOL CHILDREN IN SREBRENICA MUNICIPALITY**

HEADQUARTERS TUZLA
Stjepana Matijevića 11 (near the Square)
75000 Tuzla, Bosnia-Herzegovina
Tel./Fax: 00387-35/257 534
Mobile: 00387-61 732 027

Web: www.bosfam.ba
E-mail: bosfam@bih.net.ba

GALERRY is open every day (out of Sunday) from 9.a.m.-6.p.m.
(If you like visit Bosfam's Gallery at sunday - call us!)

BOSNIAN TRADITION
beauty and work

BOSFAM's Vision
We want our organization to be strong enough to support our members through education, so that they can learn, earn a living, and make responsible decisions for their families and themselves.

Figure 6.3. BosFam Brochure.

displacing state infrastructures and providing services that people might otherwise demand from the state.[14]

NGO proponents see the form as a way to also expand women's participation in areas of official political and economic power from which they may be excluded. Yet feminist critics and gender studies scholars have noted that while women predominate in NGOs—and as seen at TCC, which was forced to close its doors in 2006—these are not women's utopian societies, and rather should be seen as rich sites for exploring how the categories "woman / women" are produced in various contexts.[15] Even when women recipients of NGO funds strategically deploy gender essentialism, or, in what Elissa Helms has argued is "affirmative essentialism" in the case of post-war Bosnia, this may result in increased distrust of state entities and promote the fracturing of existing social supports. Further, affirmative essentialism addresses women's gendered inequality by positively emphasizing women's already-existing roles as mothers and nurturers to advance their social standing. While such approaches may initially help women to gain more public visibility and participation in regimes of power, they ultimately rely on the reproduction of limited roles through which women can achieve public recognition. In emphasizing domestic crafts and beauty, Bosfam and the agencies that fund it may be seen to rely on affirmative essentialism to improve post-war refugee women's well-being. Elmina and Nasiha are both practical people, and they believed that the focus on women's crafts and art would at least draw positive attention to Bosnia, but I wondered if they would be able to effectively communicate their political aims to keep post-war Bosnia a unified multi-ethnic country. The program began with a speech by Friedrich, from the Henrich Boll Foundation, who stood at a podium set against the backdrop of the memorial carpets the BosFam women refugees had woven with their missing male family members' names.

Friedrich told the audience that Bosnia was a place governed by "traditions of patriarchal culture" that had ignited the Bosnian Wars. He noted that more than 40 percent of women in Bosnia were "economically active" and that these women represented just the right kind of "human capital" necessary to establish a civil society guided by International Organizations (IO). Along with the IOs, these women could then model gender equality for those mired in the traditions of patriarchy. The speech was saturated in the genre of paternalist-maternalist reprimand that Leila Ahmed identifies as "colonial feminism," and that Abu-Lughod notes is central to the construction of the "Muslim woman in need of saving" that figures in discursive justifications for United States wars in Afghanistan and Iraq. Rather than draw attention to the war's origins as embedded in geopolitical struggles involving post-cold war realignments, globalizing capitalism and the widening inequality it brought

Figure 6.4. BosFam Memorial Carpet with men's names. Displayed during International Woman's Day on Capitol Hill in Washington DC, 2009. Photo by Ana Croegaert.

worldwide, the speech instead ignored the devastation wrought on the SFRY political economy by the country's opening to a free market system and privatizing its infrastructure in return for loans received from western financial institutions beginning in the early 1970s.[16] Despite ample research documenting how these dynamics put the SFRY at risk and vulnerable to political conflict, Friedrich's narrative turned on the familiar Balkanist "ancient ethnic hatreds" and virulent masculinity tropes that couched the wars in cultural terms. When Friedrich had finished his call to end the Bosnian patriarchy through a women-led civil(ized) society, Elmina introduced Beba.

Beba approached the podium and in a soft, steady voice, she briefly recounted her harrowing survival of the war, including the family members she had lost, and how she sought meaning and healing in her work with other women survivors. Then, she and Elmina invited Congresswoman Johnson to join them in front of the woven carpets, where they presented her with a square from the Srebrenica memorial rug-quilt that depicted the mineral hot springs Srebrenica was known for.[17]

The relationship to the Advocacy Project, the link to the socialist worker holiday, and the Capitol Hill venue and attendees all highlight the program's implicit political aims and suggests a more complex reading of the women's craftwork, beauty, and impartiality described above. Elmina had emphasized to me repeatedly that it was important to keep the events of Srebrenica and Prijedor present in the minds of American legislators in order to prevent RS leadership's anti-Bosniak policies and the possibility of future political violence. Thus, we can understand the co-occurrence of war testimony in conjunction with the display of the names of the dead on the carpet squares, interwoven with place-name references, in domestic items that are gifted to Americans-with-influence as political acts. Elmina and Beba sought to remind the audience of the women war widows in order to emphasize their commitment to Bosnian unification and to challenge discriminatory governance in the post-war state. In doing so, the Bosnian women were tapping into the familiar "voice" through victimhood / survivorhood frames popularized by global liberal feminism and institutionalized through international NGOs.

The NGO delegates and U.S. government officials never addressed the claim to Bosnian unification. And, despite BosFam's focus on job creation and Elmina's attempt to connect the event with women's socialist-worker status, Friedrich's speech framed the day in cultural terms of gendered victimhood and women's innate civilizing capacities. Where Beba and Elmina sought to frame their war experiences and post-conflict futures in relation to their roles as political subjects and employed workers, they were met with the Boll Foundation and the Advocacy Project delegates who emphasized women's roles as narrators of victimhood and survival, and as civilizing agents.

GIVING VOICE TO SREBRENICA AND PRIJEDOR SURVIVORS

After the Women's Day event, Nasiha invited me to another Chicago-based memorial to the Srebrenica massacres. She had helped to organize the event, working alongside some other locally based Bosnian diaspora groups. This event reflected more recent developments in the struggle for Bosnia's war survivors to gain international recognition of the atrocities they had suffered. In 2007, the ICJ issued a judgement in the genocide case against Serbia and Montenegro. While the ICJ upheld the 2004 ICTY ruling that declared the massacres at Srebrenica constituted genocide, the court ruled that Serbia had been "negligent" in failing to stop the "ethnic cleansing" in Bosnia, but could not be held responsible for the genocide.[18] In the meantime, more evidence had come to light regarding the massacres of non-Serb Bosnians in and around the Prijedor region where Nasiha and Elmina were from, and they were compelled to join efforts to spread awareness of these earlier war crimes. Enisa and Edo discouraged Nasiha from becoming involved in these memorial efforts, telling her that they were concerned for her emotional well-being because of pressures from fellow survivors, as well as possible harassment from genocide-deniers. But Nasiha felt that her memorial efforts would help to strengthen the postwar state by connecting it with the United States and with the Bosnian diaspora there.

In Loyola University's Crown Auditorium, Nasiha and her co-organizers had set the scene with hallway banners proclaiming *Srebrenica i Prijedor sva su Bosna, Bosna je sva Prijedor i Srebrenica* / "Srebrenica and Prijedor we are Bosnia, Bosnia is Prijedor and Srebrenica" emphasizing Bosnian unification, and also the shared wartime experiences of the two municipalities. At the end of the hallway was the auditorium, where the Bosnian flag and the United States flag hung side by side in front of the lectern. Next to the lectern two chairs were positioned so that they partially faced one another, as well as the audience. Behind these chairs hung a banner with the Bosnian independence fleur-de-lis flag. The stage would soon be occupied by acclaimed Bosnian writer and Chicago resident Aleksandar Hemon for his conversation with the event's headliner: journalist Roy Gutman who had won a Pulitzer Prize in 1993 for his wartime coverage of the concentration camps, including Trnopolje where Nasiha and her family were held. Before the two men ascended the stage, Nasiha stood at the podium to welcome the audience and orient us to the program. Next to Nasiha stood another young woman, whom she introduced as Almina, and told the audience that Almina was a Srebrenica survivor and would share her story. As Almina began to narrate her story in front of the two hundred people gathered in the auditorium, I realized that she looked and sounded familiar, and that she was the female teenager who had shared her survivor story years earlier at the 2005 event in Daley Plaza. Neither Nasiha, nor any of the other survivors from Prijedor, shared a personal survivor story. After Almina's story, Hemon and Gutman took the stage to engage in a writer-to-writer conversation before taking questions from the audience.

Gutman recounted his experiences documenting the wartime atrocities and reporting on them for an international audience, emphasizing the victimhood of Bosnian Muslims, and the heroic efforts of survivors. Hemon shifted this familiar narrative of victimhood by sharing a recent conversation he'd had with a Bosnian visual artist. The artist's work was based on the events at Srebrenica, and the artist asked Hemon's advice about placing his work in the United States, remarking that: "Srebrenica is a world-renowned brand." Hemon then asked Gutman, "Is this what's being produced in postwar BiH?" perhaps suggesting that genocide art, or genocide-branding, was being produced in the post-war state. Gutman offered a strange reply, "Bosnia doesn't produce much of anything at all. If Srebrenica draws people into Bosnia, that's a fine thing," overlooking Bosnia's significant agricultural production, mining, and textile industries. Hemon, taking a more direct approach, asked "Are victims using Srebrenica in a way that you find objectionable?" Gutman appeared to ponder this query and then answered, "It is a problem when victims remain victims," and went on to say that Srebrenica should be instructive, a "lesson to humanity" presumably about the occurrence and aftermath of genocide. Hemon attempted to pursue this remark by noting the significance of the market for war and for humanitarian and survivor war narratives, but Gutman didn't engage.

Hemon then directed the conversation to the thousands of women who had been raped during the same time the massacres at Prijedor and Srebrenica were taking place, and whose traumas received much less public attention or memorialization among the diaspora than had the deaths of the Srebrenica victims. Some of the audience members shifted in their seats and seemed to be uncomfortable with this reference. Gutman affirmed this concern, but offered no follow-up, and Hemon redirected the discussion to the recent discovery of a trove of documents stashed behind a false wall in Ratko Mladić's Belgrade home. The data clearly delineate a wartime chain of command between Serbia and the VRS, as well as between certain Croatian nationalists and the VRS outlining their plans to cooperate in dividing Bosnia into Croatian and Serbian territories. All parties implicated had denied such relationships, and Mladić was still at-large.[19] The question and answer session that followed the writers' discussion ended up being dominated by men, among whom were several wearing clothing and facial hair styles associated with conservative adherents of Islam, and who used the forum as an opportunity to make prolonged remarks about the persecution of Muslims rather than ask questions about Bosnia, or about the refugees living in Chicago. As with the 2005 memorial, Almina's childhood story served as the opening for the cooptation of survivors' experiences for political ethno-nationalists' platforms. This instrumental use of survivor's stories by some nationalist groups was among the reasons Edo and Enisa objected to Nasiha's involvement in the memorials. I wondered what Almina thought about telling her story in these contexts, and I approached her after the event to see if she would be willing to talk with me about her participation in the Chicago-based wartime memorials.

MAKING VOICE: BEHIND THE SCENES

Almina agreed to meet with me, and I reserved a public library room where we could talk without interruption. We met one evening after Almina had finished work at her office job, and sat next to one another on wooden chairs, my recorder on the table in front of us. While the majority of the questions I had prepared centered on how and why Almina had decided to publicly share her survival story, Almina used her responses to focus on her mother's suffering as well as her own, often linking them together. Almina's father was among the men who had escaped the Srebrenica massacres. The men of Almina's mother's family, however, were all killed in the massacres. Almina told me that the Survivors of Srebrenica group was looking for someone to share a personal survivor story at the 2005 event, and someone had recommended her. She was 19 at the time, and the only female member of the group. The men showed Almina the text for the speech they wanted her to deliver, but she decided to rewrite it because, "it didn't sound like me." Almina knew her family would also be in attendance and she especially wanted her story to resonate for her mother, Nejra.

During our conversation, Almina described Nejra as suffering from paranoia as a result of the wartime violence and loss of her family members. Her mother was very changed from how Almina remembered her, even after their arrival in the United States; Nejra had become increasingly remote and depressed over the years. In an effort to help me understand her mother's sadness, Almina drew my attention to the widely shared images of Srebrenica female mourners, pictured in the headscarf and colorful, baggy pants (*dimije*) associated with Muslim women from rural areas, often crying and pictured with images of the men they had lost:

> I mean it's sad, like, how do you, you know. . . . When you watch those videos, I mean, those women just cry, like all they do, it's all they do, all of them, it's all the same. I'm telling you, they'll sometimes say "I wish I was killed," I mean my mom will say that! And it hurts, you know? I know it's this pain speaking and not her. Sometimes she says, "I wish I died, I wish they took me."[20]

As she spoke about her mother's sorrows, Almina interspersed some of her own troubles, telling me that she had nightmares for days after hearing the loud, low-flying military aircraft at Chicago's annual "air and water" show.[21] I asked Almina if she thought telling her story at events like the Srebrenica memorials, and talking about the war with others was helpful to her, and if she thought it was helpful to her mother. In response she referenced more nightmares, and mentioned an American woman who had been encouraging her to talk about what happened:

> Sometimes, I feel it is better sometimes . . . but I'll have nightmares—I try to stay in the boundaries, then [if I talk about it] I will be having nightmares for the next four days. I was talking to this woman Ruth who I met when I came here and she . . . wanted me to talk about what happened. I told her oh my god,

I don't think I can go into certain details—[I'm] always trying to block out certain things. I don't have the perfect answer. It helps, but sometimes it opens the wound.

Almina's responses suggest that her initial impulse to share her story in public was prompted by the idea that maybe if she showed a public face of bravery, it would help Nejra to cope with her own horrific memories. Almina was also struggling with wartime memories, and further, an American woman was encouraging Almina to discuss her traumatic experiences. She told me that Ruth had even suggested Almina write a memoir about the war, although Almina wasn't sure this would be helpful. I became more aware of Bosnian refugee women's expectations that American women wanted to hear their harrowing survivor stories when I visited Zara.

On a noisy, late summer evening, bicycles, buses, and cars clamored along a busy boulevard in Rogers Park as I climbed the stairs to Zara's second floor apartment in a three-story walk-up. She met me at the door and invited me inside the small two-bedroom apartment she shared with her husband and their two teenage daughters. Her husband was still at work. Their younger daughter, Murisa, was home, and the elder daughter, Adriana, was expected to return home soon from volleyball practice. Murisa's dark brown hair fell past her shoulders, and her cheeks, arms, and thighs bore the signs of outdoor play: tanned skin, and scabbed knees. I introduced myself and Zara invited me to sit next to her on one of two comfortable well-worn couches in the front room. Zara's mother, Ilma, a friend of Ajša's, had introduced us, and I phoned the week prior to arrange a visit. An old air conditioning unit wheezed away on the windowsill of one of the two east-facing windows. Heavy fabric was also draped across the windows to keep out the heat of the daytime summer sun. Once I was seated in the dark front room, Zara took a drag on a cigarette and she told me that she had noticed the Yugoslav surname transmitted on her caller-ID when I called to schedule our meeting. I told her that I had used my friend's phone to make the call. Zara asked me where he was from and I told her that he was born in the United States, but his parents were originally from Herzegovina, the region which was also Zara's and Ilma's original home. This connection led to some discussion of Herzegovina and to the specifics of wartime destruction and postwar reconstruction in the region.[22] Then Zara offered me a popular brand of Croatian chocolates, *kraš,* and a Coke, and asked me what kinds of questions I had for her.

After I explained that I would like to understand how Zara and her family ended up in Chicago and that I was interested also in learning about what it was like to find work and housing in Chicago, Zara lit up another cigarette and launched into an almost rapid-fire delivery of her journey out of Herzegovina:

> My eldest daughter, Adriana, was four years old at the time, Murisa was not yet born. I was able to get to a refugee camp in Croatia. Later, my parents, my sister and her husband, and my younger brother joined us there. My husband remained to help defend Sarajevo. At the camp, Arab men ran an aid organization that was providing things that we could not get during the war in Bosnia, for example sugar, oil, coffee. I worked for that organization to support my whole family, since my husband stayed in Sarajevo. Soon I learned that this organization was a front for marrying Bosnian women (to Muslim men in Germany). My friend worked there too. Her husband was also in Sarajevo. We didn't know when—or if—they would return and hadn't heard from them for almost one year. It felt good to be able to help people in the camp by giving them things we hadn't had for so long. These men, the men who owned the organization, were talking to me and my friend one day and I was smoking. This man—this boss—told me that it wasn't nice for me to smoke, because I am a woman; didn't I want to put my cigarette out? I said, no, thank you very much, I do not; I like to smoke and I do not need you to tell me what you think about that. After that he kept pressuring me to let him connect me to a new husband. He said it would be better for me and my daughter, and that we would be able to leave the camp right away. It was really hard because we had no contact from our husbands. We didn't know if they were alive or not. After a while, my friend decided to do it—to marry another man—a man from Germany found by the boss at the aid organization, and she was telling me to do this too. I didn't want that, even though I could have left the country then right away. I stopped working at that organization.

Zara's narrative tumbled out so quickly that I thought she must have told it before. As I tried to keep up, inserting affirmative nods and utterances, I glanced at Murisa, who was seated to the right of Zara, to see how she might be responding to her mother's story. Murisa was looking at her hands, fingers fiddling with a wrapper that had contained one of the chocolates.

In her telling, Zara figures as a hard-working, loyal person, and a strong, even defiant, woman. She provides for her entire family as well as other needy refugees, significantly distributing sugar, oil, and coffee, staples of Bosnian hospitality that were extremely costly—and valuable—during the war because of their scarcity. She resists the invitations and demands of male outsiders, compelling as they may have been given the circumstances of war and chooses to remain with her family. Zara effectively illustrates these choices by contrasting her actions with those of her friend. And she refuses to put out her cigarette, ultimately choosing to quit working for the men who demanded she change her ways. Throughout her story, Zara uses the victim frame to emphasize survivorhood, and is able to portray herself in gendered terms that are valued among many Bosnians: as a hardworking wife, daughter, sister and mother who is loyal to her family. Her portrayal also contains characteristics that are valorized among liberal feminists: defiance of male authority, particularly of men associated with Islam. Zara made it a point to tell me that she quit working for the Islamic relief agency and began working for the local Red Cross outpost.

In addition to serving as an introduction of her family and self to me, her story may also be viewed as serving the function of socializing Murisa into womanhood. I learned later in the year that Murisa was having trouble in school. Her grades had fallen, and other students were harassing her (see chapter 7). Zara and Adis felt that Murisa needed to develop a thicker skin, to speak up when the classmates picked on her. In this story, Zara models the kinds of behaviors she hoped Murisa would develop in order to make her way through the world as an adult.

After telling me the relief agency story and discussing Zara's and her husband Adis's current employment, Zara inquired about my friend's work. Some of his cousins worked construction in Chicago's booming condominium-conversion market. Adis and his brother had worked on several building rehab projects and were interested in possibly purchasing a rental property, so she asked that I ask him to keep them in mind should he come across any interesting properties in need of reconstruction. Zara also asked after my son, whom she had learned about from Ilma, and shared the news that Adriana would soon be applying to colleges, asking that I please provide her with some information about my university. By requesting assistance, Zara recognized our interaction as one of exchange; her story would help my research and agreeing to meet with me was also a favor to her mother. She had invited me into her home and offered me refreshment, and she was thus in a position to ask me to activate my social connections on behalf of her husband and daughter, should the opportunity arise. Zara chose to tell elements of her story that she thought might be of interest to me, an American woman, and also a mother with connections to some of the larger Herzegovinian diaspora in Chicago. Although our exchange involved material elements and resources, this was not the sort of transactional market exchange most associated with capitalism, rather, it was an exchange that could serve as a basis for developing an ongoing relationship based on reciprocity.

EVERYONE HAS THEIR OWN STORY

The coincident rise of the NGO form and the prevalence of refugee narratives of victimhood created a set of openings through which Bosnian women could assert their presence as survivors and communicate their experiences to American and international audiences. The human rights gendered language of empowerment and the concept of "giving voice" established a common framework through which women's stories functioned as a recognizable currency in the aftermath of war and women's migration to Chicago. At the same time, these structures set social and material parameters that limited women's efforts to be seen as workers, and as political actors.

But everyone has their own story. This phrase indicates a different language ideology than the concept of language as "giving voice." As we have seen, giving voice implies that there is an authentic—and repressed—story that is submerged and needs to be called out by empowered people who are committed to truth-telling. There is little ambiguity or multivocality in the "voiced victim" of Bosnian women survivors as they are understood by the Bosnian group who organized the memorial in Daley Plaza, the NGO and U.S. government representatives at the Capitol Hill Bosnian International Women's Day celebration, and the American woman who tried to get Almina to discuss her traumatic experiences. By way of contrast, the belief that everyone has their own story, and that everyone should have their say renders a story as something one can choose to tell, and that this telling will inevitably also involve listening—listening to others tell their own story. Indeed, the more I heard people say this, the more I came to realize that people expected me to share my story during the myriad conversations and interviews I conducted through the course of the work for this project. Such exchanges were a way of leveling some of the inequality between me and the women refugees I came to know.

Tropes of gendered victimhood are not the only ones which Bosnians in Chicago must navigate. As immigrants simultaneously racialized as white and othered as Muslim, Bosnian war survivors had fled persecution in the former Yugoslavia only to find that ethnic, racial, and religious classification schemes also organized their social worlds in the United States. It is to these social categories and their material manifestations which we now turn.

NOTES

1. Johnson, Venice M. "Dan Žena Izbjeglica / Refugee Women's Day." Chicago: Catholic Charities of the Archdiocese of Chicago Refugee Resettlement Program: New Woman, March 2001: 5.
2. Many thanks to Selena Seferović for loaning me copies of *Nova Žena* from her personal archive.
3. The magazine makes reference to women refugees from other parts of the world, but only women's stories from the former SFRY were featured at the event, and in *Nova Žena*.
4. At the time of this writing, the official number of individuals traced to the Srebrenica genocide is 8,372. The number may be adjusted in the event that new remains

are found. The VRS went to great lengths to conceal and then move bodily remains, mixing them with others to make it more difficult to locate and identify the dead.

5. Malcolm, Noel. *Bosnia: A Short History*. New York: New York University Press, 1996[1994].

6. Šešelj had some sympathizers among the Serbian diaspora in North America, including in Chicago.

7. The Army of the Republic of Bosnia-Herzegovina (ARBiH) attempted to defend territories against "ethnic cleansing" campaigns, but they were severely under-resourced by way of comparison to the Serb-led VRS which had inherited all the munitions and artillery of the Yugoslav People's Army (JNA), who as a result were not as impacted by the international arms embargo imposed on the region. While the ARBiH also perpetrated crimes against civilians during the war, these did not even come close to approaching the systematic scale of atrocities the VRS enacted on Bosniac civilian populations in Nasiha's and Elmina's communities, and in countless others across the region (Helms, *Innocence and Victimhood*: 234).

8. Karadžić was captured in Belgrade 2008; Mladić in Lazarevo 2011.

9. At the center of memorials in Potočari is the burial of the remains of those who have most recently been identified through ongoing forensic exhumation of the mass graves (Wagner, *To Know Where He Lies*).

10. U.S. Congress June 27, 2005; Missouri state legislature July 6, 2005; city of St. Louis July 11, 2005

11. Elmina, as the ACBH representative, was met with ongoing lobbying efforts by representatives of the Serbia to garner U.S. congressional support for Bosnia's Serb "entity" to secede and unite with Serbia. Like the subjects of Coutin's work among diaspora survivors of the wars in El Salvador, Elmina, Nasiha, and other young Bosnian American women in the diaspora were determined to challenge state denials and minimizing of the Bosnian genocide (Coutin, Susan. "Re/membering the Nation: Gaps and Reckoning within Biographical Accounts of Salvadoran Émigrés," *Anthropological Quarterly* 84(4): 809–834, 2011).

12. Malcolm 1994. See Kulašić 2017 for Elmina's reflection and her grounded theory analysis for how her experiences might inform efforts to reckon with the violence of WWII and the 1990s wars.

13. The first International Women's Day was organized in New York City in 1909. During the communist era, March 8 was a state holiday for many countries. In 1975, the United Nations began observing the holiday.

14. Ferguson, James and Akil Gupta. "Spatializing States: Toward an Ethnography of Neoliberal Governmentality," *American Ethnologist* 29(4): 981–1002, 2002; Pandolfi, Mariella. "Contract of Mutual (In)difference: Governance and the Humanitarian Apparatus in Contemporary Albania and Kosovo." *Indiana Journal of Global Legal Studies* 10: 369–381, 2003; Pupovac, Vanessa. "Securing the community? An Examination of International Psychosocial Intervention." In *International Intervention in the Balkans since 1995*. P. Siani-Davies, ed. Pp. 158–171. New York: Routledge, 2003.

15. See Bernal and Grewal 2014, including Helms 2013 with a case study of women's NGOs in postwar Bosnia. Inderpal Grewal argues that NGOs operate "within transnational circuits of neoliberal power," and argues for a transnational, rather than

globalization, approach to understanding their work, and their interconnection to structures of governance (Grewal, Inderpal. *Transnational America: Feminisms, Diasporas, Neoliberalisms.* Durham, NC: Duke University Press, 2005: 4). Gender ideologies that envision women as natural agents of civilization and community are key to the NGO development strategy, and feminist scholars have traced the ways this essentialist ideology ultimately thwarts efforts that challenge gender hierarchies because it relies on neoliberal models of personhood, and lacks an intersectional approach that accounts for how gender becomes meaningful only in relation to class, sexuality, and race /ethnicity (Bernal, Victoria and Inderpal Grewal, "Introduction: The NGO Form: Feminist Struggles, the State, and Neoliberalism," in *Theorizing NGOs: States, Feminisms, and Neoliberalism.* Durham, NC: Duke University Press, 2014).

16. Woodward, Susan. *Socialist Unemployment: The Political Economy of Yugoslavia, 1945–1990.* Princeton, NJ: Princeton University Press, 1995: 152, 269.

17. Bosnia has rich mineral deposits and mining traditions (Malcolm, 1994) and in 1949 SFRY steel production was moved from Slovenia to Bosnia because of the insulation and isolation offered by the mountains (Woodward, *Socialist Unemployment*: 94).

18. In their decision, the majority justices referred to the court's earlier precedent set by Nicaragua vs. the United States (1986) in which the United States was found to be in breach of international law for supporting Contra efforts to discredit and unseat Nicaragua's 1980s democratic socialist government, but was also found not to be responsible for contra attacks against civilians, despite the fact that the United States provided training, weaponry, military assistance, and other critical support to the contra party. In February 2017, the Bosniak member of the tri-partite presidency filed an appeal of the ICJ's 2007 judgment.

19. Mladić was captured the following winter, in 2011.

20. Helms describes the prominence of this imagery in the case of Bosnian media and global reportage on the Srebrenica survivors (2013: 26–27, see also 2008).

21. The air and water show is a city and corporate sponsored annual event that takes place on the lakefront every August. The event runs on a Saturday and Sunday from 10:00 a.m. to 3:00 p.m. and showcases military aircraft that fly incredibly close to the city's skyline, and in formation over all of the outdoor recreational spaces: Soldier Field, Wrigley Field, Grant and Millennium Parks, Lincoln Park Zoo. The fighter planes are incredibly loud and fast, and certainly would provoke memories for anyone who has experienced war.

22. In Herzegovina, especially in Mostar, many Bosnian Muslims and Bosnian Catholics banded together at the beginning of the war to defend the region from VRS attacks, but when they successfully ousted the VRS, the two groups fought against each other for control of Mostar.

Chapter Seven

#BiHInSolidarity / Be in Solidarity

Bosnians' refugee-immigrant statuses, wartime victimization via anti-Muslim racism, and "off-white" appearances shaped their postwar lives in the United States. This chapter examines the racial positioning of Bosnians—how they were seen, or not seen—by Americans, and how they sought to make their Bosnian-ness known. I focus especially on the experiences of Bosnian Americans who arrived in the United States as children or teenagers during the 1990s. Their experiences illustrate how globally dispersed ideologies of race are negotiated both transnationally, and translocally. People used gestures to pan-Islamic practices, analogies of European anti-Jewish racism, and drew parallels to colonial and imperial projects to situate themselves as Bosnians in the United States by aligning themselves with the worldwide Muslim community, Holocaust survivors, and African Americans. These alignments were situational and included not only anti-racist solidarities but anti-Black racisms as well, expressed most virulently in the immediate aftermath of the murder of a young Bosnian man, Zemir Begić, in St. Louis in the wake of the non-indictment of Ferguson, MO police officer Darren Wilson for the murder of Michael Brown.

Many of Bosnians' American encounters stories focused less on Americans' perceptions of Bosnians as immigrants, and more on responses to Bosnians' Muslim identities. These encounters became such a prominent theme during my interviews and conversations with people that I started referring to them as "coming out" stories. As we have seen, the majority of Bosnian adults acquired English after their arrival to the United States, and due to the PRWORA reforms and economic necessity they often learned English on-the-job rather than in classes. Their prominent accents sometimes prompted queries from co-workers about their origins. Inevitably these questions would lead to Bosnians' refugee lives, and to the anti-Muslim racism that drove the "ethnic cleansing" that displaced them.

Nasiha recalled one such story that occurred in the early aughts while she was working as an office assistant in a municipal office. The office was staffed by women of white, Puerto Rican, and Black racial and ethnic backgrounds. One of the white women brought up religion, and this led to a discussion of the War on Terror and Muslim immigrants. According to Nasiha, she listened for a bit, but the conversation got increasingly heated as the woman who initially brought up the topic said that in her neighborhood they "had a problem with Muslims, too many were moving into the neighborhood," and, the woman said, "they keep to themselves, the women cover their heads and don't talk." Nasiha spoke up: "I am Muslim, and I had to leave my country because I am Muslim. People were killed in my country because they were Muslim." According to Nasiha, this put an end to the discussion, but it also put an end to her interactions with the co-worker: "She didn't talk to me anymore after that."

When I spoke with Elmina about her college internship at a Chicago legislator's office, she described how she thought it was important that local legislators be aware of Bosnians' particular plight,

> When I told people [at the office] parts of my story, they were shocked that I was a refugee from Bosnia. They were informed that Bosnia had survived a war, but were not aware that the majority of Bosnians who came to the United States are survivors of that war, and no one [in local government] was reaching out to them . . . and they were shocked that I was so young, I think . . . I mean, I was the first Bosnian to ever work in that office, and ended up being a translator for a lot of constituents, even though my Bosnian wasn't that good at the time. Bosnians were trying really hard to make their lives "normal" but at the end of the day, every time I attended an event directly related to the war, we were only talking about things indirectly, and amongst ourselves. Our community was not understood about why we are in Chicago. Most of us are white; we don't look like a typical minority that could be separated and identified as "Other," so people didn't really understand that about our experience. . . .
>
> Being "Other," like being turned into refugees in your own country, in Bosnia, during the war? I asked.
>
> Yeah, I wasn't thinking in terms of race [when we arrived] and people would look at Bosnians and think they, we, were white. I think Bosnians were misunderstood in terms of language, traditions, and awareness that the majority are Muslims. My dad was always asked [at his job] about his fasting for Ramadan and taking off for Bajram.[1] His English was not at a level where he could explain everything. We are stereotyped as white, and this erases the Muslim. As whites we were seen as ok when compared with other refugees and immigrants who were not white. We appreciate everything the United States has offered but see-

ing us as white erases the fact that we had no choice as to where we were going to end up as refugees.

Elmina's remarks highlight the racializing of both Muslims, and of refugees in the United States. To be Muslim is not to be white. To be a refugee is not to be white. While she acknowledged that being perceived as white came with some advantages, or at least to be viewed as "ok," this racialization also whitewashed Bosnians' experiences with being discriminated against and terrorized because they were viewed as nationally distinct and "Other" from Yugoslav Serbs and Croats. Elmina's frustrations with American racism, and with Bosnians' dissonant position in American Islamophobia led her to deepen her advocacy work.

These encounters reveal American assumptions about what Muslims "look like" and illustrate the racial and gender underpinnings of contemporary Islamophobia. These workplace encounters point to what some critical race scholars have referred to as the "off-white," "middleness," or "in-between" experiences of immigrants who do not fit American Anglo Protestant normative whiteness frameworks.[2] Notably, ethno-religious differences figure as the primary mechanisms for discrimination in these cases: European Jews, Catholics, while discrimination against Arabs, classified as "white" in U.S. racial categories, have often involved assumptions that they are Muslims. Among Bosnians in the United States, the most common referent for the Bosnian migration experience was that of European Jews.

LIKE THE JEWS?

"We are like the Jews." I heard this phrase frequently, from many different Bosnians, and yet, I was still surprised when I went to visit with Chicago's most prominent Bosnian Imam and he began his account of Bosnian migration to Chicago with "We are like the Jews." This comparison to Jewish experiences did not begin with Bosnians, but rather was introduced in European and American media whose wartime reportage referred to the genocide in Bosnia as "the largest genocide on European soil since World War II." Scholarship devoted to the appropriation of holocaust discourse in the Balkans often draws on the Nazi genocide against European Jews as a well-known illustration of collective victimhood and genocidal violence. More recently, scholars historicize the use of the concept of "genocide," coined by Polish Jewish immigrant Rafael Lemkin, by contextualizing it within the eugenics movement the Nazis drew on to justify the violence perpetrated against Jews, Roma and Sinti, Slavs, homosexuals, people with disabilities, dissidents, and other non "Aryans" during the Holocaust. Much of this work notes the truncated and Eurocentric focus in such accounts, and how this leads to a failure to delineate the relationship of genocidal violence to earlier episodes of systemic violence perpetrated in the context of settler colonialism and the trans-Atlantic slave trade. I am concerned here with Bosnians' uses of the holocaust analogy in efforts to translate their experiences to those in the United States.

In addition to western wartime media coverage that made use of the holocaust frame, Bosnians' use of this analogy arose from two features of their migration circumstances. First, Bosnians were resettled to a part of Chicago with a sizable and visible Jewish population that includes holocaust survivors and Orthodox communities.[3] These communities have been the targets of white nationalist hate groups including the National Socialist Party of America's efforts to march in Skokie in 1977, and in June 1999 when a white nationalist terrorized West Rogers Park by driving through the neighborhood during Friday prayers as he shot nine Orthodox Jews, and shot and killed Northwestern University football coach, African American Ricky Byrdsong.[4] This part of Chicago's metro-area includes several institutions that are actively engaged in public education about the holocaust and racism, including the Illinois Holocaust Museum and Education Center that opened its doors in Skokie in 2009. This history of Jewish settlement and with racist attacks established a local public sphere that was familiar with the aftermath of the holocaust and anti-Black racism.

Second, the Jewish analogy helped to address the problem of how to communicate their wartime suffering *as Muslims* by aligning themselves with another persecuted European white population rather than with other historical and contemporary persecuted Muslim populations around the world, such as Chicago's own sizable Palestinian diaspora.[5] Many people used the Jewish analogy during my interviews with them about Bosnian migration to the city. And survivors who sought to bring attention to the wartime genocide employed the references to the European context as exceptional—given the post-Holocaust setting—in educational materials for presentations about the Bosnian genocide at the Illinois Holocaust Museum and Education Center in nearby suburban Skokie.[6] Nasiha introduced a different use of the analogy in conversation one day. A popular Bosnian singer had recently performed in Chicago and she went to the concert. During the intermission, she was sitting at a table and an older Bosnian man introduced himself, and said that he was from Sarajevo, where was she from? When she replied that she was from Prijedor, he seemed to lose interest in speaking with her, and replied, "at least you're not from [a] village," before turning his back on her. She was upset by this response and asked me,

> Why do you think he said that to me? I was talking with my [American] friend Niki and she is Jewish and she told me that even though they were persecuted

during the war, German Jews looked down on other Jews from Eastern Europe—they tried to set themselves apart from them.

I replied that I was aware of such accounts of intra-Jewish race and class discrimination, and asked Nasiha if she thought her encounter with the man was similar. She replied that she thought the man was "looking down" on her, and that a lot of people from Sarajevo have never even been to Prijedor, even though it is only a four-hour drive away, because they don't think the people there "have culture," meaning that they were viewed as backward, not civilized. Nasiha used the analogy with European Jews here as a way to diagnose her countryman's rebuttal of her; although they had suffered similar types of persecution, and the same forced migration, these shared circumstances did not compel a sense of solidarity.

WHITENESS, ANTI-BLACK RACISM, AND THE QUESTION OF SOLIDARITY

The Imam's use of the analogy to Jewish experiences with forced migration drew on an assimilationist school of thought in American immigration scholarship that theorizes that "almost white" immigrants adopt American racist attitudes to establish a sense of belonging and protected "privilege."[7] For example, Karen Brodkin provides a personal account of European Jewish immigrants in the United States. Here she reflects on how her grandmother, who fled the nineteenth century pogroms in Central and Eastern Europe settled in New York City, came to adopt racist views about Black Americans as part of her efforts to "become white." Similarly, Alisse Waterston's intimate ethnography of her Polish Jewish father's emigration experiences to the Americas detail how his experiences with anti-Jewish racism in a Polish village did not prevent him from expressing anti-Black racism in Cuba, Puerto Rico, and New York.[8] In this way, Bosnians were also "like the Jews." Bosnian anti-Black attitudes often reflected pervasive American stereotypes depicting Black people as being poor and lazy.

During the fall of 2004, I attended Saturday morning Bosnian language classes for kids at TCC. One morning, seven-year-old Ena and I sat munching on donuts and waiting for Amra to convene class. We heard some loud voices outside the storefront window and looked out to see a Black woman directing two children running ahead of her to stop at the corner and wait for her to cross the intersection. "Those must be poor people," Ena said matter-of-factly. Surprised, I asked, "Why do you think so?" "They look poor," came the response. The woman wore a long dress in a bold black and white floral pattern, with a full skirt wrapped in a west African style. Her hair was coiffed softly around her head. There was nothing discernible outside of clothing, skin tone and hair texture that would distinguish the woman from me or Amra, or the running kids from Ena. I realized that, to Ena, the woman and kids "looked poor" because they were Black. I struggled to think of what to say next when Amra walked in to begin the class.

The following fall, during one of my visits to Fadila's house, I was visiting with her son-in-law Joso in the backyard. Joso's sanitation truck route was in Evanston, a north suburb that shared a border with both Chicago and Skokie, and he wanted to know, where in Evanston did I grow up? I told him my family had lived in several places in southeast and southwest Evanston. He asked, "There are a lot of Black people there? I told him that I supposed so, yes; I always grew up with Black neighbors, and with Black teachers and classmates and friends, to which Joso replied, "My friend, the guy I drive with, told me they get free houses," "What?" I said, and he responded, "Yeah, he says the government gives them free houses."

Given my loss as to how to address Ena's prejudices, I was determined to say something. I told Joso that there were no "free houses," and launched into a lengthy history of U.S. subsidized housing and racism, how white people like my grandfathers received subsidized housing through the G.I. bill that excluded most Black people due to segregation laws, and I said how great it was that Evanston has the only remaining subsidized units north of the city, and that it's really hard to get landlords to accept Section Eight vouchers.[9] Joso seemed to tune me out, and I'm not sure he believed what I was saying, although he did understand that I clearly disagreed with what his friend had told him. As had the "off-white" European immigrants in the previous studies, both Ena and Joso adopted anti-Black racialized explanations for poverty that linked and conflated race and class.

TEENAGERS

When I first met Azra in 2004, she was a freckled, bookish girl entering eighth grade. It was my first week with the youth group at TCC, and it had started to rain. This meant our original plan to go to Foster Street Beach was postponed, and we would stay inside the all-purpose activity room at the center. Some of the kids Azra's age were over in a corner giggling and teasing one another while Azra sat on a chair in the corner with her nose in a book. I went over and sat down next to her, telling her my name, and asking for hers. Without looking up from the book she mumbled something. We went through this a couple of times: me asking, Azra mumbling something down at the floor. Finally, I asked if she would lift up her face, because I was having a hard time hearing her. "Azra" she said. "Ahs-ra" I repeated the name. Hearing this her face opened up a bit, and she told me that she liked how I pronounced her name, but that she doesn't usually like to tell Americans her name because "they don't know how to say it right." Over the course of the next few weeks, I became more familiar with the kids, and on our next rain day, I visited again with Azra.

Azra's age group was clustered around a TV/VHS unit where Jackie Chan and Owen Wilson were engaged in some sort of mischief in the Hollywood film *Shanghai Knights*. Azra sat behind the other pre-teens but was not watching the film. She was reading a copy of the Qur'an, in Arabic. I sat down next to her and told her I didn't know she could read Arabic, and that it was cool that she knew three languages: Bosnian, English, and Arabic! Without missing a beat, she joked with me, "Actually, I know four languages! Bosnian, Croatian, Serbian, and English. I don't speak Arabic, but I am trying to learn the prayers in Arabic." People often joked this way about Bosnian, making fun of ethno-nationalists who claimed that the language spoken in the SFRY known as Serbo-Croatian was in fact not one language, but three, or even four depending on who you asked.[10]

When I asked Azra why she wanted to learn to pray in Arabic, she told me she wanted to learn more about Islam. She also wanted to begin wearing a head scarf, as her grandmother did, but her father forbade her to wear it outside of their home or the mosque. Some of the covered women in their neighborhood had been harassed recently, and he feared for her safety.[11] Since Azra was not allowed to cover, she had decided to devote her time to learning to pray in Arabic. In contrast to the Yugoslav nationalists' linguistic projects that sought to draw boundaries and emphasize differences within her parents' and grandparents' Bosnian language, learning to pray in Arabic offered Azra the possibility to join a large, globally recognizable, longstanding multicultural and multiracial linguistic community. Praying in Arabic was a way for her to explore and express her faith without going against her father's wishes or causing him concern.

I met Murisa later that fall, during my visit with her mother Zara, after which she occasionally participated in youth activities at TCC. Sometimes I gave her a lift home afterward and during one such afternoon ride, she was especially talkative. First, she confessed to me that she had lied about her age to some of the other girls she met at TCC that day. She had told them she was fourteen when in fact she was only twelve. "Well why did you say that?" I asked, "I'm too tall. Everyone makes too much fun of me!" she replied. Indeed, she'd grown quite a bit since I had met her the year before. Her long dark hair now hung several inches below her shoulders, and she was an inch taller than my own five feet six inches. She had also started to develop breasts and wore loose-fitting jeans and a large gray hoodie as if to camouflage her new curves, suggesting she was not yet comfortable with her more feminine figure. I acknowledged that it must be hard to be so tall at her age, but that kids often make fun of whatever differences they perceive, and she should stick up for herself. "Well, that's what my parents say, but they don't understand. I guess you don't understand either, they [kids at school] just make fun of me all the time!" she exclaimed. "About your height?" I asked, to which Murisa replied, "Because of my skin." I asked her what she meant by that and she said, "You know, like when someone says something that's stupid, they call them 'white trash.' I try and tell them 'I'm not white, I'm Bosnian!' But they don't listen." "Hmm, I see," I replied, thinking back to my days in elementary school during the 1970s when I'd heard classmates use the term. I asked Murisa who was calling her that, if they were Black kids, or white kids, or other students, "Most of them are Mexican, but you know they're not really even Mexican, they're American! My best friend Luis' parents are Mexican, but they don't even speak Spanish."

Azra's and Murisa's stories center on an all-too-familiar teenaged theme of identity—of exploring one's own identifications, and encountering others' misperceptions of one's identifications, or others' prejudices against one's identities. The girls' stories also illustrate how globally dispersed ideologies of race are often negotiated translocally. Azra, for example, modifies her desire to cover out of respect for her father's fears for her safety, fears based both in the racism they suffered as Muslims during the wars in Bosnia, and in the racism "Muslim-looking" women encountered in Chicago after the September 11, 2001 attacks. Murisa does not identify as "white," rather as "Bosnian," but is seen as white by Latinx peers at her multi-racial, multi-ethnic school where Latinx students comprised nearly sixty percent of the student body.[12]

When I asked Murisa what she knew about the phrase "white trash" she didn't know about its historical meanings, stemming from the British colonial period to refer to the landless agrarian peasants that colonial elites enlisted to settle frontier regions, or that the term is interchangeable with others such as "hillbilly," used in Chicago since at least the 1950s when poor white migrants in search of a better life left the mid-South and made their home in Uptown, near where Murisa's family now lived.[13] These newcomers were not welcomed by the city's middle class and comprised such a significant and undesirable portion of Uptown residents that by the 1960s and 1970s locals referred to Uptown as the "Hillbilly Ghetto."[14] Although she was not familiar with the term's origins, Murisa understood its negative valence in this context and tried to disassociate herself from alleged poor, stupid whiteness by claiming her Bosnian-ness.

A decade later, some 1.5-er and second-generation Bosnians continued to struggle with and debate their racialization in the United States. By this time, I was living in New Orleans, but through social media, I became aware of a heated debate about Bosnians' racial whiteness taking place online. The debate was sparked by the brutal murder of a young Bosnian man, Zemir Begić in St. Louis, Missouri. The murder occurred during the same weekend that a Ferguson, Missouri jury's non-indictment of white police officer Darren Wilson for the murder of unarmed Black teenager Michael Brown sparked protests across the United States, and the world, as part of the growing outrage at ongoing police violence against Black civilians.

A BRUTAL MURDER AND AN INVITATION TO WHITENESS

Six days after the Ferguson jury's judgment was announced, Zemir Begić, a 32-year-old Bosnian immigrant, was brutally murdered near Bevo Mill, St. Louis, 20 miles away from Ferguson. On the Saturday night that followed Thanksgiving, Zemir, his girlfriend Arijana, 22, and her aunt, were in his car; the two women had also emigrated from Bosnia. According to the police, four teenagers approached the car yelling at the people inside and pounding on the car with a hammer. When Begić exited the car in an attempt to stop them, the teens started attacking him with the hammer. He was found unconscious shortly after 1:00 a.m. Sunday, with severe injuries to his head, abdomen, and mouth. He was pronounced dead upon arrival at the hospital. Two of the four suspects were arrested shortly after the murder and identified as a 16-year-old African American male and a 16-year-old Hispanic male. Another suspect identified as a 17-year-old African American male was taken into police custody the following week. A fourth suspect identified as a 17-year-old African American male was later arrested. By fall of 2015, four out of the four suspects sought by police had been arrested and charged as adults for the murder. The following discussion is based on a hashtag ethnography of Zemir's death.[15] I draw on a sample of 110 tweets posted between the day Zemir was killed, November 30, 2014, and September 30, 2015, when all 4 suspects in the murder had been arrested and charged.[16]

Sometime during the 2000s, St. Louis superseded Chicago as home to the largest Bosniak-descent population in North America. As are most American cities, St. Louis is residentially racially segregated: South St. Louis is majority white (80 percent), and North St. Louis is majority Black (80 percent).[17] Upon their arrival to the city, Bosnian refugees were directed by resettlement agencies to the section of town that lies at the border of North and South St.

Louis, near the neighborhood where Zemir was murdered. Unlike Bosnians' settlement in Chicago's diverse racial and ethnic north side corridor, the St. Louis settlement situated Bosnian refugees in a neglected run-down interstitial zone between Black northern St. Louis, and white southern St. Louis. St. Louis lacked Chicago's longer history of resettling refugees in the wake of the 1980 Refugee Act; Bosnians were the first major wave of refugees the city had received. These different settlement patterns wrought distinctions in Bosnians' experiences, most significantly their situated-ness in the middle of St. Louis' fraught White/Black racial geography. Yet similar to Chicago, while sometimes stigmatized as immigrants, Bosnians were also lauded as bringing a desirable kind of diversity—a diversity that was not Black—to the city.[18] This celebrated Bosnian presence in St. Louis is reflected in a strip of shops along Gravois Avenue, many of which display the blue and yellow Bosnian flag, sometimes combining this with the iconic St. Louis Gateway Arch. Locals refer to this area as "Little Bosnia."

The first tweet about Begić's murder used the hashtag #JusticeForZemir and was posted that Sunday afternoon from Begić's brother Rasim's handle: "My brother did nothing wrong, innocent man killed."[19] Rasim's tweet contains a link to the local CBS affiliate KMOV's alert about the homicide investigation underway in the South City section of St. Louis. Within hours, Zemir went from being an "innocent man" to a "white man." The first reference to Zemir as "white" comes from a twitter handle, "Dizdarevic," a Bosnian surname, at 5:45 p.m. and is a reply to this question, tweeted by another Bosnian-affiliated handle, "BHDragons": "Why are the major news networks not covering the hideous murder of Zemir Begić?" Dizdarevic tweets: "because he's white killed by another ethnicity."[20] Days later, "Son of Bosnia" uses barely coded racist language to posit Bosnian immigrants as being morally superior to Black Americans by drawing on the same stereotypes that Joso did when repeating his friend's claim that "Black people get free houses." "Son of Bosnia" writes that Black people would rather "burn" than "earn," where burn refers to burning retail sites during street riots and earn refers to work.[21]

Figure 7.1. Screenshot of tweet from twitter user Sons of Bosnia (SonOf Bosnia) "#JusticeforZemir #Bosnian community wants to make this country better, we don't burn, we earn. #Nohandouts #ZemirBegic" Sons of Bosnia (SonOfBosnia) December 1, 2014.

The tweet draws on the familiar image of the (white) hard-working immigrant who will "make this country better," foreshadowing the Republican presidential campaign's 2016 slogan "Make American Great Again." From here the feed filled quickly with Anglo-sounding names, many with handles associated with white nationalist symbols and themes, and with links to far-right nationalist news sources such as Breitbart and Fox. These tweets appropriate Zemir's murder to forward an image of white victimization and the specter of Black criminality used to justify controversial policies like "stand your ground." The tweets relied heavily on the appropriation of Black political protest language, particularly that of Black Lives Matter.[22]

The hashtag #BosnianLivesMatter made its first appearance at 4:00 p.m. the afternoon of 11/30 by "Adam Jennings," and #hatecrime is used in conjunction with #JusticeForZemir at 8:30 p.m. by a female-presenting handle: "Liberty Luv N Lust." Begić's murder is used to post angry tweets at Black political leaders Al Sharpton, Jesse Jackson, and Louis Farrakhan, along with President Barack Obama and Attorney General Eric Holder. There are numerous angry references to the five Saint Louis Rams' symbolic solidarity "hands up, don't shoot" postures as they took the field against the Oakland Raiders that Sunday.[23] During the next 48 hours more tweeters with Anglo-sounding handles attach #WhiteLivesMatter, #ReverseRacism, and #BOWC ("black on white crime") to #JusticeForZemir along with false claims that "black thugs beat a white man to death," while chanting "kill the white people." Many of these tweets reposted a widely circulated image of Zemir with his girlfriend Arijana in which Arijana's hair is colored platinum blonde. This contrasted with news coverage showing Arijana with pre-platinum dark brown hair color, and one where she is wearing a headscarf in mourning Zemir's death, neither of which was picked up in the right-wing tweets. While the majority of such posts are from Anglo-handles, there are a few that come from Bosnian handles. On December 4, for example, AdmirBIH (Admir, Bosnia and Herzegovina) @admir303 (303 is a Denver, CO area code) tweets #WhiteLivesMatter with a picture of Zemir, cropped into a map of Bosnia.

No Bosnian leaders publicly endorsed the interpretation of the murder as a racially motivated hate crime; many made public statements based on police evidence that Zemir was not attacked because he was Bosnian, nor because he was an immigrant.[24] Bosnian Canadian political scientist Jasmin Mujanović weighed in on the situation in an article posted to the #JusticeForZemir hashtag by anthropologist, blogger-journalist, and former St. Louis resident, Sarah Kendzior, and her co-author Umar Lee.[25] Mujanović offers this in response to their question about whether Bosnians perceive themselves as white:

> For the time being, probably the most honest answer to the question of whether Bosnians perceive themselves as white is "we're not sure" ... I suspect,

ultimately, any definitive shift toward "whiteness" among the Bosnian population in the U.S.—when they will self-identify as "white people"—will come if or when there is a political need for it, as has historically been the case with other communities here. . . . Given the recent events in St. Louis, however, that could (unfortunately) change very quickly to a definitive "yes."

In response to the same question, Almedin, a 23-year-old Bosnian local who does not give his last name, points to Bosnians' racial ambiguity in St. Louis' clearly demarcated racial order:

"Bosnians aren't completely looked at as white, but it's different when it's a crime. No one is going to come up to you before robbing you and ask you about your ethnic background. Here, white is white, and black is black." Almedin believes that the attack was racially motivated, "black on white," and that the nonwhite teenagers mistook Begić for "white." Džemal Bijedić, a Bosnian American St. Louis police chaplain replies:

> People say black/white. I don't say this. A lot of black people are crying about this [Begić's murder]. You can't say black/white about this. We do not know yet if this is a hate crime. Everyone needs improved policing. Not all police are bad. Not all citizens are bad. No one is perfect. We have to talk as civilized people, examining the issues and seeing what we can do. We need someone to train police on how to deal with different ethnic groups, how to interact with people of different nationalities. But we are told the city does not have the money.

In the final paragraph, Kendzior and Lee describe visiting the memorial four days after the murder, when "a black, middle-aged couple approached, holding a teddy bear and a balloon. With tears in their eyes, they placed the items at the memorial and walked away."

The objects and images associated with Zemir's memorial bear the familiar hallmarks of memorials to the sudden deaths of young people. There are stuffed animals, balloons, and flowers, and a poster signed by mourners, including a New Testament bible verse: "Greater love has no one than this: to lay down one's life for one's friends" (John 15:13). The bible verse references Arijana's report that Zemir was attacked while trying to protect her and her aunt.

The article includes photos that depict a variety of scenes: Zemir and Arijana together in which Arijana has dark brown hair, and sports short jean cut-offs and a tank top as well as the one of Arijana with her head covered. In another photo, we see a festive Zemir holding an empty champagne flute. One image captures Zemir's father looking weary in the family's modest living room, and we learn that the family had limited means, and relied on a "Go Fund Me" campaign to finance funerary and burial expenses. Although no posts from Arijana appear on the #JusticeForZemir hashtag, and no Bosnian

Figure 7.2. Screenshot of tweet showing a sidewalk memorial for Zemir Begić in St. Louis Bevo Neighborhood. Sarah Kendzior (sarahkendzior) December 12, 2014.

Figure 7.3. Screenshot of tweet showing a photo of young mourners with R.I.P. sign for Zemir Begić. Francis Flandro (Fflandro) December 3, 2014.

women are interviewed in Kendzior's and Lee's article, it is noteworthy that the most antiracist arguments are forwarded by two young Bosnian women based in Chicago. Sisters Ida and Tea Sefer are social justice educators and activists who belong to Zemir's and Arijana's generation.

#BiHInSOLIDARITY / BE IN SOLIDARITY

Amidst the flurry of hate posts that followed Zemir's murder, a young female Bosnian American from Chicago, Ida Sefer, tweeted: "I have to be really honest. Zemir's death is really triggering for me, as it is for many other Bosnians" and introduced the hashtag #BiHInSolidarity.[26]

Figure 7.4. Screenshot of tweet from twitter user Ida (idddaaa23): "I have to be really honest. Zemir's death is really triggering for me, as it is for many other Bosnians. #JusticeforZemir #BiHInSolidarity" December 1, 2014.

Sefer is a 1.5-er who lives in Chicago and is an educator and social justice organizer. She created the #BiHInSolidarity hashtag in an attempt to provide a justice-focused online space for Bosnian Americans to grieve Begić's death and counter the white supremacist material permeating #JusticeForZemir. The first three letters of the hashtag, BiH, is the abbreviation for Bosnia's postwar country name: Bosnia i Herzegovina / Bosnia and Herzegovina. The hashtag then, reads "Bosnia i Herzegovina in solidarity." But if you know Bosnian *and* English, the hashtag carries an additional pronunciation and meaning. In Bosnian, "i" is pronounced as a hard "e" as in "she" and when "h" ends a word, it is pronounced with a nearly silent aspirated "h." Thus, bilingual Bosnian and English speakers know to pronounce the #BiHInSolidarity hashtag as "Be In Solidarity."

The reason Begić's death is "triggering" for Sefer, and for other Bosnian Americans, is because Zemir is a Bosnian Muslim man who was brutally murdered with no apparent cause. As we have seen, the circumstances of the wartime genocide meant that the remains of many of the civilians killed—most of whom were male—have yet to be identified and properly mourned, leaving families and friends with little sense of closure.[27] This lack of closure is exacerbated by the reality that many of those who orchestrated the wartime "ethnic cleansing" have escaped prosecution, and that some are even celebrated locally as war heroes rather than war criminals. Although four suspects were arrested and charged for Zemir's murder less than one year later, only two suspects had been arrested when the twitter hashtag was loudest.

This context of absent men and their survivors' senses of injustice is essential to understanding the ways in which Bosnian Americans responded to Begić's death and made use of the #JusticeForZemir hashtag as a forum to debate their racialized belonging in the United States. Indeed, it is in the absence of justice in the face of state aggression that Bosnian Americans such as Ida and Tea locate common ground with Black Americans and articulated an antiracist account of Begić's murder. Three days after the murder, Tea Sefer, sister to Ida, published an "Open letter on Ferguson" with the Bosnian/English bilingual blog, *Chicago Raja*:[28]

> The inherited and first-hand history of racial and ethnic conflict that Mike Brown and Zemir Begić carried are shockingly similar. Both the Black community and Bosnian community have lost thousands of young men and boys at the hands of a military and government set out to eliminate them, we have both survived a history of slavery and colonization, both are resilient and have fought to protect their families.

Sefer goes on to point out differences among Black American experiences and those of Bosnian Americans, including their migration histories to the United States, and then acknowledges Bosnian experiences of victimization and writes that there is "no excuse" for Bosnians to jump on the racist white supremacy bandwagon:

> What I can say is that there is deeply embedded trauma in the Bosnian community. We are a community of people who have not had the chance to bury our dead from the war and who have not learned our lesson about conflict or hatred. We are also being used by white supremacists who are using the murder of Zemir as a reason to justify the killing of Mike Brown retroactively. We are being used as a backdrop to prove that 'anyone can succeed in America if you try hard enough' as a way to dismiss the hundreds of years of oppression and genocide committed against Black people in the United States. We are being pinned against each other because, right now, our whiteness is convenient and a perfect tool to fuel anti-Black hate. We are enough to trust for now. But as soon as the going gets tough, as soon as a Bosnian commits a crime, the rhetoric switches back to anti-immigrant, Islamophobic racism. When we stop being useful, we are no longer the picture-perfect example of assimilation in the United States, we are the *dirty Muslims* mainstream media and white supremacists wanted to deport post 9/11. (emphasis added)

When I read Sefer's essay, I was struck by the references to the perception that Americans view Bosnians as "dirty" immigrants and Muslims.[29] These were the same kind of references that Mia, Jasmila, and Tajma, women of

Sefer's parents' generation, had made back in 2004. I was reminded also of the more recent conversation I had with Amer with whom I had discussed the feature film *In the Land of Blood and Honey*, a fictional drama based on wartime Sarajevo. After he'd recounted the refugee stereotype of the "poverty stricken women with headscarves" (see introduction) he went on to say, "I don't think people understand . . . they think Islam is at the back door; they don't understand how Bosnians [Bosnian Muslims] have been displaced. . . ."

Amer's remarks illustrate the particular place in which his generation finds themselves in the United States social order. For many Bosnians, Begić's murder tapped into their recent history with gendered anti-Muslim violence; for them his death was another event in a series of persecutions that began with the 1990s political violence and were motivated by ethno-nationalist movements against Bosnian Muslims. And, anti-Muslim discrimination continued upon their arrival to the United States during the heightened Islamophobia that has accompanied the country's ongoing wars in Iraq and Afghanistan. The American readings of the murder as a "Black on White hate crime" incorporate Bosnians into an American Black/White binary that flattens Bosnian-ness into "whiteness" thereby effacing their experiences with war and ethno-national persecution.

FUTURES

Bosnian refugees' struggles to situate themselves within the United States show they must contend with deeply entrenched U.S. racism, particularly anti-Black racism. Yet Yugoslavia, writes Catherine Baker, "has been as entangled in global raciality as any other part of the planet."[30] Bosnians' efforts to fit in show that they draw on Yugoslav-era understandings of national difference that are linked to ethno-religious identifications and colonial histories, and refugees reworked these understandings in the context of the politics of racialization in the United States. These are not necessarily conscious re-workings, as are the sisters' social media activism, but rather are negotiated in the minutiae of everyday life: the interpretation of passersby, a schoolmate's comments, and conversations with co-workers. It is in these micro-interactions that Bosnians discover the racialized meanings of Whiteness and Blackness in the United States. Yet, it is not only skin color, nor their refugee-immigrant statuses that shape Bosnians's experiences in America; rising American Islamophobia intersects with gender, race, class, and ethnicity in ways that often confounded Bosnians' efforts to make themselves known to those outside of their communities.

Significantly, the sisters draw attention to a particular gendered and generational demographic loss shared among Bosnian refugees and Black Americans: the loss of men. Fathers, sons, brothers, uncles, husbands, friends, cousins are missing. For Bosnians this loss occurred during a protracted period of wartime, but the aftermath will be felt for generations to come. Among Black Americans, this loss has occurred through centuries of legalized state-sanctioned violence in the form of enslavement, followed by racial segregation, followed by criminalization and mass incarceration. The aftermath will be felt for generations to come. And women are left to contend with the loss and to memorialize the dead.

At first glance, the sisters' anti-racist campaign may be understood as belonging to a long history of non-Blacks' appropriations of Black experiences with difference, oppression, and resistance to forward their own cause.[31] Yet I suggest their campaign may also be seen as a process of cross-racial cultural appropriation through appreciation and identification.[32] In the case of Bosnian references to Black experiences, this means learning and passing on the history of Black resistance, as well as how their own histories with violence and oppression are both distinct from and relate to those of Black Americans.

Of course, as Mujanović points out, Bosnians' racial identifications will be varied, and will depend on local, national, and transnational politics. Whether or not appreciation for and identification with Black experiences become manifest in Bosnians' material and social lives remains to be seen. In the meantime, Bosnian refugees' experiences with living in the United States unsettle the Black/White binary and reveal the fragility of the racial edifice. Their efforts to communicate their refugee experiences with war and migration reveal the racial elements of United States Islamophobia that denies the existence and presence of European Muslims. In showing the lie of racial artifice, they also draw attention to the limits of assimilationist immigration models and invite the expansion of already-existing conceptualizations of citizenship and belonging.

NOTES

1. Bajram feasting marks the end of the month of Ramadan fasting.

2. Brodkin, Karen. *How the Jews Became White Folks and What That Says About Race in America.* New Brunswick, NJ: Rutgers University Press, 1998: 1–2.

3. Hasidic Judaism is a mystical Orthodox sect that has its roots in eighteenth century romantic movements in Central and Eastern Europe. As do some Muslim women, Hasidic women cover their hair as a sign of their faith and piety although they typically use wigs and not headscarves to do so.

4. The ACLU represented the NSPA in their suit against the village of Skokie, and the Supreme Court found in favor of the NSPA. However, the city of Chicago granted the NSPA a permit to march in Chicago, thus sparing the residents of Skokie. At the

time, Chicago's mayor was Michael Bilandic, whose parents had emigrated from Yugoslavia. The 1999 shooter drove back downstate Indiana, shooting and killing Korean graduate student Won Joon-Yoon who was on his way to church. The killer committed suicide before the police apprehended him.

5. Notably, Louise Cainkar's research on Muslim experiences with Islamophobia in Chicago, after September 11, 2001, shows that anti-Muslim attacks were more prevalent in suburbs where Arab Muslim constituted a sizable minority, than in city neighborhoods such as Bridgeview, with its sizable Black American and Palestinian Muslim populations (Cainkar, Louise. "Space and Place in the Metropolis: Arabs and Muslims Seeking Safety," *City & Society*. 17(2): 181–209, 2005).

6. Skokie is a suburb immediately adjacent to Chicago's north border and is home to a large Jewish Holocaust survivor population and their descendants. National and international attention turned to Skokie in 1977–1978 when the Nazi-affiliated National Socialist Party of America planned to parade in Skokie after the city of Chicago denied them a permit to hold a demonstration in Marquette Park. After a prolonged legal battle, Chicago issued the permit and the parade through Skokie was never held.

7. A robust body of scholarship documents this dynamic. See, among others, di Leonardo, Micaela. *The Varieties of Ethnic Experience: Kinship, Class, and Gender among California Italian-Americans*. Ithaca, NY: Cornell University Press, 1984; Guglielmo, Thomas A. *White on Arrival: Italians, Race, Color, and Power in Chicago, 1890–1945*. Oxford: Oxford University Press, 2003.

8. Waterston's father was from the village of Jedwabne in Poland and left just prior to the horrifying massacre of the remaining Jewish population at the hands of their Polish Catholic peers (Waterston, Alisse. *My Father's Wars: Migration, Memory, and the Violence of a Century*. New York: Routledge, 2014).

9. "Section Eight" is a federal program for subsidized rental housing.

10. Serbo-Croatian was standardized around the shtokavian Herzegovinian variant in the nineteenth century and is written in both cyrillic and latin scripts. The variants do not correspond to national territorial borders and are mutually intelligible.

11. As we learned earlier, the majority of Chicago's Muslims live in the south side of the city, and in the southwest suburbs, areas with longstanding Muslim communities. While the north side is more racially diverse than is the south side, the south side is home to a larger and more diverse Muslim population. See Cainkar 2009 for a discussion of Chicago's Muslim population particularly in relation to Muslims who identify as Arab. In addition to the post-September assault on the south side Bridgeview mosque, a north side Assyrian Church had been fire-bombed, and an arson fire was set at the South Side Arab American Community Center in 2002; both acts were deemed anti-Muslim hate crimes targeting Chicago's Arab community, regardless (or ignorant) of their faiths. There have been ongoing situations of public opposition to mosques in Chicago area suburbs, including Naperville (2011) and Palos Park (2016).

12. At the time, Murisa's school racial/ethnic demographics were reported as 57 percent hispanic, 15 percent Black, 13 percent Asian, and 11 percent white. None of the Bosnian kids she knew went to her school.

13. See Nell Irvin Painter, *The History of White People*, and Nancy Isenberg's *White Trash* for historiographies of the term "white trash." Uptown had become the

site of newly vacant housing due to middle-class "white flight" to the suburbs. John Hartigan similarly found "hillbilly" used as an intra-racial class distinction between "old-timer" white residents and those who migrated from Appalachia during the migration described in note #14.

14. See Maly and Leachman (Maly, Michael T. and Michael Leachman. "Rogers Park, Edgewater, Uptown, and Chicago Lawn, Chicago," *Cityscape: A Journal of Policy Development and Research* Vol 4(2): 131–160, 1998); and Guy (Roger Guy, *From Diversity to Unity: Southern and Appalachian Migrants in Uptown Chicago, 1950–1970*, Lexington Books, 2009) for accounts of this south-north migration, also known as the "hillbilly highway," a phrase coined by musician Steve Earle (Guy 2007: 4, 14). The mid-south included primarily the Appalachian regions of Kentucky, North Carolina, West Virginia, Eastern Tennessee. As many as 70,000 people arrived in Chicago during this migration. In the 1950s, Chicago Tribune reporter Nancy Browning wrote a series of articles sensationalizing these migrants centered on stereotypes of drunken violent feuding.

15. Bonilla, Yarimar and Jonathon Rosa. "#Ferguson: Digital Protest, Hashtag Ethnography, and the Racial Politics of Social Media in the United States." *American Ethnologist* 42(1): 4–17, 2015.

16. I followed tweet links, and coded them for references to race, ethnicity, immigration, and religion. The majority of tweets were in English. Thanks to Callie Dorsey for assistance with coding.

17. Tighe, Rosie J. and Joanne P. Ganning. "The Divergent City: Unequal and Uneven Development in St. Louis." *Urban Geography* 36(5): 654–673, 2015. See also McCarthy, Patrick and Tom Maday. *After the Fall: Srebrenica Survivors in St. Louis*. St. Louis: Missouri Historical Press, 2000.

18. According to some cultural geographers and city planners, Bosnian refugee-migrants are credited with the "revitalization" of the neighborhood in the aftermath of post-WWII racialized urban development policies that directed resources in ways that guaranteed suburban–urban race-coded housing segregation and labor segmentation (Hume, Susan E. "Two Decades of Bosnian Place-Making in St. Louis, Missouri." Journal of Cultural Geography 32(1): 1–22, 2015).

19. Rasim, Begic, "My brother did nothing wrong, innocent man killed," Twitter. November 30, 2014.

20. BHDragons, "Why are the major news networks not covering the hideous murder of Zemir Begić?" Twitter. November 30, 2014.; Dizdarevic, "because he's white killed by another ethnicity." Twitter, November 30, 2014.

21. SonOfBosnia, "Community wants to make this country better, we don't burn, we earn," Twitter. December 1, 2014.

22. The tweets must be seen as part of the broader conversation taking place in the United States about race and structural violence that crystallized around the Black Lives Matter movement established by three Black women in the wake of a Florida jury's 2013 decision, based on that state's controversial "stand your ground" policy, not to indict another white man, George Zimmerman, for killing another unarmed African American teenager, 17-year-old Trayvon Martin. Alicia Garza, Opal Tometi, and Patrisse Cullors are the BLM founders. One of them is the daughter of

immigrants. Their organizing modality relies on intersectional approaches to feminism, sexuality, and racism.

23. The city's National Football League team. It was said that Brown was in this posture when shot by Officer Wilson, but more significantly, the gesture references the countless previous instances in which Black people have been in nonthreatening and vulnerable positions when advanced upon and killed by police officers and vigilante racist enforcers such as members of the Klu Klux Klan.

24. The ACBH (Advisory Council for Bosnia and Herzegovina) posted this statement on December 1: "ACBH Outraged Over Brutal Attack of Bosnian American," *Advisory Council for Bosnia and Herzegovina,* December 1, 2014, http://www.acbih.org/acbh-outraged-over-brutal-attack-of-bosnian-american-in-st-louis/

25. Kendzior, Sarah. "There's Another Community in St. Louis Upset Over a Senseless Killing," *Quartz,* December 11, 2014, https://qz.com/308348/theres-another-community-raging-in-ferguson-over-a-senseless-killing/

26. Idddaaa23, "I have to be really honest. Zemir's death is really triggering for me, as it is for many other Bosnians," Twitter. December 1, 2014.

27. Wagner, To Know Where He Lies.

28. "Raja" in Bosnian meaning Muslim believers/faithful, but when used colloquially, it references more generally "the people," "the folk," During the Ottoman period, "raja" referred to lower status members of the empire; neither the enslaved, nor the upper classes. Sefer, Tea, "Bosnia and Herzegovina in Solidarity: An Open Letter on Ferguson," *Chicago Raja,* December 14, 2014, http://www.chicagoraja.net/?p=38911

29. Ten days later, Arnesa Buljusmić published her essay, "How White Supremacist media pundits used the Begić murder to create a Black on white racist agenda, and how the Bosnian American community played in to it" to the online issue of Islamic Monthly, a Boston-based English-language print and web-based publication aimed at Muslims living in the United States. After recounting her distress at learning of Begić's death, she writes:

> The next day I followed up on the news of Zemir Begić's murder and noticed a disturbing pattern. White supremacists, neo-Nazi, and ultra-conservative websites began posting about the murder. Zemir Begić, a Bosnian Muslim immigrant, suddenly became the poster child for "black on white" crime, with all of these articles referencing Begić's attackers as of the Latino and Black race. The irony was seemingly lost on those who were using Zemir Begić's murder to further promote their own racism and anti-blackness. In any other circumstance, these same pundits would consider Zemir Begić *a terrorist, a dirty immigrant and a barbaric Muslim*. The same people who are hardly advocates of immigrants or Muslims, were expressing their love and solidarity with the Bosnian community to further their own racist agendas. Certain members of this same Bosnian community joined in and supported the black on white framing of the brutal murder. [emphasis added]

Buljusmic, Arnesa, "Ferguson, Zemir Begic, The Agenda of White Supremacists and Bosnian Americans," *The Islamic Monthly*, December 4, 2014, http://www.theislamicmonthly.com/ferguson-zemir-begic-the-agenda-of-white-supremacists-and-bosnian-americans/

30. Baker, Catherine. *Race and the Yugoslav Region: Postsocialist, Post-Conflict, Postcolonial?* Manchester University Press, 2018: 1.

31. Brodkin makes note of this phenomenon when discussing Jewish immigrants' and their descendants' romantic uses of Black protest histories.

32. I am drawing here on Nitasha Sharma's work. The second-generation desi hip hop artists Sharma interviews make this distinction by emphasizing the discipline they develop through hip hop to build knowledge and spread awareness of their own circumstances by drawing on a body of work innovated by Black artists, to show respect for that work by naming and acknowledging their artistic influences, and through dedication to furthering the genre through skillful performance and by teaching it to others (Sharma, Nitasha. *Hip Hop Desis: South Asian Americans, Blackness, and a Global Race Consciousness*. Durham: Duke University Press, 2010: see esp pp. 269–299).

Gathering Grounds: A Reflection

On July 11, 2017, five women stood over gas-fired camping stoves situated atop three folding tables arranged in a "U" shape at the southern edge of Chicago's Daley Plaza. Car traffic clogged Washington Street behind the women while a lunchtime steppers' set played at the opposite end of the plaza. Amidst the din and bustle of office and service workers, shoppers, and municipal employees, two men quietly worked on either side of the stove setup, collecting water in large plastic containers from the public spigot, and offering bottled water and sandwich snacks to the women working over the stoves. One of the women, Anela, smoothed her light brown hair and pulled it back to the nape of her neck, securing it with a hairband so it wouldn't fall in her face when she checked the flames on her gas burners, a motion she would repeat a hundred times over the course of the next four hours.

The water in the aluminum pot on the right burner had not yet boiled, freeing her up to prep a džezva etched with slender copper dashes in a motif that resembled the feathered heads of wheat stalks. She tilted the džezva's mouth toward her at a ninety-degree angle and ladled in spoonfuls of finely ground coffee until the grounds hit the center of the džezva's inner base. Anela glanced at the water again. Boiling! She moved the pot with the boiling water over to the left burner, just until the bubbles stopped. Once the water had calmed a bit, she poured enough hot water into the džezva with coffee to fill it nearly to the top, gave the grounds and water a gentle stir, set the spoon to the side, and placed the džezva onto the still-hot right burner. She watched. As soon as the coffee liquid began to bubble and climb toward the džezva's lip, she removed the džezva and set it on a towel next to the stove. She poured in a tiny bit of water that remained in the other pot in order to help the coffee grinds settle. Anela motioned to another young woman, pixie haired Danira, that the coffee was ready.

Danira picked up the džezva and took several steps over to a growing circle of small porcelain cups clustered on the granite ground in the center of the plaza. She knelt down next to a young girl whose hair was styled in an afro-puff framed by a hairband of pink flowers and began to explain what she, Anela, and the rest of us were doing with the coffee, "We are pouring coffee in these cups to help remember someone who has died." "So, we can't drink it?" the girl asked. "No, since they are dead and can't drink their coffee, we are going to leave it in there, just for today, to help remind us of them when they were alive." The girl seemed to ponder the idea. "My uncle Jason died," she said. "Want to pour a cup for him?" Danira offered. "Yes" replied the girl. Together, Danira and the girl poured the dark liquid into two of the small cups, setting them down among those already assembled. Danira placed the džezva to the side for others to use and the girl rejoined her mother and two younger girls at the outer edge of the growing collection of fildžani.

Since 2006, Bosnian American artist Aida Šehović has collaborated with the Bosnian diaspora to facilitate a participatory art installation she calls ŠTO TE NEMA in a public square in a North American or European city.[1] The one-day installation is always on July 11, to commemorate the VRS mass executions of Bosnian Muslim men and boys at Srebrenica. Volunteers prepare Bosnian coffee for all of the individuals who have been identified and reburied and engage passersby to pour a coffee into fildžani, which have been donated by survivors in Bosnia and in the diaspora. Participants may not drink the coffee and are instructed to place the coffee cups on the ground. Over the course of the day the collection of cups takes up more and more paved space as each fildžan is set next to another.

Šehović's "recurring monument" reworks the public square through the practice of Bosnian coffee preparation that is most often done at home. As

Figure C.1. ŠTO TE NEMA Chicago 2017. Photo by Ana Croegaert.

we've seen, while men sometimes prepare prava kafa, women are the primary brewers. Šehović is deliberately inviting participants and passersby to engage in a domestic social activity in a public plaza, and thereby to temporarily collapse any pre-conceived divisions between inside and outside, private or public space. By centering the installation on hosting practices that are typically women's domain, Šehović also centers women's lives.

Thus, although the core scale of ŠTO TE NEMA is structured around the cups that honor the individual men and boys killed at Srebrenica, the installation subtly accentuates the experiences of women refugees. In our volunteer training Šehović reminded us that it was like we were "welcoming people into our home" when we invited passersby to pour the coffee. The installation is intended to encompass all survivors of the war, and to engage other communities that have either experienced genocide or want to raise public awareness regarding stopping genocide.

The monument's title, "ŠTO TE NEMA," is a Bosnian phrase that translates literally as "Why aren't you here?" but is better understood in this context as "Wish you were here. . . . Why haven't you returned?" The phrase is also the title of a well-known song in the Bosnian Balkan lyrical poetry art form *sevdah / sevdalinka* that tends to focus on melancholy sensibilities, such as longing for a loved one. The lyrics are based on a poem published by Aleksa Šantić in 1897. Although *Što te nema* was first recorded by a male author, sevdah songs were often composed and performed by women; one of the most popular versions of *Što te nema* is that of Jadranka Stojaković, recorded in the 1980s. In pairing this phrase with the practice of brewing and serving Bosnian coffee, the project suspends time in place. Because prava kafa is used, the associated sensory pleasures of ćejf may be stimulated among some participants, but since you are prohibited from drinking the coffee, there is no ćejf here and you are redirected to the sense of melancholia associated with sevdah. This melancholy space offers participants the possibility of engaging feelings of loss and of mourning in shared public space.

The installation also creates a space that neither emphasizes "voice," nor insists on a unifying, spoken narrative of victimization or oppression. It is a space made of improvised conversations centered on themes: the facts of the Srebrenica genocide, the invitation to learn more about the Yugoslav wars and their aftermath, the preparation and serving of Bosnian coffee in memory of those who are no longer alive to savor it. It is a space of sensory reflection: the sounds and smells of coffee preparation, the sights of embellished and enamel džezve and porcelain fildžani painted with flowers or silver filigree patterns. And this occurs in the midst of the din of daily life. Šehovic has rejected offers to brand and market ŠTO TE NEMA, and, in marked contrast to the Srebrenica memorial staged in the same plaza in 2005 (chapter 6), there are no political signs or paraphernalia such as flags permitted at the installation. These decisions may reduce the installation's legibility for passersby and even for volunteer-participants, and this is precisely the point. This is what makes ŠTO TE NEMA an artwork. Strangers pass through on their way to a work meeting, school, shopping, a doctor's appointment. Some of them stop, but many do not. This also invokes a feature of trauma—that one may experience immense suffering while others are simultaneously seemingly oblivious to the injuries one is subject to.

The reach of the wartime and genocidal violence involves so much more than the physical violation of a body, whether through sexual violence, killing, or maiming. It involves the absences of loved ones, the gaps in schooling and work. It involves the destruction of cherished places. It involves the assault on social ties, on social life. ŠTO TE NEMA provides a much-needed space to mourn these losses while being reminded of all that remains through the enactment of generosity via Bosnian coffee.

Nearly two decades following their arrival in Chicago, many refugees of the Yugoslav wars have experienced the sort of "successes" Nasiha highlighted in her post-performance rejoinder to the *Necessary Targets* discussion panelists (chapter 1). Some have earned college degrees, have "good jobs," own property, operate businesses. At the same time, rising white supremacist ideology coupled with Islamophobia and anti-refugee nativism adversely affects Bosnian Americans' material and social well-being.

While individual suffering can never be "twinned" to use Sontag's metaphor, the genocide against Bosnian Muslims during the 1990s wars is not a unique case. The empowerment of hatred and racism through state mandates and institutions has recurred throughout the modern era, as has institutional support for the denial of genocide. At the time of this writing, the Bosnian genocide is being actively denied by government representatives in parts of Bosnia and Serbia and among their diaspora. Survivors contend with both overt and covert intimidation when they memorialize the war-dead in parts of Bosnia—sometimes they are met with stone-throwing and threats of violence, and sometimes they are simply denied the permit necessary for staging a public event.

At the same time that some people in Bosnia and elsewhere engage in genocide denial, the wartime assaults against Bosnian Muslims are being celebrated among globally dispersed white supremacists engaged in a distinctly Islamophobic ideology. The assailant who in 2019 attacked two mosques in New Zealand, killing 49 people was listening to a Serb war song when he televised his horrific attacks. The song, recorded during the 1990s wars, praises the political leader of the VRS, a convicted war criminal.[2] The New Zealand killer claimed to be motivated by the assailant who murdered

77 people in Norway in 2011; the Norwegian assailant valorized the same Serb war criminal as an anti-Muslim crusader, defending "Christian Europe" against "Muslim invaders."[3] Overt champions of white supremacist ideology are not the only international figures engaged in actively obscuring the facts of genocide and diminishing survivors' accounts. In November 2019, the Nobel committee awarded the prize for literature to Austrian writer Peter Handke who has been a vocal apologist for Serb war crimes. The decision prompted outrage from literary figures around the world and among the Bosnian diaspora, but the award committee stood by their decision.

In light of these developments, Šehović has altered her 2020 installation plans. Šehović has fostered strong collaborative relationships with activists and artists living in Belgrade in the hopes of mounting the 2020 installation—the final iteration of the monument in its "ephemeral form"—in Serbia's state capital. Late in 2019, Šehović announced that she had decided to move the 2020 installation site from Belgrade to Potočari, the memorial and burial ground dedicated to the Srebrenica victims. While the installation was relocated in part due to safety concerns, the primary reason ŠTO TE NEMA will go to Potočari for its final staging is because the Women of Srebrenica Association requested Šehović bring it there, to them. The collective act of gathering to prepare Bosnian coffee and placing coffee cups in a public square to honor the dead makes ŠTO TE NEMA a quiet resistance to intimidation and threats and offers a nurturing space to those harmed by the 1990s political conflicts in Bosnia.

Understanding how Bosnian women navigate the many gathering grounds of their lives in the United States: those that bring people together for resistance and mourning, community and dissention, love and conflict helps bring into view some of the most challenging dynamics of our time. Their efforts to sustain and nourish transnational families illustrate the contours of global economic hardship in the context of intensive neoliberal capitalism wherein women continue to shoulder the majority of household and affective labor, in addition to their wage work. Women's struggles to be addressed as more than victims, but rather as workers, political actors, creative beings bring to light the biases structuring many humanitarian and non-governmental organizations, as well as ethno-nationalist political projects. Yet women's conscious coupling of socialist symbols with anti-Islamophobia discourse, as in the celebration of BosFam's work on Capitol Hill, and the sisters' hashtag activism in response to the murder of Zemir Begić sheds light on how connecting postsocialist and postcolonial perspectives may be politically generative.[4] As people around the world are forced from their homes due to political conflict that is simultaneously local, transnational, and global, the question of how to effectively build progressive political alliances demands responses. Bosnian women's experiences of living with the injuries of conflict, genocide, and displacement, and with the loss of home, status, and social ties emphasize the centrality of nuanced connections across identity and difference to the creation of progressive political projects. Such projects necessarily require imagining more expansive conceptions of citizenship and belonging in order to realize durable collective futures.

NOTES

1. The artist purposefully titles the project in all-caps. https://stotenema.com/.
2. Sentenced to life in prison for the genocide in Bosnia.
3. Mujanović, Jasmin, "Why Serb Nationalism Still Inspires Europe's Far Right," *Balkan Insight*, July 5, 2019, https://balkaninsight.com/2019/03/22/why-serb-nationalism-still-inspires-europes-far-right/.

Hajdarpašić, Edin, "Perspective: How a Serbian War Criminal Became an Icon of White Nationalism," *Washington Post*, March 20, 2019, https://www.washingtonpost.com/outlook/2019/03/20/how-serbian-war-criminal-became-an-icon-white-nationalism/.

4. See for example Chari, Sharad, and Katherine Verdery. "Thinking Between the Posts: Postcolonialism, Postsocialism, and Ethnography After the Cold War," *Comparative Studies in Sociology and History* 51(1): 6–34, 2009.

Bibliography

Abu-Lughod, Lila. "The Cross-Publics of Ethnography: The Case of the 'Muslim-woman.'" *American Ethnologist* 43(4): 595–608, 2016.
———. *Do Muslim Women Need Saving?* Cambridge, MA: Harvard University Press, 2013.
Agamben, Giorgio. *State of Exception*. Translated by Kevin Atrell. Chicago: University of Chicago Press, 2005.
———. *Homo Sacer: Sovereign Power and Bare Life*. Palo Alto, CA: Stanford University Press, 1998.
Agić, Senad. *Immigration and Assimilation: The Bosnian Muslim Experience in Chicago*. Lima, OH: Wyndham Hall Press, 2004.
Ahmed, Leila. *Women and Gender in Islam: Historical Roots of a Modern Debate*. New Haven, CT: Yale University Press, 1992.
Alcoff, Linda Martín. "What Should White People Do?" *Hypatia* 13(3): 6–26, 1998.
Alexander, Ronelle. *Bosnian, Croatian, Serbian, a Grammar: With Sociolinguistic Commentary*. Madison: University of Wisconsin Press, 2006.
Appadurai, Arjun. "Theory in Anthropology: Center and Periphery," *Comparative Studies in Society and History* 28(2): 356–361, 1986.
Archer, Rory, Igor Duda and Paul Stubbs. "Bringing Class Back In: An Introduction." In *Inequality and Discontent in Yugoslav Socialism*, Archer, Rory, Igor Duda and Paul Stubbs, Eds. New York: Routledge, 2016.
Arendt, Hannah. *The Origins of Totalitarianism*. New York: Schocken Books, 2004 [1948].
Baker, Catherine. *Race and the Yugoslav Region: Postsocialist, Post-Conflict, Postcolonial?* Manchester University Press, 2018.
Bakić-Hayden, Milica and Robert M. Hayden. "Orientalist Variations on the Theme 'Balkans': Symbolic Geography in Recent Yugoslav Cultural Politics." *Slavic Review* 51, Spring 1992.
Ballinger, Pamela. "Definitional Dilemmas: Southeastern Europe as 'Culture Area'?" *Balkanologie* 3(2): 73–91, December 1999.

Banwell, Cathy, Jane Dixon, Sarah Hinde, and Heather McIntyre. "Fast and Slow Food in the Fast Lane: Automobility and the Australian Diet." In *Fast Food/Slow Food: The Cultural Economy of the Global Food System*. Richard Wilk, Ed., 219–240. Lanham, MD: AltaMira, 2006.

Bateson, Gregory. *Steps to an Ecology of Mind*. New York: Ballantine Books, 1972.

Berdhal, Daphne. *Where the World Ended: Reunification and Identity in the German Borderland*. Berkeley, CA: University of California Press, 1999.

Bernal, Victoria and Inderpal Grewal. "Introduction: The NGO Form: Feminist Struggles, the State, and Neoliberalism." In *Theorizing NGOs: States, Feminisms, and Neoliberalism*. Durham, NC: Duke University Press, 2014.

Besteman, Catherine. *Making Refuge: Somali Bantu Refugees and Lewiston, Maine*. Durham, NC: Duke University Press, 2016.

Bockman, Johanna. "The Political Projects of Neoliberalism." *Social Anthropology* 20 (3): 310–317, 2012.

———. *Markets in the Name of Socialism: The Left-Wing Origins of Neoliberalism*. Stanford, CA: Stanford University Press, 2011.

Bonfiglioli, Chiara. "Gendering Social Citizenship: Textile Workers in Post-Yugoslav States." *The Europeanisation of Citizenship in the Successor States of the Former Yugoslavia*. Working Paper 2013/30. Edinburgh: University of Edinburgh School of Law, 2013.

Bonilla, Yarimar and Jonathon Rosa. "#Ferguson: Digital Protest, Hashtag Ethnography, and the Racial Politics of Social Media in the United States." *American Ethnologist* 42(1): 4–17, 2015.

Bourdieu, Pierre. *Distinction: A Social Critique of the Judgement of Taste*. Richard Nice, trans. Cambridge, MA: Harvard University Press, 1984.

Briggs, Charles. *Learning How to Ask: A Sociolinguistic Appraisal of the Role of the Interview in Social Science Research*. New York: Cambridge University Press, 2012.

Bringa, Tone. *Being Muslim the Bosnian Way*. Princeton, NJ: Princeton University Press, 1995.

Brković, Čarna. "The Everyday Life of a Homo Sacer: Enclave Urbanism in Podgorica, Montenegro." *Südosteuropa* 66(1): 10–26, 2018.

Brodkin, Karen. *How the Jews Became White Folks and What That Says About Race in America*. New Brunswick, NJ: Rutgers University Press, 1998.

Buechler, Hans, and Judith-Maria Buechler. "The Bakers of Berburg and the Logics of Communism and Capitalism." *American Ethnologist* 26(4): 799–821, 1999.

Butorović, Amila. "Islam in the Balkans." *Oxford Bibliographies Online*. New York: Oxford University Press, 2009.

Cainkar, Louise. "Space and Place in the Metropolis: Arabs and Muslims Seeking Safety," *City & Society*. 17(2): 181–209, 2005.

———. "Homeland Insecurity: The Arab American and Muslim American Experience After 9/11." New York: Russell Sage Foundation, 2009.

Center for Justice and Accountability. "Torture and Ethnic Cleansing in the Bosnian War," Last accessed July 3, 2018.

Chari, Sharad, and Katherine Verdery. "Thinking Between the Posts: Postcolonialism, Postsocialism, and Ethnography After the Cold War," *Comparative Studies in Sociology and History* 51(1): 6–34, 2009.

Clemetson, Lynette. "Bosnians in America: A Two-Sided Saga." *The New York Times*. New York City, April 29, 2007.

Coles, Kimberly. *Democratic Designs: International Intervention and Electoral Practices in Post-War Bosnia-Herzegovina*, Ann Arbor, MI: University of Michigan Press, 2007.

Collier, Stephen. "Neoliberalism as Big Leviathan, or . . .?" *Social Anthropology* 20(3): 310–317, 2012.

Collins, Jane. "What/Where Is the Working Class?" paper presented at *Mellon Humanities Without Walls Global Work and Working-Class Community* in the Midwest Symposium, Evanston, IL: Northwestern University, 28 Sept. (2014).

———. "The Specter of Slavery: Workfare and the Economic Citizenship of Poor Women." In *New Landscapes of Inequality: Neoliberalism and the Erosion of Democracy in America*, Jane Collins, Micaela di Leonardo, and Brett Williams, Eds., 131–152. Santa Fe, NM: School of American Research, 2007.

Comaroff, John and Jean Comaroff. *Ethnography and the Historical Imagination.* Philadelphia: Taylor & Francis, 1992.

Conquergood, Dwight. "Performance Studies: Interventions and Radical Research." *TDR* 46(2): 145–156, 2002.

cooke, miriam. "The Muslimwoman." *Contemporary Islam* 1: 139–154, 2007.

Coutin, Susan. "Re/membering the Nation: Gaps and Reckoning within Biographical Accounts of Salvadoran Émigrés," *Anthropological Quarterly* 84(4): 809–834, 2011.

Čapo, Jasna. "Ethnology and Anthropology in Europe: Toward a Trans-National Discipline," *Cultural Analysis* 13(2014): 51–76, 2015.

Crenshaw, Kimberle. "Mapping the Margins: Intersectionality, Identity Politics, and Violence against Women of Color," *Stanford Law Review* 43(6): 1241–1299, 1991.

Cushman, Thomas. "Anthropology and Genocide in the Balkans: An Analysis of Conceptual Practices of Power," *Anthropological Theory* 4(1): 5–28, 2004.

Davis, Dana-Ain and Christa Craven. *Feminist Ethnography: Thinking Through Methodologies, Challenges, and Possibilities*. Lanham, MD: Rowman & Littlefield, 2016.

Davis, Dana-Ain. "Manufacturing Mamies: The Burdens of Service Work and Welfare Reform among Battered Black Women." *Anthropologica* 46(2): 273–288, 2004.

De León, Jason. *The Land of Open Graves: Living and Dying on the Migrant Trail*. Berkeley: University of California Press, 2015.

di Leonardo, Micaela. *Exotics at Home: Anthropologies, Others, American Modernity*. Chicago: University of Chicago Press, 1998.

———. di Leonardo, Micaela. *The Varieties of Ethnic Experience: Kinship, Class, and Gender among California Italian-Americans*. Ithaca: Cornell University Press, 1984.

Du Bois, W. E. B. *Darkwater*. New York: Harcourt, Brace and Company, 1920.

Durkheim, Emile. *The Division of Labour in Society*. W. D. Halls, Trans. New York: Free Press, 1997.

Elyachar, Julia. "Empowerment Money: The World Bank, Non-Governmental Organizations, and the Value of Culture in Egypt," *Public Culture* 14(3): 493–513, 2002.

Ensler, Eve. *Necessary Targets: A Story of Women and War*. New York: Villard Books, 2001.

Espiritu, Yén Lê. "Toward a Critical Refugee Study: The Vietnamese Refugee Subject in US Scholarship." *Journal of Vietnamese Studies* 1(1–2): 410–433, 2006.

Fanon, Franz. *The Wretched of the Earth*. C. Farrington, trans. New York: Grove Weidenfeld, 1991.

Ferguson, James and Akil Gupta. "Spatializing States: Toward an Ethnography of Neoliberal Governmentality." *American Ethnologist* 29(4): 981–1002, 2002.

Fleming, K. E. "Orientalism, the Balkans, and Balkan Historiography." *The American Historical Review* 105(4): 1218–1233, 2000.

Fouron, Georges and Nina Glick Schiller. "All in The Family: Gender, Transnational Migration, and the Nation-State." *Identities* 7(4): 539–582, 2001.

Franz, Barbara. "Bosnian Refugees and Socio-Economic Realities: Changes in Refugee Resettlement Policies in Austria and the United States." *Journal of Ethnic and Migration Studies* 29(1): 5–21, 2003.

———. *Uprooted and Unwanted: Bosnian Refugees in Austria and the United States*. College Station: Texas A&M University Press, 2005.

Friedman, Victor. "Observing the Observers: Language, Ethnicity, and Power in the 1994 Macedonian Census and Beyond." In *Toward Comprehensive Peace in Southeast Europe: Conflict Prevention in the South Balkans*, Report of the South Balkans Working Group of the Council on Foreign Relations Center for Preventative Action. New York: The Twentieth Century Fund Press, 1996.

Gagnon, Phillip Jr. *The Myth of Ethnic War: Serbia and Croatia in the 1990s*. Ithaca: Cornell University Press, 2004.

Gal, Susan. "A Semiotics of the Public/Private Distinction." *Differences: A Journal of Feminist Cultural Studies* 13(1): 77–95, 2002.

Gal, Susan and Gail Kligman. *The Politics of Gender after Socialism: A Comparative Historical Essay*. Princeton, NJ: Princeton University Press, 2000a.

———. *Reproducing Gender: Politics, Publics, and Everyday Life after Socialism*. Princeton, NJ: Princeton University Press, 2000b.

Gilmore, Ruth. "Fatal Couplings of Power and Difference: Notes on Racism and Geography." *The Professional Geographer* 54(1): 15–24, 2002.

Gilroy, Paul. *The Black Atlantic: Modernity and Double Consciousness*. Cambridge, MA: Harvard University Press, 1993.

Goffman, Erving. *Frame Analysis: An Essay on the Organization of Experience*. New York: Harper and Row, 1974.

Gomberg-Muñoz, Ruth. *Becoming Legal: Immigration Law and Mixed-Status Families*. Oxford: Oxford University Press, 2017.

Grewal, Inderpal. *Transnational America: Feminisms, Diasporas, Neoliberalisms*. Durham, NC: Duke University Press, 2005.

Grigoryeva, Angelina. "When Gender Trumps Everything: The Division of Parent Care Among Siblings." *The Center for the Study of Social Organization (CSSO)*, Working Paper #9, April 2014.

Guglielmo, Thomas A. *White on Arrival: Italians, Race, Color, and Power in Chicago, 1890–1945*. Oxford: Oxford University Press, 2003.
Guy, Roger. *From Diversity to Unity: Southern and Appalachian Migrants in Uptown Chicago, 1950–1970*. Lanham, MD: Lexington Books, 2007.
Hajdarpašić, Edin. *Whose Bosnia? Nationalism and Political Imagination in the Balkans, 1840–1914*. Ithaca, NY: Cornell University Press, 2015.
Halilovich, Haris. *Places of Pain: Forced Displacement, Popular Memory and Translocal Identities in Bosnian War-torn Communities*. Oxford: Berghahn, 2013.
Hansen, Karen Tranberg. "Introduction," In *African Dress: Fashion, Agency, Performance*, Karen Tranberg Hansen and D. Soyini Madison, Eds. New York: Bloomsbury, 2013.
Hartmann, Heidi I. "The Family as the Locus of Gender, Class, and Political Struggle: The Example of Housework." *Signs* 6(3): 366–394, 1981.
Harvey, David. *A Brief History of Neoliberalism*. Oxford: Oxford University Press, 2005.
———. "Globalization and the Spatial Fix." *Geographische Revue* (2): 23–30, 2001.
———. *The Condition of Postmodernity: An Enquiry into the Origins of Cultural Change*. Cambridge, MA: Blackwell, 1990.
Hattox, Ralph. *Coffee and Coffeehouses: The Origins of a Social Beverage in the Medieval Near East*. Seattle: University of Washington Press, 1985.
Helms, Elissa. *Innocence and Victimhood: Gender, Nation, and Women's Activism in Postwar Bosnia-Herzegovina*. Madison: University of Wisconsin Press, 2013.
———. "The Gender of Coffee: Women and Reconciliation Initiatives in Post-War Bosnia and Herzegovina." *Focaal: Journal of Global and Historical Anthropology* 75(Summer): 17–32, 2010.
———. "East and West Kiss: Gender, Orientalism and Balkanism in Muslim-Majority Bosnia-Herzegovina." *Slavic Review* 67(1): 88–119, Spring 2008.
Hochschild, Arlie. *The Second Shift*. New York: Viking, 1989.
Hockenos, Paul. *Homeland Calling: Exile Patriotism and the Balkan War*. Ithaca, NY: Cornell University Press, 2003.
Hromadžić, Azra. *Citizens of an Empty Nation: Youth and State-making in Postwar Bosnia and Herzegovina*. University of Pennsylvania Press, 2015.
———. "Discourses of Trans-Ethnic Narod in Postwar Bosnia and Herzegovina." *Nationalities Papers* 41(2): 259–275, 2013.
———. "'Once We Had a House': Invisible Citizens and Consociational Democracy in Post-War Mostar, Bosnia and Herzegovina." *Social Analysis*, 56(3): 30–48, 2012.
Hume, Susan E. "Two Decades of Bosnian Place-Making in St. Louis, Missouri." *Journal of Cultural Geography* 32(1): 1–22, 2015.
Hunleth, Jean. *Children as Caregivers: The Global Fight Against Tuberculosis and HIV in Zambia*. New Brunswick, NJ: Rutgers University Press, 2017.
International Commission on the Balkans. "The Balkans in Europe's Future." Sofia, Bulgaria: Centre For Liberal Strategies, 2005.
International Crisis Group. "Bosnia's Precarious Economy: Still Not Open For Business." Balkans Report No.115, August 7, 2001.

Isenberg, Nancy. *White Trash: The 400-Year Untold History of Class in America.* New York: Penguin Books, 2016.

Jackson, Michael. *The Wherewithall of Life: Ethics, Migration, and the Question of Well-Being.* University of California Press, 2013.

Jansen, Stef. "Troubled Locations: Return, the Life Course, and Transformations of 'Home' in Bosnia-Herzegovina." *Focaal: Journal of Global and Historical Anthropology* 49: 15–30, 2007.

———. "The Privatization of Home and Hope: Return, Reforms, and the Foreign Intervention in Bosnia-Herzegovina." *Dialectical Anthropology* 30: 177–199, 2006.

———. "Misplaced Masculinities: Status Loss and the Location of Gendered Subjectivities Among 'Non-Transnational' Bosnian Refugees." *Anthropological Theory* 8(2): 181–200, 2007.

Johnson, Kirk. "Anti-Bosnian Backlash Feared in Utah." *New York Times.* New York, February 15, 2007.

Johnson, Venice M. "Dan Žena Izbjeglica/Refugee Women's Day." Chicago: Catholic Charities of the Archdiocese of Chicago Refugee Resettlement Program: *New Woman*, March 2001.

Kidron, Carol. "Toward an Ethnography of Silence: The Lived Presence of the Past in the Everyday Life of Holocaust Trauma Survivors and Their Descendants in Israel," *Current Anthropology* 50(1): 5–27, 2009.

Kingfisher, Catherine and Jeff Maskovsky. "The Limits of Neoliberalism," *Critique of Anthropology* 28(2): 115–126, 2008.

Kleinman, Arthur, Veena Das, and Margaret Lock. *Social Suffering.* Berkeley: University of California Press, 1997.

Kolind, Torsten. "In Search of 'Decent People': Resistance to the Ethnicization of Everyday Life among the Muslims of Stolac." In *The New Bosnian Mosaic: Identities, Memories, and Moral Claims in a Post-War Society*, Xavier Bougarel, Elissa Helms, Ger Duizings, Eds., 123–140. Burlington, VT: Ashgate, 2007.

Kulašić, Elmina. "Inherent History: Memories and Intergenerational Search for Missing Family Members in Bosnia and Herzegovina." *The International Journal of Conflict and Reconciliation* 3(1), 2017.

Le Normand, Brigette. "The Gastarbaiteri as a Transnational Yugoslav Working Class." In *Inequality and Discontent in Yugoslav Socialism,* Archer, Rory, Igor Duda and Paul Stubbs, Eds. New York: Routledge, 2016.

Longinović, Tomislav. *Vampires Like Us: Writing Down "The Serbs."* Belgrade: Belgrade Circle Journal, Belgrade Displaced Series, 2005.

Lowe, Frederick H. "A Light in the Darkness: The Heroism of a Bosnian Refugee." Chicago: *Chicago Reader* February 2, 1999. News and Politics, Our Town.

Madison, Soyini D. *Critical Ethnography: Method, Ethics, and Performance.* Los Angeles: Sage, 2012.

Malcolm, Noel. *Bosnia: A Short History.* New York: New York University Press, 1996[1994].

Malkki, Liisa. "Refugees and Exile: From 'Refugee Studies' to the National Order of Things." *Annual Review of Anthropology* 24: 495–523, 1995.

———. "Speechless Emissaries: Refugees, Humanitarianism, and Dehistorization," *Cultural Anthropology* 11(3): 377–404, 1996.

Mallon, Mary T. "Development Amidst a Fragmented Community." M.A. thesis, Graduate Program in Intercultural Studies, *Wheaton College*, 1997.

Maly, Michael T. and Michael Leachman. "Rogers Park, Edgewater, Uptown, and Chicago Lawn, Chicago." *Cityscape: A Journal of Policy Development and Research* Vol 4(2): 131–160, 1998.

Maskovsky, Jeff "Critical Anthropologies of the United States," In *Handbook of Sociocultural Anthropology*. James Carrier and Deborah Gewertz, Eds. London: Berg Press, 2013.

Mbembe, Achille. "Necropolitics." Libby Meintjes, trans. *Public Culture* 15(1): 11–40, 2003.

McCarthy, Patrick and Tom Maday. *After the Fall: Srebrenica Survivors in St. Louis*. St. Louis: Missouri Historical Press, 2000.

Menjívar, Cecelia. *Fragmented Ties: Salvadoran Immigrant Networks in America*. Berkeley: University of California Press, 2000.

Metz, Nina. "Lana Has Week to Prove Itself." *Chicago Tribune*: Chicago, 2004.

Meznarić, Silva and Jelena Zlatković Winter. "Forced Migration and Refugee Flows in Croatia, Slovenia, and Bosnia-Herzegovina: Early Warning, Beginning and Current State of Flows." *Refuge* 12(7)1–5, February 1993.

Mollica, Richard. *Healing Invisible Wounds: Paths to Hope and Recovery in a Violent World*. Nashville, TN: Vanderbilt University Press, 2009[2006].

Nguyen, Mimi Thi. *The Gift of Freedom: War, Debt, and Other Refugee Passages*. Durham, NC: Duke University Press, 2012.

Nikolić-Rištanović, Vesna. *Women, Violence, and War: Wartime Victimization of Refugees in the Balkans*. Budapest: Central European University Press, 2000.

Ong, Aiwha. *Buddha is Hiding: Refugees, Citizenship, the New America*. Berkeley: University of California Press, 2003.

Painter, Nell Irvin. *The History of White People*. New York: W. W. Norton & Company, 2011.

Pandofli Pandolfi, Mariella. "Contract of Mutual (In)difference: Governance and the Humanitarian Apparatus in Contemporary Albania and Kosovo." *Indiana Journal of Global Legal Studies* 10: 369–381, 2003.

Peck, Jamie. *Work-Place: The Social Regulation of Labor Markets*. New York: The Guilford Press, 996.

Petrini, Carl. *Slow Food Nation: Why Our Food Should Be Good, Clean, and Fair*. New York: Rizzoli ex libris, 2007.

Pupovac, Vanessa. "Securing the community? An Examination of International Psychosocial Intervention." In *International Intervention in the Balkans since 1995*. P. Siani-Davies, Ed., 158–171. New York: Routledge, 2003.

Ralph, Laurence. *Renegade Dreams: Living Through Injury in Gangland Chicago*. Chicago: Chicago University Press, 2014.

Ranney, David. *Global Decisions, Local Collisions: Urban Life in the New World Order*. Philadelphia, PA: Temple University Press, 2003.

Rasza, Maple and Nicole Lindstrom. "Balkan is Beautiful: Balkanism in the Political Discourse of Tudjman's Croatia." *East European Politics and Societies* 18(4): 628–650, 2004.
Razack, Sherene. "Stealing the Pain of Others: Reflections on Canadian Humanitarian Responses." *The Review of Education, Pedagogy, and Cultural Studies* 29:4(375–394), 2007.
Roberts, Dorothy. *Killing the Black Body: Race, Reproduction, and the Meaning of Liberty*. New York: Vintage, 1998.
Saltaga, Fuad. *Muslimanska Nacija u Jugoslaviji: Porijeklo, Islam, Kultura, Povijest, Politika*. Sarajevo: *Institut za Proučavanje Nacionalinih Odnosa*, 1991.
Schwartzman, Helen B. "The Significance of Meetings in an American Mental Health Center." *American Ethnologist* 14(2): 271–294, 1987.
Sharma, Nitasha. *Hip Hop Desis: South Asian Americans, Blackness, and a Global Race Consciousness*. Durham, NC: Duke University Press, 2010.
Singer, Audrey, and Jill H. Wilson. "Refugee Resettlement in Metropolitan America," Migration Information Source. March 1, 2007, last accessed 9.20.2019, http://www.migrationpolicy.org/article/refugee-resettlement-metropolitan-america.
Skrbiš, Zlatko. *Long-Distance Nationalism: Diasporas, Homelands, and Identities*. Brookfield, VT: Ashgate, 1999.
Sontag, Susan. *Regarding the Pain of Others*. New York: Farrar, Straus, and Giroux, 2003.
Sorabji, Cornelia. "Islamic Revival and Marriage in Bosnia." *Journal of Muslim Minority Affairs* 9(2): 331–337, 1988.
———. "Bosnian Neighborhoods Revisited: Tolerance, Commitment and Komšiluk in Sarajevo." In *On the Margins of Religion*. Joao de Pina Cabral and Frances Pine, Eds., 97–112. Oxford: Berghahn Books, 2003.
Stack, Carol. *All Our Kin*. New York: Basic Books, 1974.
Stephen, Lynn. *Transborder Lives: Indigenous Oaxacans in Mexico, California, and Oregon*. Durham, NC: Duke University Press, 2007.
Sugarman, Jane. "Imagining the Homeland: Poetry, Songs, and the Discourses of Albanian Nationalism." *Ethnomusicology* 43/3 (Fall 1999): 419–458.
Thompson, E. P. *The Making of the English Working Class*. Toronto: Penguin Books, 1991.
Tighe, Rosie J. and Joanne P. Ganning. "The Divergent City: Unequal and Uneven Development in St. Louis." *Urban Geography* 36(5): 654–673, 2015.
Todorova, Maria. *Imagining the Balkans*. Oxford: Oxford University Press, 2009.
Trouillot, Michel-Rolph. *Silencing the Past: Power and the Production of History*. Boston: Beacon Press, 1995.
Vološinov, V. N. *Marxism and the Philosophy of Language*. Translated by Ladislav Matejka and I. R. Titunik. New York: Seminar Press, [1929] 1973.
Wacquant, Loic. "The Penalization of Poverty and the Rise of Neo-liberalism." *European Journal on Criminal Policy and Research* (9): 401–412, 2001.
Wagner, Sarah. *To Know Where He Lies: DNA Technology and the Search for Srebrenica's Missing*. Berkeley: University of California Press, 2008.
Warner, Michael. *Publics and Counterpublics*. New York: Zone Books, 2002.

Waterston, Alisse. *My Father's Wars: Migration, Memory, and the Violence of a Century*. New York: Routledge, 2014.
Weick, K. E. *Sensemaking in Organizations*. Thousand Oaks, CA: Sage Publications, 1995.
Wilk, Richard. "From Wild Weeds to Artisanal Cheese." In *Fast Food/Slow Food: The Cultural Economy of the Global Food System*. Richard Wilk, Ed., 13–30. Lanham, MD: Altamira, 2006.
———. "'Real Belizean Food': Building Local Identity in the Transnational Caribbean." *American Anthropologist* 101(2): 244–255, 1999.
Williams, Brett. *Debt for Sale: A Social History of the Credit Trap*. Philadelphia, PA: University of Pennsylvania Press, 2004.
Wilson, Ara. *The Intimate Economies of Bangkok: Tomboys, Tycoons, and Avon Ladies in the Global City*. Berkeley, CA: University of California Press, 2004.
Winland, Daphne. "The Politics of Desire and Disdain: Croatian Identity between 'Home' and 'Homeland.'" *American Ethnologist* 29(3): 693–718, 2002.
Woodward, Susan. "The Political Economy of Ethno-Nationalism." *Socialist Register*, 2003.
———. *Socialist Unemployment: The Political Economy of Yugoslavia, 1945–1990*. Princeton: Princeton University Press, 1995.
Yanagisako, Sylvia Junko, and Jane Fishburne Collier. "Toward a Unified Analysis of Gender and Kinship." In *Gender and Kinship: Essays Toward a Unified Analysis*. Jane Fishburne Collier and Sylvia Junko Yanagisako, Eds., 15–50. Stanford, CA: Stanford University Press, 1987.
Yurchak, Alexei. *Everything Was Forever, Until It Was No More*. Princeton, NJ: Princeton University Press, 2006.
Žarkov, Dubravka. *The Body of War: Media, Ethnicity, and Gender in the Break-up of Yugoslavia*. Durham: Duke University Press, 2007.
———. "The Body of the Other Man: Sexual Violence and the Construction of Masculinity, Sexuality, and Ethnicity in Croatian Media." In *Victims, Perpetrator or Actors? Gender, Armed Conflict and Political Violence*. Caroline O. N. Moser and Fiona C. Clark, Eds. London: Zed Books, 2001.
Zavella, Patricia. *I'm Neither Here nor There: Mexican Quotidian Struggles with Migration and Poverty*. Durham: Duke University Press, 2011.
Zulfić, Muharem. *100 godina Bošnjaka u Čikagu*. Chicago: Džemijetul Hajrije, 2003.

Index

Abu-Lughod, Lila, 16

Balkan:
    "balkanize," 99;
    nomenclature, 98–99, 113n4
Balkanism, 99–100, 113n5;
    conceptual inspiration and distinction from Orientalism, 113n6
Begić, Zemir:
    murder of, 141, 149–56
Black Lives Matter, 151
Brown, Michael:
    murder of, 141, 149

ćejf, 85–91, 165
Chicago:
    history of Bosnian migration to, 48–49;
    manufacturing job losses, 33;
    memorializing Bosnian genocide, 119–25, 130–32, 163–66;
    refugee agencies, 28, 35;
    translocal anti-racism, 154–55
coffee, 18–19;
    Bosnian brands, 78;
    and džezva (pl. džezve) and fildžan (pl. fildžani), 47;
    "the real coffee" / "prava kafa," 75–77;
    "slow" coffee as commodity, 88–89, 135;
    social history of and religious ritual, 78–81;
    social ritual, 85–88;
    in ŠTO TE NEMA nomadic monument and memorial, 163–66
Collins, Jane, 33
The Community Center (TCC), 1, 9, 13, 28, 35–41, 81–85, 107, 145–47
critical ethnography, 11–12

Daley Plaza, *122, 164*
debt, 45–46, 51, 55, 57–59
di Leonardo, Micaela, 11
domestic violence, 106–9, 111, 115n27

ethnicity:
    "ethnic cleansing," 2, 138n7, 142, 154;
    "ethnic wars," 19, 28–31;
    ethno-nationalism, 30–31;
    in the S.F.R.Y. "national key," 30;
    and Volags, 36
Espiritu, Yén Lê, 16

feminism:
    colonial feminism, 128–29;
    Eve Ensler, 38;
    feminist anthropology, 48;
    liberal feminism 118–19, 130

gender, 13;
  gender-based violence, 101;
  gender, place, and space, 165;
  men, 47–49, 50, 79;
  and NGOs, 36, 119;
  separation during genocide, 122–23;
  stereotypes of, 101–6, 110–11, 129;
  women, 35, 38, 74, 78, 81–82, 90
genocide, 2, 22n6, 98, 120, 123–25, 130–31, 154–55, 165–66;
  genocide denial, 98, 112, 131, 166;
  Holocaust analogy, 143–44;
  Rafael Lemkin, 143

Helms, Elissa, 31, 106, 128

Injured Life, 3, 7–8, 23nn10–13
Internally Displaced Persons (IDP), 15
International Commission on the Balkans, 99–100
International Court of Justice (ICJ), 97–98, 123, 130, 139n18
International Criminal Tribunal for Yugoslavia (ICTY), 19, 97–98, 123–24, 130
International Monetary Fund (IMF), 4, 19, 30, 46
Islam:
  Arabic as pan-Islamic language, 147;
  head scarf, 147;
  sevap, 55–57;
  zikir / dhikir, 78–79

kuća:
  significance of home, moral economy, 46–48, 50, 60n10

Madison, Soyini, 12
militias:
  Army of the Republic of Bosnia and Herzegovina (ARBiH), 98, 123–24, 138n7;
  Army of Republika Srpska (VRS), 4–5, 22n8, 31, 64, 93n11, 121, 123–24, 132, 138n7, 166;
  Croatian Defense Council (HVO), 64, 70n4;
  Yugoslav People's Army (JNA), 98, 112, 138n7
moral economy, 48, 57
Mostar, 3, 47, 53, 57, 64–67

neoliberalism, 32–35, 37;
  and Personal Responsibility and Work Opportunity Reconciliation Act of 1996 (PRWORA), 33, 44, 141;
  and "precarity fix," 34;
  and socialism, 34;
  and "spatial fix," 33–34;
  and Workforce Investment Act of 1998, 33
Non-Aligned Movement (NAM), 29
Non-Governmental Organizations (NGOs), 36, 40, 106, 119, 126–30;
  International Non-Governmental Organizations (INGOs), 126, 138n15;
  non-profit, 35;
  Volag as a form of, 36

Prijedor, 2, 22n6, 39, 56, 112, 125, 130–32
Post-Traumatic Stress Syndrome (PTSD), 11, 24n17
public:
  counterpublic, 97, 112n1;
  public sphere, 112n1, 144;
  public square, 164–65

racialization:
  as part of "assimilation," 143;
  of Muslims, 143;
  of poverty, 32–33, 148;
  of refugees, 142–43;
  "welfare queen," 32–33;
  "white trash," 148;
  whiteness, 142–43, 150, 150–56.
  See also racism

racism:
  anti-Black, 32, 40, 145–46, 150–56;
  anti-Muslim, 30, 142–43, 155–56, 166–67;
  anti-Jewish, 145;
  White supremacist ideology, 166.
  See also racialization
rape, 3, 5, 17, 118, 132;
  media depictions of, 101–4;
  stigma of, 106.
  See also sexual violence
refugee, 15–17, 37–40;
  1980 Refugee Act, 27;
  racialization of, 142–43;
  refugee resettlement, 13, 27, 38, 40, 100.
  See also Internally Displaced Persons (IDP) and Temporary Protected Status (TPS)
remittances, 30, 45–46

Sarajevo, 3, 39–40, 46, 66, 93n11, 145
sexual violence, 5, 6, 10, 36, 105–6, 166.
  See also rape
socialism:
  "laissez-faire socialism," 28;
  "market socialism," 28;
  Yugoslav late twentieth century, 12, 91, 29–32
Socialist Federal Republic of Yugoslavia (SFRY), 1, 12–13, 29–34, 78, 84, 156
Sontag, Susan, 39–40
Srebrenica:
  1995 genocide, 3, 10, 22n6, 98, 112, 119, 123–24, 130;
  memorial quilt presentation on Capitol Hill, 2009, 130;
  memorials to 1995 genocide, 119, 163;
  survivors in St. Louis 120, 149–50
Stolac, 63–71
Structural Adjustment Programs (SAPs), 30

Temporary Protected Status (TPS), 4
Todorova, Maria, 99, 113n4, 113n6
translocal, 141, 148
transnational, 64, 67, 79, 119, 141, 157;
  and NGOs, 122–24;
transnational family, 61n20;
  "transnational social fields," 45, 59, 59n1
Trnopolje concentration camp, 4–5, 7

United Nations Protection Force (UNPROFOR), 123

Voluntary Agency (Volag), 1, 13, 28.
  See also The Community Center (TCC)

Woodward, Susan, 4, 30–31
World Bank (WB), 4, 9, 29, 30, 46, 99

Yugoslavia. See Socialist Federal Republic of Yugoslavia (SFRY)

A number of key participants appear across the chapters in this book. To help orient the reader, the following is a list of names (pseudonyms) and the initial pages in which the participant appears:

Ajla (mother = Safija), 63–71
Almina, 131–34
Amina, 73–75
Hana (mother = Vehida, husband = Damir), 43–45
Edita (daughter = Lejla), 108–10
Elmina, 109–10
Enisa (daughter = Nasiha), 3–6
Fadila (son-in-law = Joso), 49–55
Nasiha (mother = Enisa, husband = Edo), 1–6
Selma, 88–91
Zara (daughter = Murisa), 134–36, 147

About the Author

Ana Croegaert is a sociocultural anthropologist whose research centers on gender, performance, and inequality. She has published on a range of topics including refugee migration, coffee rituals, contested public space, street parades, monuments and memorials, and racism.

www.ingramcontent.com/pod-product-compliance
Lightning Source LLC
Chambersburg PA
CBHW050906300426
44111CB00010B/1406